ONE MINUTE SCRIPTURE STUDY IN THE NEW TESTAMENT

KRISTEN WALKER SMITH AND CALI BLACK

ISBN 978-1-4621-4444-0

Cover art and book format by Nichelle Schmidt
Copy editing by Tasha Bradford

www.oneminutescripturestudy.com

To my amazing BYU roommate, Rachel Willis Gwin,
and my Book of Mormon professor, Todd Parker.
Thank you for helping me discover the
joy of the scriptures over 20 years ago!

– *Kristen*

To my parents who have always been the
ultimate examples of how to love the scriptures!
And to Kyle for being the best example
of Christlike love and encouragement.

– *Cali*

WELCOME!

Have you been looking for a way to dive into the New Testament that is both simple and fits your busy schedule? We are Kristen Walker Smith and Cali Black, and we're beyond excited to help you study the scriptures this year!

You may know us as the co-hosts of the popular Latter-day Saint podcast "One Minute Scripture Study," where we apply the scriptures to real life in short, bite-sized episodes.

Both of us have a lot of things in common: We love chocolate, we each have three kids, and we love telling stories to make the scriptures come alive. Most importantly we are obsessed with making sure each study session improves who we are, even if it's just a little bit. That's why you'll see our signature "takeaway of the day in five words or less" at the top of each page! These take aways are invitations to act on what you've learned and felt.

On the pages of this book, you'll notice that we take turns sharing the truths we've learned from the New Testament. You'll always be able to find our name at the bottom of each day's devotional, so you know which one of us wrote it!

No matter your age or familiarity with the gospel, you'll find something simple but valuable on each page, and we can't wait to get started. We are so excited to join you in your study, and thank you for coming closer to Christ with us in the New Testament, one minute at a time!

— Kristen & Cali

BOOK LAYOUT

This book is meant to be a 365+ day study of the New Testament. We tried to keep each day's devotional short enough that you can do your study in just one to two minutes a day! The format of the book is explained below.

YOUR READING IS BROKEN DOWN INTO DAYS 1 - 357, PLUS AN INTRO & 15 DAYS THAT COVER EASTER AND CHRISTMAS.

EACH DEVOTIONAL HAS A TAKE AWAY IN FIVE WORDS OR LESS. THESE ARE GREAT TO PONDER!

EACH DAY'S FOCUS SCRIPTURE IS LISTED AT THE TOP.

THE REFERENCED SCRIPTURE IS IN BOLD FOR EASY READING!

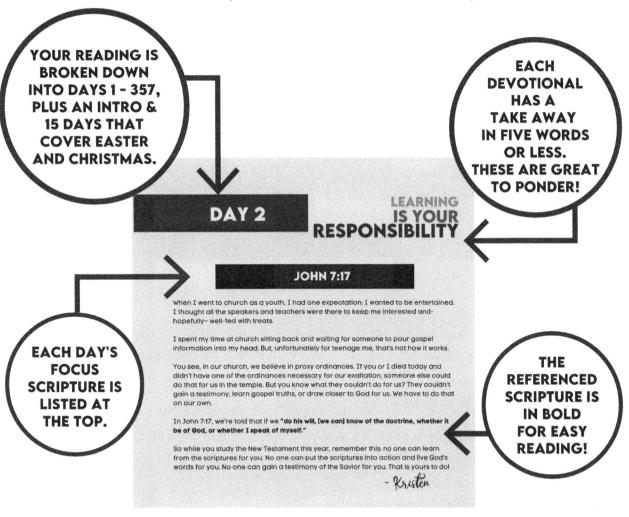

DAY 2

LEARNING IS YOUR RESPONSIBILITY

JOHN 7:17

When I went to church as a youth, I had one expectation: I wanted to be entertained. I thought all the speakers and teachers were there to keep me interested and- hopefully- well-fed with treats.

I spent my time at church sitting back and waiting for someone to pour gospel information into my head. But, unfortunately for teenage me, that's not how it works.

You see, in our church, we believe in proxy ordinances. If you or I died today and didn't have one of the ordinances necessary for our exaltation, someone else could do that for us in the temple. But you know what they couldn't do for us? They couldn't gain a testimony, learn gospel truths, or draw closer to God for us. We have to do that on our own.

In John 7:17, we're told that if we **"do his will, [we can] know of the doctrine, whether it be of God, or whether I speak of myself."**

So while you study the New Testament this year, remember this: no one can learn from the scriptures for you. No one can put the scriptures into action and live God's words for you. No one can gain a testimony of the Savior for you. That is yours to do!

- Kristen

NOW LET'S GET STARTED . . .

THE BIG PICTURE

The New Testament can be broken into four main sections: the biography of Jesus' life, the history of the Church's establishment, the letters of the apostles, and a revelation about the end of days.

SECTION 1 (BIOGRAPHY): The story of Jesus Christ's birth, life, death, resurrection, and ascension into heaven. <u>This includes the books of Matthew, Mark, Luke, and John.</u>

SECTION 2 (HISTORY): The history of how the apostles and early Christians established and spread the Church. <u>This includes the book of Acts</u> which can be divided into two sections. Chapters 1-12 are the acts of Peter, and chapters 13-28 are the acts of Paul.

SECTION 3 (LETTERS): Epistles (or letters) of encouragement and instruction from the apostles to individuals and congregations of Christians all over the world. <u>This includes the books from Romans to Jude</u>-- that's 21 of the 27 books in the New Testament!

SECTION 4 (REVELATION): The end of the New Testament is the record of John's vision of the end of the world and Christ's ultimate victory over evil. <u>This includes the book of Revelation.</u>

On the next page is a basic overview of the entire story of the New Testament.

1 Jesus' birth is foretold.

2 Jesus is born in Bethlehem.

3 Jesus' family flees to Egypt after King Herod decrees the death of all baby boys. They return to Nazareth a few years later.

4 Jesus teaches in the temple at twelve years old.

5 Jesus is baptized by His cousin, John the Baptist.

6 Jesus fasts for 40 days and is tempted in the wilderness.

7 Jesus performs His first miracle-- turning water into wine-- at a wedding feast in Cana.

8 Jesus calls His disciples.

9 Jesus performs miracles, teaches, and shares parables.

10 During Passover week, Jesus enters Jerusalem and has the Last Supper.

11 Jesus suffers in Gethsemane, is tried and convicted, and is crucified. He is resurrected three days later.

12 On the Day of Pentecost, the gift of the Holy Ghost is given to the apostles.

13 The apostles lead the church with Peter, James, and John at the head.

14 Christians are persecuted and some -- including Stephen-- are killed.

15 Saul is called to repentance and becomes Paul.

16 Peter receives a vision in which he learns that the gospel should go to Gentiles as well as Israelites.

17 Paul goes on missions to spread the gospel.

18 All of the apostles are killed and the keys of the priesthood are taken from the earth.

As you study the New Testament this year, you can refer back to this chart to figure out where you are in the big picture.

DAY 1

LUKE 18:22

The Savior invited those who listened to Him to **"Come, follow me."** He didn't say, "Come, listen to me." His invitation was one of action! So how do we apply that to our scripture study?

Before we dive into this year of study together, I'd like to share a simple technique my family loves to use. Imagine yourself holding a sword that is pointing to the sky. After reading the scriptures, look up at the sword tip and ask, "What was the POINT of that? What is God trying to teach me through this scripture?"

Next, look at your hand on the imaginary sword's handle and ask, "What does this have to do with my PERSONAL life?" Consider how well you're living the principle you just studied.

And last, look at the blade of the sword and ask yourself, "How can I add POWER to what I learned by taking action with it?"

As you understand the POINT of the scriptures, what they have to do with your PERSONAL life, and then figure out how to add POWER by taking action, you will actively follow Jesus instead of just listening to Him. And that is the kind of scripture study that can change your life in just minutes a day!

— Kristen

DAY 2

JOHN 7:17

When I went to church as a youth, I had one expectation: I wanted to be entertained. I thought all the speakers and teachers were there to keep me interested and– hopefully– well-fed with treats.

I spent my time at church sitting back and waiting for someone to pour gospel information into my head. But, unfortunately for teenage me, that's not how it works.

You see, in our church, we believe in proxy ordinances. If you or I died today and didn't have one of the ordinances necessary for our exaltation, someone else could do that for us in the temple. But you know what they couldn't do for us? They couldn't gain a testimony, learn gospel truths, or draw closer to God for us. We have to do that on our own.

In John 7:17, we're told that if we **". . .do his will, [we can] know of the doctrine, whether it be of God, or whether I speak of myself."**

So while you study the New Testament this year, remember this: no one can learn from the scriptures for you. No one can put the scriptures into action and live God's words for you. No one can gain a testimony of the Savior for you. That is yours to do!

– Kristen

DAY 3

ASK AND SEEK FOR YOURSELF

LUKE 11:10

Isn't it funny to think about prophets as little babies? But it's true! Just like everyone else, even prophets needed to be toddlers, kids, and teenagers!

This is also true spiritually: everyone has to start at the beginning! Even great prophets, loving leaders, and brilliant gospel teachers were born with no spiritual understanding. Everyone has to gain a testimony and learn the truth on their own.

But how?

The Savior teaches in Luke 11:10 that the first step is to ask. **"For every one that asketh receiveth; and he that seeketh findeth; and to him that knocketh it shall be opened."**

If we look for more knowledge of Jesus, if we look for a greater understanding of the New Testament, and if we look for spiritual growth, then our Savior promises us that it will be given to us. But He won't give it to us just because we want it. It takes work! It takes asking, seeking, and knocking.

Are we willing to put in the work to know the truth for ourselves?

– Cali

DAY 4

ACTS 17:11

I was walking into one of my classes in college when my phone started ringing. My best friend was calling, and she had the best news ever– she had just gotten engaged! I was so excited for her and wanted to ask a million questions, but I needed to get to my class on time, so I told her I'd call her back later.

As I sat in my physical science class, my brain was not focused at all! I knew I was supposed to be in class, but my brain wasn't ready to learn anything that day. Sure enough, my professor picked that day to do an in-class quiz, and I completely bombed it.

We can't just be in the right place in order to learn; our minds have to be engaged, too! Isn't that the same with our gospel learning? I can sit down, open my scriptures, scan the pages, and close the book, thinking I've studied my scriptures for the day. But if my mind isn't invested in what I'm doing, it doesn't help me much!

In Acts 17:11, we learn, **"These were more noble than those in Thessalonica, in that they received the word with all readiness of mind. . . ."** Their minds were ready! Taking just a minute before we open the scriptures to prepare our minds can make all the difference in our learning!

– Cali

DAY 5

MATTHEW 13:23

In high school, I used to dread getting graded essays back from my teachers. Even if most of the comments were good, any little suggestion, comment, or question made me feel as if I had completely messed up. I wanted my essay to be good just as I had written it!

I've learned that one of the best qualities is humility. It's the ability to take corrections with grace, and it's the ability to admit that we've been wrong. In the famous parable of the sower, our Savior teaches: **"He that received seed into the good ground is he that heareth the word, and understandeth it."**

Learning new principles, scriptures, and attributes of the Savior can be difficult if our hearts are hardened with pride and unwilling to change. But if we soften the ground with some humility, showing the Lord that we are willing to do whatever it takes to change, then the seed will always find good ground!

– Cali

DAY 6

YOU CAN MAKE A DIFFERENCE!

1 TIMOTHY 4:12

I want you to imagine something that I'm sure has never happened in your home: It's time for family scripture study, but no one seems to want to do it.

Some people are hiding in their bedrooms. Others are slouching on the couch staring at their phones. And to be honest, you don't feel like studying the scriptures either.

Now, in this totally fictional example, what do you do? Do you go to your room and use the extra time to scroll through social media? Or do you take responsibility for your whole family by being the one who makes sure scripture study happens?

Even though it might seem like someone else should take the lead on family scripture study, you have the power to do it too. You don't have to wait for someone else to call the family together. You can do it! The scriptures invite us to **". . .be thou an example of the believers,"** including in your own home!

– Kristen

DAY 7

HEBREWS 4:12

In the Old Testament, the Israelites were bitten by venomous snakes and offered a simple solution to save them. If they looked at the brass serpent Moses held up, they would be saved. And yet, in the Book of Mormon, we discover that many people refused to look because it seemed too easy.

Well, what if I told you that there was a simple way for you to be 59% less likely to look at pornography, 228% more likely to share the gospel with others, 30% less likely to feel lonely, and 61% less likely to smoke or drink?* Would you do it, no matter how simple? I hope so because there is a way to reap all these benefits with just minutes of effort a week.

That way is reading your scriptures at least four times a week. It sounds simplistic, but it has been proven through science and the Spirit. Hebrews 4:12 tells us, **"For the word of God is quick, and powerful, and sharper than any twoedged sword. . . ."**

It might sound too simple, but will you try it out this year? Will you make a goal (alone or with your family) to study the scriptures at least four times a week?

– Kristen

*"Bible Engagement & Social Behavior: How Familiarity & Frequency of Contact with the Bible Affects One's Behavior," Arnold Cole, Ed.D. Pamela Caudill Ovwigho, Ph.D., The Center for Bible Engagement.

DAY 8

MATTHEW 1:3, 5, 6

The New Testament starts with a seemingly dull family history: **"And Judas begat Phares and Zara of Thamar. . . and Booz begat Obed of Ruth. . . and David the king begat Solomon. . . . "**

Are you falling asleep yet? Don't! Because here is the fantastic thing. This family history tells the story of Jesus Christ's lineage, and that story is packed with awkward, inappropriate, and embarrassing stories. Jesus' family line included people who were deceptive, manipulative, and committed the worst of all sins. And yet, Christ was none of those things. In fact, He was the only perfect person to ever live on the earth.

Despite His earthly family history, Jesus lived up to the best of His heavenly family history and did not allow His ancestors' mistakes to define Him.

I love this reminder that no matter what our family– past or present– might look like, we get to determine our own story. And like Christ, we can make that story magnificent!

– Kristen

DAY 9

MATTHEW 1:21

When I was six years old, my mother asked me to carry a jar of mayonnaise into the garage. I held the jar in between my little hands and carefully went down the three steps into the garage. Suddenly I tripped and fell onto the hard concrete floor, and the mayonnaise jar smashed into pieces. One of those pieces became lodged in the base of my right pointer finger and blood began to pour from it.

I screamed for help, and my mom came running. She quickly realized this was a severe injury and took me straight to the hospital, where a doctor stitched my finger back together. That day I was not embarrassed to go to the hospital. In fact, I was desperate to go! I knew that was the only place my finger could be healed. And so I gladly went and allowed the doctors to fix my hand.

Why do you think we are happy to let a doctor heal our broken bodies, but we are hesitant to let the great Physician heal our souls? In Matthew 1:21, we are told that **"Jesus . . . shall save his people . . . ."** The Greek word in this sentence that is translated as "save" is σῴζω or "sozo" and can just as easily be translated to mean "to make well, heal, restore to health." What if instead of feeling ashamed when we come to Christ with our sins, asking for help to "save" us, we came to Him as our master Physician and asked Him to "heal us, make us well, and restore our spiritual health"? There is truly no shame in asking the master Healer for help!

- Kristen

DAY 10

BLESSINGS ALWAYS COME FROM PRAYING

LUKE 1:13

When I was five, my parents shared the devastating news that my dad was sick and might die. As soon as I heard this news, I went into my bedroom and returned a few minutes later, telling my parents, "Don't worry, Daddy will be fine. I just said a prayer."

Two years later, as a seven-year-old, I attended my dad's funeral. He had not been fine. The illness had taken hold of his body, and, despite two years of prayers, fasting, and blessings, he had died. At the time, I thought my prayers hadn't worked and that God simply didn't care.

Zacharias might have felt the same way. He and his wife Elizabeth prayed for many years for a son, yet that blessing had not come. But one day, as Zacharias was in the temple, an angel came to him and said, **"Fear not, Zacharias: for thy prayer is heard. . . ."** After years of waiting, God was answering Zacharias' prayer in just the way he'd hoped!

But what about those times when God doesn't answer our prayers the way we want? Does it mean God doesn't hear us or doesn't care? After years of asking myself that question, here is what I've learned. God answers every single prayer. Sometimes that is by giving us exactly what we request, and many times it is by giving us the strength to endure when our request is denied. Either way, our prayers are heard and answered by a loving God!

— Kristen

DAY 11

ASK CURIOUS QUESTIONS

LUKE 1:34

Has your life ever gone in a completely different direction than you had hoped or expected? When I first got the strong impression to quit my job that I loved so much, my brain wanted to turn to an "accusing" mindset. "Oh, I'm supposed to quit my job? Really? What will I do next? How is this going to work?" I wanted the Lord to answer all of my questions, and if He wouldn't, then I felt like I had good reason to be frustrated.

But don't you just love Mary's strong example? When she learned about a future that she very much had not expected for herself, she didn't turn accusatory. Instead, she turned curious. **"How shall this be?"**

I've found much more connection with God when I've focused on asking my questions with a "curious" mindset instead of an "accusing" mindset. "Oh, I'm supposed to quit my job? Wow, that is scary but I'm really interested to see what exciting things You have planned for my life next. Is there anything I need to do right now to help the plans go forward?"

In fact, I think our questions to the Lord tend to reveal a lot about our heart! Are we showing faith and trust or doubt and distrust with our questions about God's answers?

— Cali

DAY 12

LUKE 1:37

I love watching cooking competition shows. It fascinates me that the cooking show contestants are always given challenges that seem impossible: Cook with those ingredients? In that time frame? With that weird twist thrown at them? I always think, "There's no way they can actually do that!" And yet, they pretty much always accomplish their challenge.

I've also had plenty of projects to complete or deadlines to hit that seem impossible! And yet, when the time runs out, I've somehow made it happen.

On a much grander scale, do we actually believe what the angel Gabriel said to Mary? **"With God nothing shall be impossible."** Nothing is impossible with God! Not just cooking competitions or school deadlines but tasks that really seem impossible: forgiving someone for something that seemed unforgivable, fulfilling a church calling that seems overwhelming, learning how to enjoy motherhood, becoming a friend to someone you don't get along with, or learning a new skill at any age.

What seems truly impossible to you right now? When we turn to the Savior, I've learned that He can make anything possible.

— Cali

DAY 13

GIVE YOUR DREAMS TO GOD

LUKE 1:38

I was 19 years old when I got engaged to the love of my life. I had such big plans for us to start a family together, travel the world, and be insanely wealthy and happy. I would imagine that Mary, the mother of Jesus, had her own girlish plans like I did. She probably dreamed of the family that she and Joseph would start together, of the kind of home she would help create, of the happy future they would share.

And yet all of those dreams would have come crashing down when an angel told her that her life was taking a drastic turn. She was to become the mother of the Savior but it would be before her marriage took place. What would Joseph do? He likely wouldn't marry her, and she might find herself ostracized by her society and left to raise this child alone. What a different and horribly bleak future lay before her!

And yet, in answer to the angel, Mary said, **"Behold the handmaid of the Lord; be it unto me according to thy word."** No hesitation, no holding back, Mary was willing to do what God asked of her, no matter the consequences.

Are you and I willing to give up our own dreams and accept God's plans? Do we seek His will even if it is in direct opposition with our own? That's something worth considering today!

— Kristen

DAY 14

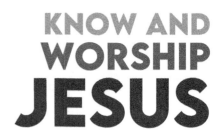
KNOW AND
WORSHIP
JESUS

LUKE 1:46

I've given birth to three little babies. Each time that I am pregnant, I try to do my due diligence to create a strong bond with my babies while they are still growing within me. I've sung songs, read books, and narrated my day, hoping that the little developing baby can hear my voice and learn to trust me before they are even born!

This is why I think it is one of the coolest things ever that Mary already had such a strong relationship with her Savior, before He was even born! Her encounter with the angel Gabriel was clearly not the first time that she had learned about a Messiah who would come to save the world. When speaking with her cousin Elizabeth, the pregnant Mary testified, **"My soul doth magnify the Lord. . . ."**

Mary had a strong relationship with her Savior before she learned about her unique role as His earthly mother! She already worshiped Him, knew about Him, and trusted Him.

No matter what callings, roles, or situations we will have here on the earth, we are always qualified enough to have a personal relationship with Jesus Christ!

— Cali

DAY 15

DON'T ACCEPT GOSPEL SPOON FEEDING

MATTHEW 2:4, 8

My first year away from home was, to be honest, spiritually shocking. I had grown up in a wonderful home where I was taught the gospel diligently. Good, daily spiritual habits had been ingrained in me thanks to wonderful parents. So it came as quite a surprise when I got to college and didn't have anyone feeding the gospel to me. I stopped studying my scriptures. My prayer habit started to decrease, and even my church attendance suffered. I quickly realized that even though I had been surrounded by the gospel my whole life I had never sought out a testimony for myself.

This is similar to what King Herod, ruler of Judea, did when he heard that a "King of the Jews" was born. He wanted to know about this possible enemy so he gathered his scribes and chief priests and **"...demanded of them where Christ should be born."** When wise men came to see the "King of the Jews," Herod **"...sent them to Bethlehem and said, Go and search diligently for the young child; and when ye have found him, bring me word...."** Herod wanted to know about Jesus, but he wasn't about to take action himself. Instead, he demanded information from others and was satisfied with that. Do we ever do the same? Do we sit in church or family scripture study and let others feed us the gospel? Or are we anxiously engaged in the learning process? I can say from personal experience, our active participation in seeking Jesus is 100% necessary to grow our own powerful testimonies.

— Kristen

GO WITH HASTE AND PONDER

LUKE 2:16, 19

Have you ever realized that you need entirely opposite directions at different moments in your life? One day recently, I was trying to clean and organize our house while also taking care of my kids. My kids repeatedly insisted I come "play house" with them, and I kept saying "no" because I was busy cleaning. Finally, the Spirit whispered, "Slow down, and go play with your kids." But then, on another day, I found all sorts of mindless things to distract myself with, and the Spirit whispered, "Get up and get some stuff done!"

I see these same opposites of QUICKLY and SLOWLY in our Savior's birth story. After hearing the angel, the shepherds **"came with haste"** to see the Savior and worship Him. Where do we need to add more "haste" in our lives? Where do we need to stop thinking about the logistics, the "what ifs," the things that seem more urgent at the time, and just GO?

And on the other hand, Mary kept all these things and **"pondered them in her heart."** Pondering requires slowing down and potentially even stopping other activities. When do we need to get off our phones, turn off the music, and just read, ponder, and pray without any time restrictions? Which do you need more of right now? To move a little faster or to slow down? The Spirit can always help us know which way to go!

— Cali

DAY 17

LUKE 2:20

Every time I upgrade my cell phone, I feel like I have the most incredible new gadget in the world! It looks so sleek, and whatever the new features are seem incredible. I want to show my new phone off to everyone and talk about the camera quality!

And then fast forward a month, and I've completely lost the "awe" with my phone. It doesn't seem quite so special or exciting anymore.

Look at how the shepherds reacted after seeing baby Jesus: **"And the shepherds returned, glorifying and praising God for all the things that they had heard and seen, as it was told unto them."**

They had come with great speed, and they left worshiping Jesus! Do we find that same kind of awe and joy in the Savior?

Sometimes when life gets serious and challenging, it's hard to remember that having the ability to worship our Savior should fill us with so much happiness and joy! How can you still find ways to be in "awe" of Jesus?

— Cali

DAY 18

LUKE 2:43

One time, my daughter got lost in our church building. She was three years old at the time and left me in the chapel, confident that she could find the way to her classroom on her own. By the time I realized she was missing, I couldn't see her in the chapel.

It took about two minutes to figure out where she was, get her calmed down, and take her to her correct classroom.

So can you imagine three days? Three whole days. **"The child Jesus tarried behind in Jerusalem; and Joseph and his mother knew not of it."**

I'm sure that Joseph and Mary panicked. I'm sure they felt fear. I felt panic and fear in that moment when I realized I didn't know where my sweet little daughter was!

But the answer to panic and fear is the same answer that Joseph and Mary were able to find: Jesus. Jesus brings peace, and He calms our fears. In those scary moments, when everything seems to be going wrong, we can find peace in the Savior, just like His parents did.

– Cali

DAY 19

DO THE
FATHER'S
BUSINESS

LUKE 2:49

Twelve-year-old Jesus taught His parents a beautiful lesson about His primary purpose on earth. When they found their son talking with and listening to the doctors in the temple, Jesus said, **"Wist ye not that I must be about my Father's business?"**

I remember volunteering for a political campaign a few years ago. While volunteering, I surprisingly felt overwhelmed with the Spirit. I felt a strong impression that what I was doing, while it didn't seem "spiritual," was actually a really good thing my Father in Heaven wanted me to do.

What other good things can we do with our time that might contribute to our being about our Father's business? I have found spiritual confirmations while getting a good education, caring for family members, excelling at work, having quality family time, and strengthening my talents. I think it's important to consider what it looks like to NOT be about our Heavenly Father's business, too. What is wasting my time? What is distracting me from the important stuff? What is driving the Spirit away?

Whatever I choose to do, I hope my Savior can see that I am always trying to be about my Father's business.

– Cali

DAY 20

LUKE 2:51

What is the difference between something being secret and something being sacred?

Growing up, I kept a lot of secrets. I knew who my best friend had a crush on. I didn't tell my mom about the candy stash I kept under my bed. And I tightly guarded my sister's secret about her most embarrassing moment. Why did I keep those secrets? Mostly because I would embarrass someone if I told them, or I would get someone in trouble. That is very different from the reason we don't speak about sacred things.

When Mary came home from her visit to the temple with her family, the scriptures say that Jesus' **"mother kept all these sayings in her heart."** It wasn't that no one COULD know what she felt or experienced, but that it was so precious to her she guarded that knowledge carefully and likely only shared it with those who SHOULD know.

Similarly, we don't share all of the details about the temple, not because it's embarrassing or would get anyone in trouble, but because it requires spiritual preparation to really "get" it. It is not a secret experience, but it is a sacred one. And like Mary, we guard that knowledge carefully because it is so precious to us.

— Kristen

DAY 21

DON'T SKIP LEG DAY!

LUKE 2:52

Have you ever seen a "Don't skip leg day" meme? Usually, it shows a man with a hugely muscular upper body whose humorously thin and untoned legs are poking out of a pair of shorts. It's a strange sight, but it teaches an important lesson: balance is essential to our growth!

The scriptures tell us that **"Jesus increased in wisdom and stature, and in favour with God and man."** In other words, He grew spiritually, physically, intellectually, and socially. Now imagine how different Jesus' mission would have been if He had only grown spiritually but ignored His physical health or intellectual and social skills.

Jesus used His physical health to help Him endure a forty-day fast. He used His social skills to relate to small children as well as Pharisees. He used His intellectual skills to outsmart even the shrewdest critics. Jesus was well-rounded, making Him an incredibly powerful teacher, friend, and example.

So the question for us is, what's our leg day? What's the thing we consistently put off doing? Today let's consider what we can do to be more well-rounded disciples of Christ and avoid growing to excess in some areas while shrinking in others.

– Kristen

DAY 22

JOHN 1:1

I took my first ballet class as an eighteen-year-old and was unprepared for the tights, leotards, and full-length mirrors. In each class, I would look at myself in the mirror and think, "You look nothing like a ballerina. You can't move like a ballerina. You look ridiculous."

Then one day, a professional ballerina came to class and practiced with us. As I watched her, I began to pretend that I was her. In my head, I would tell myself, "I am a professional ballerina. I move gracefully and look elegant as I dance."

And guess what? My technique and my presence improved overnight simply by changing the words I said to myself. When I began to think, talk, and act like a ballerina, I began to dance like one!

John wrote, **"In the beginning was the Word, and the Word was with God, and the Word was God."** Jesus Christ was that "Word," and He created the universe through the power of His words. He made mountains, rivers, animals, and planets with His words. What we say has significant power to create our experiences. We need to remember that God uses His words to lift, create, and improve. We should do the same! We cannot bully ourselves into becoming like God!

– Kristen

DAY 23

JOHN 1:8

Before a recent Disneyland trip, I went into full research mode. I made lists of all the places we needed to eat. I found itineraries to help us get the shortest wait times on all the rides. I learned which events were worth attending and which ones were a waste of time. And the trip went awesome! Everyone in my group kept turning to me with questions or looking to me for advice. I felt like my preparation paid off!

John wrote about John the Baptist when he said: **"He was not that Light, but was sent to bear witness of that Light."** It was John the Baptist's foreordained purpose to prepare followers for and then bear witness of Christ.

How can we be like John the Baptist? Christ couldn't just come into the world without having someone prepare the way. How can we better prepare for the things that matter most?

I'm probably not the only one who gets a million times more out of Sunday meetings when I do my scripture study to prepare. I feel refreshed after taking the sacrament when I readied my mind beforehand. I feel a greater purpose and direction when I prepare to start my day with a personal prayer. We can find small ways each day to prepare to add more spiritual light into our lives, just like John the Baptist!

– Cali

DAY 24

JOHN 1:10

I have a friend who has made it a point to never complain about the weather. Where I live in Arizona, there are certain summer months where it is very socially acceptable to complain about the scorching heat. However, this friend has always felt strongly that she would rather show gratitude than complain about the heat. She told me that anytime someone starts to complain about the triple-digit forecast, she begins a prayer of gratitude in her heart for being able to live in Arizona.

In his writings, John did not want us to forget one critical role the Savior had: Creator! **"He was in the world, and the world was made by him, and the world knew him not."**

Before Jesus Christ ever stepped foot on this earth, He created it. The power that He displayed long before being born into Bethlehem is incomprehensible.

We have a huge opportunity each day to show a little more gratitude for the world that Jesus created for us. Whether it's getting outside more often, being grateful for the beauty of the world in our prayers, being respectful of the waste we put into the world, or feeling gratitude for the area of the earth we live in, humbly recognizing Jesus Christ as the creator of this earth is a powerful way to worship Him!

– Cali

DAY 25

JOHN 1:12

One of my favorite Primary songs has always been "I Am a Child of God." I love to sing the lyrics that remind me I am Heavenly Father's daughter– they are powerful! This is why, when John 1:12 says that we can **"become the sons [and daughters] of God,"** it can be a bit confusing. Aren't we already? God is the Father of our spirits after all; He created us!

Well, it turns out that being a son or daughter of God is more than a matter of spiritual DNA. It is a matter of choosing to be spiritually "born again" by entering into covenants with Him.

When I was young, I would often proudly stand by my mother as people complimented her on her intelligence, strength, and kindness. I felt lucky to be her daughter because I had her DNA– I'd naturally become just like her, right?
But when I moved away from home, I realized I wasn't much like my mother at all. I struggled to keep my testimony strong, I was self-centered, and I wasn't all that smart either. I had to choose to become all the good things my mother embodies, and it took a lot of work! In fact, I'm still working on it.

God asks us to do the same with Him. He asks that we decide to become like Him so we can indeed be called His sons and daughters!

– Kristen

DAY 26

BE BORN
AGAIN
TODAY

JOHN 1:13

What is a significant spiritual memory that you will never forget? For me, it involves a testimony meeting at Young Women's camp being surrounded by trees and countless stars. But maybe for you, it was a moment on your mission, an experience at the temple, or a lesson at home.

While those big spiritual moments are eternally powerful, I've realized we can't live our lives drawing from a single experience when we felt the Spirit.

Some religions emphasize a one-time experience of being "born again." John wrote about this saying, **"Which were born, not of blood, nor of the will of the flesh, nor of the will of man, but of God."** But we know we need constant spiritual experiences to stay close to the Lord! In other words, we must be "born again" almost daily!

Have you been spiritually born of God yet. . . today?

If we haven't felt that spiritual moment yet, what can we do to invite the Spirit, draw closer to God, or renew our righteous desires today?

– Cali

DAY 27

BELIEF IS A GIFT

JOHN 1:36-37

Growing up, I always wished I had the gift of tongues. I thought it would be great to impress my friends by saying a sentence in Russian, another in Mandarin, and another in French. The gift of tongues– in my teenage opinion– was the best of all the spiritual gifts.

Now that I'm a bit older, I have recognized that many spiritual gifts are much more helpful than showing off my linguistic abilities. Some of Jesus' disciples manifested one such gift.

In John, we read the story of John the Baptist recognizing the Savior for who He truly was and saying, **"Behold the Lamb of God!"** Standing nearby were two men– likely John the Beloved and Andrew– who heard what John had said. Then the scriptural record states, **"and they followed Jesus."**

Without hearing a sermon, without seeing a miracle, simply with faith in someone else's testimony, they decided to follow Jesus. Later they learned for themselves. Later they interacted one-on-one with the Savior of the world and came to have their own burning testimonies. But at first, they had the gift of believing in the testimony of others– and that gift made all the difference!

– Kristen

DAY 28

JOHN 1:39

I've learned that you can't force a toddler to eat anything. No matter how much I may beg, bribe, or cheer, my kid is the one who has to decide whether or not they will take the bite and chew. They have complete agency on what they will do with their food.

Christ and Philip both say this simple phrase: **"Come and see."**

Unfortunately, no one can "come" nor "see" for us. We have to be the ones to use our agency to come closer to Christ and to see what He sees.

On the other hand, we can't force anyone around us, including our own children, to "come and see." The Savior performed miracles here on the earth and still needed to invite others to come and see what He had to offer. He couldn't force anyone to believe in His divine role, and neither can we.

Luckily, we can always focus on ourselves.

How will we come a little closer to the Savior and see a little more clearly what He has to offer, and how can we gently extend the same invitation to others?

— Cali

DAY 29

LOOK INWARD NOT OUTWARD

MATTHEW 3:7

Keeping the Sabbath day holy used to be the easiest commandment in the world for me to keep! Don't go shopping on Sunday and go to church? Check! Done. Super simple.

And then I started to learn how nuanced "keeping the Sabbath day holy" could be! Is my heart in the right place on Sundays? Am I filling the day with good things that draw me closer to my Savior? Am I serving others? Am I teaching my children? Am I avoiding media that drives away the Spirit? I realized that I couldn't rely on my outward actions to prove whether or not I was keeping this commandment.

Guess what the Pharisees and Sadducees did? They prided themselves on how strictly they kept every commandment and law. John the Baptist showed his frustration toward them: **"But when he saw many of the Pharisees and Sadducees come to his baptism, he said unto them, O generation of vipers, who hath warned you to flee from the wrath to come?"**

Are we putting our value in what we do rather than where our hearts are? It happens! But we can learn from the Pharisees and Sadducees that our hearts matter the most.

– Cali

DAY 30

MATTHEW 3:11

When I turned eight years old, I was so excited to be baptized. I couldn't wait for the chance to be 100% clean like a brand new baby. Honestly, the day's confirmation part was just an afterthought. I didn't get why the gift of the Holy Ghost mattered all that much.

But eight-year-old Kristen didn't understand the power of the Holy Ghost to make long-lasting change. John the Baptist explained to his followers that Jesus wouldn't just baptize people with water, **". . . he shall baptize you with the Holy Ghost, and with fire."**

That word "fire" is so instructive. The cleansing part of baptism is a temporary thing. As soon as we sin after baptism, we are no longer clean— until we repent. The baptismal ordinance is absolutely necessary, but the part most of us focus on, the cleansing portion, is not permanent.

That is why we need the baptism of fire— because it purifies us so that we no longer <u>want</u> to sin and become unclean. The Holy Ghost works <u>in</u> us and <u>with</u> us to change how we see, speak, and feel. He doesn't simply remove our sins; He changes us, so we no longer desire to sin!

- Kristen

DAY 31

MATTHEW 3:17

I once heard a teacher say that the Spirit usually whispers three different things to us while we listen to a spiritual message or read our scriptures: 1) something we should start, 2) something we should stop, and 3) something we should continue. This blew my mind because I think the third one is often overlooked.

Do you think God is pleased with anything you are doing in your life right now? Sometimes we focus so much on becoming better people that we forget we are already doing great things!

When Jesus chose to be baptized, God the Father expressed how pleased He was with His son's actions. **"This is my beloved Son, in whom I am well pleased."** It was the ultimate, divine 'pat on the back'. God knew He didn't need to correct anything that was going wrong, and He instead wanted to draw attention to what was already going right.

What is something good you are doing right now that you can continue to do? If you come up a little blank, try taking this question to the Lord in prayer and see what comes to mind. When we ask God what things we should CONTINUE doing, we give Him a chance to show us personally what He approves of in our lives.

— Cali

DAY 32

MARK 1:9-11

This is going to sound a bit over the top, but my husband and I were extremely excited when our son– who previously showed no interest in sports– signed up for the middle school cross country team. It was like we were brand new parents again! We started buying all the gadgets and researching what all the experts had to say. We were ecstatic. I signed my son up for a private training session with his cross country coach, hired a sports psychology coach to help him learn mental toughness, and took him to the local running store to buy the correct shoes for his stride despite the painful price tag.

Was it a bit much on our part? Totally! But with the combined help of his coaches, his dad, and me, he excelled. That is why I am grateful for the clarification the scriptures provide about who we have supporting us in our spiritual race of life. At Jesus' baptism, He went into the water, and then, **". . .he saw the heavens opened, and the Spirit like a dove descending upon him; And there came a voice from heaven, saying, Thou art my beloved Son, in whom I am well pleased."**

These verses make it clear that we don't just have one God helping us make it home to Him: we have a Heavenly Father, a Savior, and the Holy Ghost! And with the help of all three of these amazing Beings, we can have more than just a "good" life; we can have an excellent one!

- Kristen

DAY 33

WORK TO STAY CLEAN

MARK 1:41

I've noticed that my son always seems to be messy! No matter when we last ate food, he probably has something smeared on his cheek and crumbs in his hair. His hands are usually sticky, and there might also be colored marker streaks on his arms. But he doesn't seem to care! I'm constantly wiping, washing, and scrubbing, and he usually gets more annoyed with me trying to clean him than he does with the mess itself.

When the Savior saw a man with leprosy, the man pleaded for the Savior to clean him. **"And Jesus, moved with compassion, put forth his hand, and touched him, and saith unto him, I will; be thou clean."**

The man recognized his disease and desired to become clean! This meant that the Savior could heal him. But "be thou clean" also sounds like a command or invitation to keep up the washing in the future. The Lord won't come and cleanse us of our sins against our will. He works where He is invited and believed.

I know that as my little boy grows and matures, he will start washing his own hands or cleaning up his spills after eating. He'll learn not only how to become clean but how he can maintain that cleanliness throughout the week. And in the same way, the Savior can cleanse us spiritually and invite us to stay clean in the future!

– Cali

DAY 34

HAVE PATIENCE WITH ROUGH EDGES

LUKE 3:5

"I'm really awkward." "I'm just a late person." "I couldn't stay calm any longer." "I completely messed up." Life is messy, and we often act pretty messily, too! In Luke 3:5, we learn that through Christ, **"Every valley shall be filled, and every mountain and hill shall be brought low; and the crooked shall be made straight, and the rough ways shall be made smooth."**

If the Savior can make mountains to be brought low, He probably can take away bad habits or annoyances that we have too. Jesus can help us become more patient. He can make up for the awkwardness we feel when talking to someone new. He can help us have compassion instead of constantly criticizing. He can help us kick that habit of gossiping.

Every little crooked and rough way on our souls will eventually be made smooth! But just like a river carving its way through a mountainside, this process takes time. These changes usually happen inch by inch, day by day, even year after year.

Are we willing to stick with the Lord through the entire process? The "way that we are" isn't how we will stay because mountains constantly change. But we can trust and have faith that eventually, one day, in this life or the next, all of our rough ways will be made smooth.

— Cali

DAY 35

LUKE 3:8

I have to admit that I spent much of my growing years with a slight sense of superiority. Whenever I got into a spiritual discussion with someone, my goal was to prove how much more I knew than they did because I had access to the fullness of the gospel. I was pompous and downright annoying. Luckily, in my twenties, I was introduced to a Christian friend who attended a non-denominational church. She was so humble and kind that I was compelled to listen rather than prove a point whenever we had spiritual discussions.

Over the course of many of these conversations, I realized something that shocked me: she knew Jesus and loved Jesus better than I ever had. Despite my membership in what I had always been so proud to call the "one true Church," she had been living a more Christlike life than I had. I realized that being a member of the true church wasn't enough. I had to become like Jesus for that membership to mean much of anything.

John the Baptist warned the prideful Israelites, **". . . begin not to say within yourselves, We have Abraham to our father: for I say unto you, That God is able of these stones to raise up children unto Abraham."** In other words, don't get complacent because you belong to the right church. Who you actually are is what matters to God.

— Kristen

DAY 36

MATTHEW 4:1, 10

Have you ever read the account of Jesus being **"led up of the Spirit into the wilderness to be tempted of the devil"**? Satan's efforts seem almost pitiful. How did he think he could win by encouraging Jesus to eat bread or throw Himself off the temple?

But Satan had thousands of years to prepare for this moment, and if he could get Jesus to commit just one little sin, the entire Plan of Salvation would be ruined! So instead of taking these temptations at face value, could they be about something else? Instead of the temptations being about eating bread, owning the world, or converting people quickly, perhaps it was a temptation of self. Maybe it was the temptation for Jesus to– just one time– ignore God's will and use His gifts, talents, and abilities for His own good and glory.

Are we ever tempted to do that? Do we want to use our time and gifts to serve ourselves more often than we serve God?

If so, Jesus' response to Satan's last temptation is incredibly instructive for us. He said, **"Get thee hence, Satan: for it is written, Thou shalt worship the Lord thy God, and him only shalt thou serve."** Jesus refused to capitulate to Satan's temptations because He had one God. It wasn't Himself or His own comfort; it was and always will be Heavenly Father.

– Kristen

DAY 37

COMMUNE
WITH
GOD

MATTHEW 4:2

"When was the last time you had a conversation with God?" I had a Sunday School teacher ask that question, and I couldn't stop thinking about it. My prayers up to that point had mainly been listing off a bunch of things I'm grateful for, followed by a bunch of stuff I want.

But the idea of having an actual conversation with God during my prayers sounded interesting! That is what it really means to "commune"– talking with God in an intimate and personal way. I decided to try it that night. Instead of just talking, I also tried listening and responding. It was an incredible experience, and it has become something I've continued to try to include in my prayers ever since!

Christ communed with God, too! **"And when he had fasted forty days and forty nights, and had communed with God, he was afterwards an hungered, and was left to be tempted of the devil."** Christ, our perfect example, left the crowds and His friends to be alone and commune with God. What can we do better to make time to commune with God regularly? Get up a little earlier? Stay up later? Set a specific time? Be more flexible? Even though this can be tricky to find time for, we can follow the Savior's example of making time to be alone, even when other people need and want our help.

– Cali

DAY 38

MATTHEW 4:10

I recently made it a personal goal to spend less time on my phone during the day. But even though I had made the goal, I found that whenever I had a spare moment, I'd pull my phone out of my pocket and start scrolling.

I realized that the only way I was going to improve was if I got rid of the temptation! I plugged my phone into the charger in a different room, and my success rate suddenly improved!

It's not a sin to be tempted. Christ, the perfect person, was tempted in three different ways.

But we can always control how we react to those temptations. The Savior gave us the perfect example. He responded with: **"Get thee hence, Satan."**

He got rid of the temptation. He asked it to leave. He made it so that He wouldn't have to endure the temptation for too long. And we can try this too! What is your biggest temptation right now that you've been trying to resist? How can you work to eliminate the temptation instead of trying to resist it all the time?

– Cali

DAY 39

LUKE 4:1, 32

I can still remember the moment the Spirit left the room. I was sitting on my couch chatting with a friend who wasn't a member of the Church. She asked me a question about the gospel that I didn't have an answer to, so I started sharing my personal thoughts on the matter.

I could literally feel the moment I stopped speaking with the Spirit and started speaking from my head. I finished my sentence and then didn't say anything else on the matter. I realized I didn't have the Holy Ghost ratifying what I was saying, so it wasn't worth saying.

The power of the Holy Ghost in our missionary work is essential. The scriptures tell us that **"Jesus being full of the Holy Ghost . . . was led by the Spirit . . . And [the people] were astonished at his doctrine: for his word was with power."** Jesus spoke with the power of the Holy Ghost, and it was so impressive that the people who heard were astonished! Not just impressed, not just touched, but astonished!

I love this reminder that it's not our job to convert people. It's not our job to change them. All we can do is seek the Spirit when we share the gospel. The Spirit does the hard work of reaching others' hearts so that they can feel the power of our words.

– Kristen

DAY 40

LUKE 4:3, 9

Middle school was rough for me. I struggled to find my place, felt uncomfortable in my skin, and desperately wanted others to like me. Because of this, I spent a lot of time thinking, "If I buy this shirt, I'll look cute, and everyone will like me!" Or, "If I'm funny enough that people laugh, then I'll become popular!" If. If. If.

I think "if" might be one of Satan's favorite words because he always uses it on us. "If you're really free, why do you have to keep commandments?" "If you wear the new (totally immodest) fashion trends, you'll finally be popular and happy." "If you want that boy/girl to like you, you better loosen your standards."

In fact, when Satan was trying to tempt the Savior, he used an "if" temptation. He said twice, **"If thou be the son of God. . . ."** and then offered a temptation to "alleviate" that doubt.

But that is not how God speaks to us. Our God is NOT a God of doubt but a God of confidence. At Jesus' baptism, God didn't say, "This might be my Beloved Son if He makes the right choices." No! He said, "This is my beloved Son, in whom I am well pleased" (Matthew 3:17). So when you and I find ourselves doubting our worth and our identity, we can be sure of who is talking. . . and it's definitely not our loving Father!

- Kristen

DAY 41

LUKE 5:11

The Savior personally invited Peter, Andrew, James, and John to come and join Him in His ministry. Their response? **"And when they had brought their ships to land, they forsook all, and followed him."**

They forsook (forgot) all the little things they were occupied with in their fishing, and they followed Jesus. What a great formula for turning to the Lord! Forsake and follow.

Would Jesus have more room in your life if you forgot about all of your temptations, distractions, or worries? Would it be easier to remember Him if you stopped worrying about all the ways you fall short? Forsaking can be so freeing!

And with that freedom comes more energy to follow the Lord! We can get up and act as He would. We can find someone new to serve today, and we can help Him work more miracles!

– Cali

DAY 42

EVEN WHEN IT'S UNCOMFORTABLE

LUKE 5:31

The year 2012 was a tough one for me. I was dealing with untreated Obsessive Compulsive Disorder, I'd recently had a miscarriage, and I was now pregnant and terribly ill. Suffice it to say, I was not on my A-game; but to put it more bluntly, I was a mental, emotional, and physical mess. Luckily for me, I was assigned to wonderful visiting teaching sisters.

They came over with surprise meals, ate lunch with me, talked me into park play dates, insisted on watching my son so I could go to doctors' appointments without him, and even got me to go out for a girls' night. No matter how awkward, uncomfortable, or off-putting I was, they would not give up on me and brought so much light into my very dark life. To this day, though I don't have contact with them, I consider these women two of my best friends. They understood the words of the Savior when He said, **"They that are whole need not a physician; but they that are sick."**

I'm sure I wasn't a lot of fun to be around. I'm sure they had plenty of other people they would have enjoyed hanging out with more. But physically, emotionally, and mentally, I was sick, and despite my best efforts to hide it, they seemed to know it. They ministered to me and loved me just as the Savior would. And for that, I will always be grateful.

- Kristen

DAY 43

FOCUS ON BUILDING FAITH

JOHN 2:23-24

The story of the Israelites escaping Egypt always confused me. They had walked across the Red Sea with walls of water on each side. They had seen the ten plagues that helped them gain their freedom. They had sign after sign to prove that the God of Israel was real and powerful, yet they still struggled to believe.

During Jesus' life, He performed miracles that astonished people. The scriptures tell us that **". . . many believed in his name when they saw the miracles which he did. But Jesus did not commit himself unto them. . . ."**

That word "commit" is interesting. It is translated from the Greek word Πιστεύω which we would pronounce as "pisteuō" and means to have faith or trust in something or someone. Jesus didn't trust in the people who were converted by His miracles because– as we can see from the ancient Israelites– miracles aren't what lead to lasting conversion.

It turns out that it is simple faith– faith to read our scriptures every day, faith to say our prayers, faith to attend Church every week– that leads to the greatest miracle of all: complete conversion to Jesus Christ.

– Kristen

JOHN 3:14

Every time I read the story of Moses raising the brass serpent, I get a bit angry. In the face of death, many Israelites were too stubborn to turn their heads in the hopes of being saved!

I'm afraid I'm sometimes a little like those stubborn Israelites. Sometimes I ignore the things that can most easily "save" me– regular scripture study, prayer, temple attendance– because I'm looking for a solution that "makes sense."

The truth is that salvation through Jesus doesn't make sense to the logical mind!

It can't be that easy. It can't be possible that a perfect Brother like He is would give up His life to save mine. But it's true. **". . . as Moses lifted up the serpent in the wilderness, even so must the Son of man be lifted up. . . ."**

So, even though it might not make sense, we need to do all the little things the Savior asks us to do. We need to attend church, read our scriptures, pray daily, serve others, and more. They might seem inconsequential on their own, but those small actions added together will help keep us on the covenant path back to our Savior.

– Kristen

DAY 45

One time, I was feeling sick. It wasn't anything terrible, just a small cold; but I realized that battling this minor cold made almost every aspect of my day more difficult. When it was time for me to pull out my scriptures, I complained in my head. It wasn't because I didn't want to, but because I felt so "blah" from dealing with the sickness all day!

I had some back and forth in my head about whether or not I should read my scriptures because I knew I would feel a little better afterward. And then, I thought, "Wait! Christ can help me." I said a small prayer asking for help to have the DESIRE to read my scriptures, and then I got off the couch. And guess who pretty quickly had a strong desire to read her scriptures and had a super meaningful study session? It was awesome!

"Whosoever believeth in him should not perish, but have eternal life." Sometimes the "perishing" that Jesus saves us from is real and dramatic. But more often than not, we need to be saved from a day where we just feel "blah" and unmotivated. Living in a fallen world, the Savior can keep us from perishing in whatever difficult circumstances we find ourselves in, no matter how small they may seem! We just need to believe and ask.

— Cali

DAY 46

SEND A VALENTINE TO GOD

JOHN 3:16

Have you ever received a fantastic Valentine's Day gift from someone you love? My absolute favorite Valentine's Day gifts probably don't look that exciting to anyone else. I remember when my mom ding-dong-ditched some of my favorite cereal on our porch with a corny note. I remember laughing and watching a movie with my husband. I remember a sweet hand-drawn picture from one of my kids. I loved them all because they showed how much that person cared about me in a simple and sincere way.

God has given us the best Valentine's gift ever! It is truly unmatchable and perfect. This gift also shows a significant sacrifice on the Father's part to give us this gift. **"For God so loved the world, that he gave his only begotten Son, that whosoever believeth in him should not perish, but have everlasting life."** Heavenly Father loves us so much that He sacrificed His only begotten Son so that we could become what He ultimately wants us to become. Unlike earthly gifts that sometimes fall short of our expectations, the gift of Jesus Christ will never leave us wanting for anything else!

And if a big "thank you" doesn't feel quite adequate to show God the Father how you feel about this perfect gift, then we can give our own valentine back to Him! What could we possibly give to our Heavenly Father? "If ye love me, keep my commandments." (John 14:15)

— Cali

DAY 47

JESUS
WILL COME
TO HELP

JOHN 4:4

Christ was traveling. **"And he must needs go through Samaria."**

But guess what? Christ did NOT need to go through Samaria! In fact, the Jews avoided Samaria because the Samaritans were considered such religious and political outcasts.

So why did Christ feel like He needed to go through Samaria? That's where He met the woman at the well and declared His divinity to her in a moment when she needed to know of His love. Jesus knows our life situations. He knows where we are and what we need in each moment. He felt compelled to be in Samaria at that well, no matter how little sense it made to anyone else.

So what does that mean for you and me? Christ feels the need to come to each of us in our circumstances and in our troubles. He wants to come to us, just as we are, as we go about our daily routine.

Jesus wants to help us. And so we can expect Him to be near even in those mundane moments when we seem just to be getting our daily water at the well.

— Cali

DAY 48

BELIEVE OTHERS OR EXPERIENCE YOURSELF

JOHN 4:39, 42

The woman that Christ had met at the well bore a strong testimony of Jesus to the people in Samaria. People seemed to have two main responses to her powerful words. First, some Samaritans believed in the Savior purely after hearing the woman's testimony! They even begged the Savior to stay with them for a couple of days to teach them. **"And many of the Samaritans of that city believed on him for the saying of the woman, which testified, He told me all that ever I did."**

The second group of Samaritans had to wait until they heard the Savior and felt the Spirit themselves. Then they were converted, too. **"And said unto the woman, Now we believe, not because of thy saying: for we have heard him ourselves, and know that this is indeed the Christ, the Saviour of the world."**

We know that these are actually two different spiritual gifts. Some people are given the gift of believing in other people's words, and others are given the gift of knowing through the Spirit. Which group would you have been in? Do you know which gift you have? Is it easy for you to believe other people's testimonies and spiritual experiences? Or do you need to search out the truth yourself? Or maybe a combination of both? We all can have the same end result of full conversion to the Savior, but it's okay to take different paths to get there, just like the Samaritans!

– Cali

DAY 49

JOHN 4:50, 53

When my oldest son was in fifth grade, he participated in a three-day school camp in the woods of Colorado. Sending him off was such a strange feeling. He had no phone, so I had no direct access to him for three whole days. No matter how much I wanted to talk to him, make sure he was eating his vegetables, or check that he was getting enough sleep, the distance between us left me powerless! This is one of many reasons I find it so amazing that Jesus' influence in our lives isn't affected by distance.

Jesus was in Galilee when a man came to him, desperate for the Savior to heal his dying son. The trip would take almost an entire day, but the man still hoped that the Savior would arrive in time to provide a miracle. However, Jesus didn't come with the man. He told him, **"Go thy way; thy son liveth."** The man, believing his words, left immediately for home. The next day when the father reached home he was greeted by his servants, who told him that his son had been healed. Quickly he asked them when it had happened and when they told him, **"the father knew that it was at the same hour, in which Jesus said unto him, Thy son liveth. . . ."**

Jesus was a day away, yet He healed this young boy. This means we don't need to be in Christ's presence for Him to heal us. Like this father, we simply have to believe for Christ's healing power to take hold in our lives.

– Kristen

DAY 50

BE WILLING TO WAIT

MATTHEW 5:12

Would you eat one marshmallow now or two marshmallows later? I can already tell you that one of my kids would choose to wait for the two marshmallows, and the other would gobble up the first one before I even finished the question.

Let's consider this marshmallow experiment in the spiritual sense. Has it ever seemed like people who leave the church have a lot of good things going on in their lives? People stop living the commandments one by one or leave the church altogether; and they seem super happy, successful, rich, and indulgent. When that happens, I think a part of us goes, "huh."

But Christ has told us that this is what happens! People do "find joy" in things other than the gospel. Not lasting, peaceful happiness, but some immediate joy. And in Matthew 5:12, Christ teaches, **"Rejoice, and be exceedingly glad: for great is your reward in heaven."** Are we "spiritually mature" enough to not need our rewards right now? Can we wait and endure? Can we find joy in our journey? Can we be okay with being persecuted and poor if that is part of our path?

If we can endure some time feeling a little hungry right now looking at the marshmallow that others are enjoying, then later we can receive unspeakable rewards in heaven!

— Cali

DAY 51

MATTHEW 5:14

I once worked as a recruiter for a temporary employment agency in Washington, D.C. I had several wonderful coworkers but quickly discovered that I was the only member of the Church among them.

When my coworkers found out about my Church membership, they started asking me questions about the Church, our doctrine, and especially about things they thought were "weird."

Without intending to, I became the resident expert on all things Christian and The Church of Jesus Christ. It sometimes made me uncomfortable, but it also reminded me of what the Savior said: **"Ye are the light of the world. A city that is set on a hill cannot be hid."** I find it interesting that Jesus didn't say "shouldn't be hid," but "cannot be hid." And I have found it to be true!

Once you join Christ's church, it's as if you have crossed a line and have become His representative. We must be ready to share that light, our knowledge, and our testimony at all times– not only in what we say but in how we act!

As members of Christ's church, we cannot hide our light, so it is our job to ensure our light always points others to Jesus!

– *Kristen*

DAY 52

REMOVE YOUR STUMBLING BLOCKS

MATTHEW 5:29

I became friends with someone my mom was concerned about during my childhood. I can still remember the day my mom and I sat in front of my school, and she asked me to end this friendship. At first, I was offended– I loved this person! I thought they were great! But as we drove away from the school, I had another feeling come into my heart: my mom was right.

I slowly pulled back from this friendship and became friends with a new group of wonderful people. As the years continued on, I began to see the wisdom of my mom's request: my dear friend continued making poor choices until they were trapped by them. While I hoped I would have been strong enough to choose my own path even if we had still been close friends, I wasn't sure I would have.

It turns out that my mom had given me the same advice that the Savior gave to His followers, **". . . if thy right eye offend thee, pluck it out, and cast it from thee. . . ."** The original Greek word that was translated as "offend" actually has a much deeper meaning. The word σκανδαλίζω (skandalizó) means to put a stumbling block or impediment in the way. So the Savior was saying that if you see a stumbling block in your path, get rid of it, rather than forcing yourself to climb over it!

– Kristen

DAY 53

MATTHEW 5:43-44

My teacher at church invited the class to think of the person who made them feel the most angry. I immediately had a name come to mind. The teacher then invited us to try to sincerely pray for that person. I was shocked to discover that I couldn't do it! I was so angry that I couldn't even say a prayer on their behalf.

I worked for a long time to have my heart softened toward this individual. When I got to the point where I could sincerely pray for them, I realized that even though this person hadn't changed, I had changed for the better.

When Christ preached His Sermon on the Mount, He first talked about the lower law. **"Ye have heard that it hath been said, Thou shalt love thy neighbour, and hate thine enemy."** Doesn't the world teach that lower commandment all the time? Love everyone, but hate the people who aren't nice to you.

But Christ teaches us the higher law. This is the law He hopes the more spiritually mature individuals will follow. **"But I say unto you, Love your enemies, bless them that curse you, do good to them that hate you, and pray for them which despitefully use you, and persecute you."** When we love our enemies, it doesn't change them; it changes us!

— Cali

LUKE 6:2

Christ made a lot of traditional Jewish leaders angry with His apparent disregard for the "rules of the Sabbath." **"And certain of the Pharisees said unto them, Why do ye that which is not lawful to do on the sabbath days?"**

Jesus had gotten food for His hungry disciples and used His healing power to restore a withered hand on the Sabbath. I can't help but think of what these people who criticized Him missed out on because they were focused too much on the rules! Had miracles been avoided because of their devotion to the Law over the Lord?

What blessings might we miss out on during the Sabbath because we are more concerned about following the rules (or even about appearing to follow the rules)? Are we missing out on visiting others and having uplifting and meaningful interactions with them? Are we missing out on purposeful family time? Are we missing out on additional personal gospel study? Are we missing out on redeeming our ancestors? Are we missing out on devoting more time to our callings? Are we resting too much on the Sabbath instead of making it the Lord's day? Christ showed the Pharisees that they were missing out on so much goodness because they were too concerned with the rules! So how could your Sabbath day be a little more about doing what Jesus would do?

— Cali

DAY 55

LUKE 6:12-13

I am not fantastic at praying. I'm great at remembering to pray, but the content and feeling of my prayers leave much to be desired.

In fact, I often find myself at the end of a prayer having no memory of what I said. Have you ever felt the same? It is a weakness I am working on constantly because I know that prayer is powerful. Jesus, who had such a close relationship with God that He always did His Father's will, still felt the need for prayer as He prepared to call His disciples.

The scriptures tell us that, **". . . he went out into a mountain to pray, and continued all night in prayer to God. And when it was day, he called unto him his disciples: and of them he chose twelve, whom also he named apostles."**

I love this reminder that even the Savior of the world needed hours of prayer to make an important decision. I also love this unspoken example that prayer can be so meaningful that it becomes an hours-long conversation with our Father rather than a few sleepy moments before hopping into bed.

I think we could all seek to pray more like Jesus!

– Kristen

DAY 56

DON'T BECOME BEAM-FOCUSED

LUKE 6:41-42

When teaching the Sermon on the Mount, the Savior said, **"And why beholdest thou the mote that is in thy brother's eye, but perceivest not the beam that is in thine own eye? . . . cast out first the beam out of thine own eye, and then shalt thou see clearly to pull out the mote that is in thy brother's eye."**

Every time I have read that, I've thought about how often I have focused on someone's faults without realizing that I have plenty of my own to work on. But is the opposite true as well?

I have a dear friend who is constantly lifting me. Every time we chat, she tells me how wonderful I am, how fun I am, how everything-good-you-can-think-of I am. Can you tell why I love to be with her?! I feel the same way about her, and I often try to tell her so, but she rarely believes me. She is sure that she is lazy, dull, out of style, and so many other awful things that she can't accept my honest compliments. She is so aware of the beam in her own eye (aka her perceived faults) that she can't see all the great things I can see.

So, should we recognize the beams in our own eyes? Yes! But should we become so focused on them that we can't see anything else? Not at all! God loves us, beams and all, and so should we.

— Kristen

DAY 57

PEOPLE SHOULD COME BEFORE POSSESSIONS

MATTHEW 6:19-21

Last summer, our family borrowed my brother-in-law's four-wheeler and trailer for a camping trip. We thought it would be a blast to ride the four-wheeler around the woods and explore.

It was loads of fun until I tried to drive the four-wheeler off the trailer on the second day. The trailer tipped, and the four-wheeler's wheels went crashing through the wood bottom of the trailer. It was a scary moment, and I felt awful about the damage I'd caused.

When my husband called his brother to tell him what happened, his first question was, "Is Kristen okay?!" It was such a relief that the cost of repairing the trailer didn't matter to him nearly as much as my safety!

The Savior said, **"Lay not up for yourselves treasures upon earth . . . But lay up for yourselves treasures in heaven . . . For where your treasure is, there will your heart be also."**

That brings up a great question: do we ever become possessed by our possessions? Do we ever treat them as more important than the people in our lives?

– Kristen

DAY 58

DON'T WASTE TIME WORRYING

MATTHEW 6:34

One of the things about having anxiety is that you spend a lot of time thinking about the past and the future.

I have spent hours agonizing over a past conversation and all the things I should or should not have said. Or I've spent hours worrying about an upcoming event and all the awful things that might happen. Anxiety basically means a lot of wasted time living in the land of "what ifs."

Jesus spoke to His disciples, saying, **"Take therefore no thought for the morrow: for the morrow shall take thought for the things of itself. Sufficient unto the day is the evil thereof."**

I love this reminder that, while proper planning for life is good, we don't need to waste our lives worrying about the past or the future. They will take care of themselves, and our worrying about them won't make them any better!

– Kristen

DAY 59

MATTHEW 7:14

I used to think the Celestial Kingdom would have maybe a dozen people. I was sure that it was pretty near impossible to get into whether you were a member of God's church or not. Reading the words that Jesus taught, **". . . strait is the gate, and narrow is the way, which leadeth unto life, and few there be that find it,"** just seemed to confirm my thinking.

I thought that if both the gate and the pathway were so narrow, it could only fit a very few people in eternity– even if there were a lot of us on the covenant path in mortality.

That is why I was so excited the day I read the words of Elder Bruce R. McConkie, who said, ". . . If you're on [the covenant] path and pressing forward, and you die, you'll never get off the path. There is no such thing as falling off the straight and narrow path in the life to come."*

Did you catch that? If you and I are on the covenant path when we die, we will not leave it! That is just about the best news ever! So is the Celestial Kingdom possible for you and me? Absolutely! It's not only possible, it's entirely probable if we can just stay on the path until the day we die!

– Kristen

* Bruce R. McConkie, "The Probationary Test of Mortality," Address given at Univ. of Utah, Jan. 1982, p.2; See JD 1:6

DAY 60

MATTHEW 7:16

I want you to imagine that you're walking in an orchard filled with a variety of fruit trees. As you're walking through the orchard, you decide that you want an orange; which tree would you go to? An orange tree– right! Let's say you change your mind and decide you want an apple; which tree would you go to? An apple tree– right!

A tree is known by the fruit it produces. And so are we.

When Jesus taught the Sermon on the Mount, He said that **"Ye shall know them by their fruits."**

This is an excellent opportunity to consider what our fruits are. If someone wanted to feel loved and understood, would they come to you? If they needed help for a job no one else would help with, would they know they could count on you? Would they seek you out if they wanted to feel uplifted by kindness?

Today is a great day to consider what fruits you're producing and what people know they can expect from you.

– Kristen

DAY 61

MATTHEW 7:23

It's pretty easy to say, "Let's serve and love everyone!" It's a lot more difficult to love the person who said something rude about your spouse or to serve someone when you don't feel like you have any extra time.

Jesus tells us that if we think we can just say the right answers without taking action, He will say, **"I never knew you."** Take a look at the footnote for Matthew 7:23 to see what Joseph Smith translated "I never knew you" to mean. Jesus really wants us to know Him!

Do we only know ABOUT the Savior, or are we increasingly coming to know Him? Can we answer all the questions about what Jesus would do, or are we out there actually doing what He would do?

I have found that when I actually try to apply all of His teachings, especially the powerful ones we have been studying in the Sermon on the Mount, I feel like I know Jesus even more! If we want to get to know Jesus on a more personal level, we need to try doing the things He would be doing!

— Cali

DAY 62

MATTHEW 7:25

Arizona has the best monsoons in the summertime! If you've never experienced a monsoon in the desert, it's always a surprise what kind of storm you will get. Sometimes the monsoon starts with a big dust storm, lowering visibility and covering everything with a thin layer of dirt. Other times, the wind is intense, uprooting trees and flipping trampolines. And other times, the rain seems never-ending, flooding parks and streets.

In our spiritual lives, monsoons and other types of storms are unavoidable. The Savior teaches that the rain will come, the floods will rise, and the wind will blow, no matter what. At different times in our lives, we'll have more rain where trials keep pouring in. Other times, the wind will blow, making it hard to stay focused on the gospel. And other times, the flood waters rise, almost suffocating us with competing priorities. Some people have bigger and scarier intense storms that pass in a flash. Others have storms that brew for a long time. But we all have them!

The difference, of course, is Christ. **"And the rain descended, and the floods came, and the winds blew, and beat upon that house; and it fell not: for it was founded upon a rock."** We can go through hard things with Him or without Him. We don't need to lose faith just because the storm comes; He said it would. But Jesus will love us and help us grow through it.

— Cali

DAY 63

MATTHEW 7:29

When President Russell M. Nelson was first called as the President of The Church of Jesus Christ of Latter-day Saints, I remember being impressed as he spoke. He had always been a great speaker, but suddenly he had this spiritual power that I could feel in every word he said! A friend reminded me that what I was noticing was the mantle of his calling which gave him new authority to speak and prophesy to the entire world.

After Christ gave His beautiful Sermon on the Mount, the people listening to Him were astonished because He taught with authority. **"For he taught them as one having authority, and not as the scribes."**

We can teach and speak with authority, too! When we pray, ponder, read the scriptures, and connect with God often and in meaningful ways, then we can act and give guidance with true godly authority.

Whether it's for your calling at church, conversations with your children, or seeking revelation for yourself, you can act and speak with the authority of God when you make and keep priesthood covenants!

— Cali

DAY 64

GOD'S GOODNESS IS IMMEDIATE

MATTHEW 8:3

During my teenage years, I had an undiagnosed food intolerance that eventually left me only able to eat white rice, white bread, and rice cereal. I hated it! Can you imagine life without ice cream, pizza, or even vegetables for years?!

In frustration, I would read stories in the scriptures like that of the leper who approached the Savior, begging for Him to perform a healing miracle. Jesus recognized the faith in this good man, laid His hand on him, and **"... immediately his leprosy was cleansed."**

I longed to have lived during the time of Jesus so that I could approach Him and receive "immediate" healing. I didn't know or realize that even though my healing was not immediate, His blessings were.

As I waited for my miracle, God blessed me with increased faith. He blessed me with amazing friends who didn't mind going out to eat only at places that served rice. He blessed me with daily joy to make up for the frustrations of my eating restrictions.

Without realizing it, I was being blessed by God's immediate goodness even while waiting for a still-to-come miracle of healing.

– Kristen

DAY 65

BALANCE
HUMILITY AND
FAITH

MATTHEW 8:8, 10

Would you say that you're someone who can't stop feeling unworthy every time they fall short of perfection? Or are you someone who feels more pride and brushes off addressing the weaknesses they have?

I think one of the greatest mysteries in life is finding the balance between recognizing and understanding the magnitude of our weaknesses and not wallowing in feelings of unworthiness!

In my interpretation, the centurion in Capernaum seems to find this balance pretty well! I see a man who is very aware of his shortcomings and sins: **"Lord, I am not worthy that thou shouldest come under my roof."** But he still approaches the Savior and asks for a miracle! Christ then says, **"I have not found so great faith, no, not in Israel."**

I think the centurion got something right. He allowed his weaknesses to humble him, but he didn't let them stop his approach to the Savior, filled with faith and ready for a miracle. How can we find a better balance?

– Cali

BE
HEALED AND
MINISTER

MATTHEW 8:14-15

It's one of the shortest exchanges we read about, but Christ's interaction with Peter's mother-in-law is quiet and powerful! **"And when Jesus was come into Peter's house, he saw his wife's mother laid, and sick of a fever. And he touched her hand, and the fever left her: and she arose, and ministered unto them."**

As far as the record shows, no words were exchanged. (Of course, it's possible there were, but I like to imagine there weren't.) Maybe she wanted to be healed in her heart, but she couldn't voice that. She didn't want to sound selfish or self-important. But Jesus saw her, blessed her, and she was healed. What an intimate, compassionate moment! And then what did she do? She ministered. She probably spoke to them and testified of our Savior. That is amazing. But I also think of another definition of the word "minister." I like to think she lived a beautiful, healthy life filled with serving others after this point.

She used her silent healing to go and do even more of God's will. She was healed and chose to use her healing to become an extension of the Savior. Just like this important woman, we can choose to ask for blessings and then use those blessings to go out and bless others! In this way, Jesus knows He is healing more than one person when He blesses us.

— Cali

DAY 67

MATTHEW 8:19

My oldest son does not like change. And yet, because of our family's frequent moves, he had to attend five elementary schools in four states.

Each time we planned to move again, I had to ask my sweet son to trust me that the move was right, even though the change to a new school would be hard. And he did trust me. Though it was difficult for him, he didn't complain and simply had faith that we were doing what was best for our family.

My son's faith reminds me of the scribe who came to Jesus and said, **"Master, I will follow thee whithersoever thou goest."**

This man trusted that Jesus would never lead him astray. He didn't ask for a guarantee of comfort or safety; he simply promised to go wherever Jesus went.

Likewise, the Lord might ask us to follow Him into uncomfortable places. He might ask us to follow Him into situations where we are scared, sad, or anxious. But as long as we follow Him, we are on the right path and are never alone.

— Kristen

DAY 68

MARK 2:27

My mom was a strict Sabbath observer. We had very set rules on what movies we could watch, what we could do, and what we could listen to.

Honestly, I kind of hated it. I hated feeling so restricted and thought my mom and Heavenly Father were stopping me from having fun.

I didn't realize that my mom and Heavenly Father were providing me with exactly what I needed: a day off from the world's influence. Every Sunday was almost like a reset button. It was a reminder of what mattered most and where my priorities should be.

This is something the Pharisees in Jesus' day didn't understand. They accused Jesus, who performed miracles on the Sabbath, of disobedience to God's law. In response, the Lord told them, **"The sabbath was made for man, and not man for the sabbath."**

In other words: this is the day to remember what matters most and where your priorities are. The Pharisees' priority was the law, while Jesus' priority was on doing what God called Him to do. Perhaps we could each look at our own Sabbath observance and see if we're using it as a day to prioritize what matters most.

– Kristen

DAY 69

MARK 4:38, 40

Every time I read the news, my heart aches. There is pain, suffering, violence, and injustice everywhere. And for some it might seem like, if there is a God, He has abandoned His children.

Have you ever felt that way? Jesus' disciples sure did.

They found themselves on a boat in the middle of a frightening storm while Jesus slept. In anguish, they called out to Jesus, saying, **"Master, carest thou not that we perish?"**

Immediately, Jesus stood and miraculously calmed the storm, reproving His disciples, asking, **"Why are ye so fearful? how is it that ye have no faith?"**

And perhaps He asks the same question of us. Do we believe that Jesus could calm every emotional, physical, mental, and spiritual storm around us? If so, then why are we so fearful?

Each of us is in His hands. He cares deeply about what happens to us. Whether He chooses to calm the storms around us or not, He cares very much whether or not "we perish."

– Kristen

CHRIST HAS COMPASSION ON YOU

LUKE 7:13

Jesus saw a dead young man being carried out of town, followed by his widowed mother and many other people. He approached the grieving mother.

"And when the Lord saw her, he had compassion on her, and said unto her, Weep not." He then performed one of the most amazing miracles of all, showing His power over death as He raised this young man back to life.

But I invite you to reread that verse from Luke. This time, put your name in it. Think about your life. What is troubling you? What has made you shed tears recently? The Lord already knows what is troubling your heart. Whether or not you have been bringing it to your Heavenly Father in prayer, He knows. And He already has compassion for you. And He is telling you to stop feeling that despair and to have some faith because miraculous things are going to happen. All because He loves you.

It might be a miraculous change of circumstances. It might be a quiet but miraculous change of mindset. It might be a miraculous and healing conversation with someone. Since our Savior quite literally knows what we are going through, He can have genuine compassion. And guess what always seems to follow Christ's pure compassion? Miracles.

— Cali

DAY 71

MATTHEW 9:12

I had a health situation a couple of years ago that involved spending a LOT of time with doctors! I went through many different tests, met with specialists, and ended up in the hospital for an emergency surgery where I spent even more time with doctors. It was the most time I had ever spent in the hospital or with physicians in my life!

Like my physical ailment, the Lord knows that we need some extra time healing our souls when we have spiritual difficulties. He taught the Pharisees, **"They that be whole need not a physician, but they that are sick."** But guess what Jesus had just been doing with these people who were spiritually suffering? He hadn't been preaching a long sermon to them, and He hadn't been telling them a list of everything they were doing wrong. He was eating with them! Eating with them was His first step in healing those with spiritual wounds.

Christ sits with us when we feel spiritually run-down, and our hearts are heavy. He performs miracles even when we have sinned. He calms the storm even when we are filled with fear.

Repenting and changing become a bit easier when we feel loved! Christ often follows this pattern with us. And we can help reach out to those who are sick around us to show love in any way that we can!

— Cali

DAY 72

MATTHEW 10:1

I had to teach a lesson at church about service.

As I prepared, I reflected on how I had learned the importance of service. Story after story popped into my mind of watching my parents, teachers, and leaders and observing how they helped others. And then I laughed! Here I was trying to teach a lesson about service when the best way to learn about it is actually by watching others serve.

In Matthew 10, Christ calls all twelve of His disciples. **"And when he had called unto him his twelve disciples, he gave them power against unclean spirits, to cast them out, and to heal all manner of sickness and all manner of disease."** He gave them the priesthood power to serve and perform miracles!

But how did these disciples know how to use their priesthood power appropriately? They had just watched the Savior do all of these same things! He lived it and then invited them to do the same. Are we asking people in our lives to be kind and patient but not giving them an example to follow? Are we asking people we love to study the scriptures without modeling what meaningful scripture study can look like? The best lesson we can ever teach is how we live our lives.

– Cali

GOD CAN
FILL YOUR
MOUTH

MATTHEW 10:20

During one of my sessions teaching at Especially For Youth (EFY), a beautiful young girl approached me. She spoke to me humbly and earnestly and asked a question I could tell had been on her heart for a long time. She asked me quietly, "I don't want this to sound conceited, but I sometimes worry that people tell me I'm so good and always doing the right thing. But it's not hard for me. I don't even want to do the wrong thing. It's just always been easy. I feel guilty that people think I'm good when that's just how I am."

As I looked into her eyes, I felt a flood of the Spirit and found words pouring out of my mouth that I hadn't planned or thought of: "Don't you realize that you lived for thousands of years before this life? Do you think you spent those thousands of years being lazy? No! You worked hard to become the kind of person and spirit you are now. Who you are now is a consequence of who you worked hard to become before."

As I bore my witness to this sweet girl, I knew it was not me who had spoken but the Spirit. Jesus taught that this is possible for those who preach His gospel. He told His disciples, **"For it is not ye that speak, but the Spirit of your Father which speaketh in you."** We don't have to be scared to open our mouths and teach. When we are open to the Spirit, God will help us know what words to say.

– Kristen

DAY 74

CHOOSE YOUR FOCUS CAREFULLY

MATTHEW 10:30

Have you ever wondered how it's possible that "...the very hairs of your head are all numbered"?

For years it confused me how God could be aware of so many things without being overwhelmed by it all. But then I realized something. Even though God is aware of the hairs on our heads, it doesn't mean He's paying rapt attention to them. We don't understand how His perfect mind works, but it is highly likely that He can be aware of many things without giving them His complete focus.

I think this is a God-like characteristic we all need to emulate.

There is so much noise, so much information, and so many opinions fighting for our attention. We are drowning in information! Every minute of the day, over 4 million YouTube videos are watched, over 103 million spam emails are sent, over 3.5 million Google searches are conducted, and The Weather Channel receives more than 18 million forecast requests.*

To survive spiritually, we need to be aware of those voices but not give them our focus and instead keep our focus on God.

– Kristen

*May 2018 www.forbes.com

DAY 75

MATTHEW 10:40

I sat down in my Living Prophets class at BYU, ready to learn about all of the modern presidents of the Church from Joseph Smith to President Monson. I was surprised to discover that I was completely wrong! Instead, we spent the entire semester focused on the 15 current living people that we sustained as prophets, seers, and revelators: the apostles and members of the First Presidency! We studied their lives, most popular messages, and most recent General Conference talks.

It was awesome! And it strengthened an area of my testimony that I had never even focused on before: the apostles are special witnesses of Jesus Christ who have the authority to preach to the entire world! Jesus taught His disciples about this special relationship. **"He that receiveth you receiveth me, and he that receiveth me receiveth him that sent me."** Listening to our apostles and prophets today is just like listening to Jesus. And when we listen to Jesus, we are listening to God.

This also reminds me of why General Conference is so important! It's more than just a nice time to listen to messages from church leaders. We are quite literally getting instruction from our Savior, Jesus Christ! Pretty cool, right? And any time we share those talks and messages with other people, we extend that same powerful witness of the Savior. When we receive doctrine from the apostles, we receive doctrine straight from the Lord!

— Cali

DAY 76

MARK 5:27

I remember sitting in my classroom the morning of my first day as a school teacher. I was terrified! Would I be able to handle my own classroom?

The bell rang, and I could hear kids starting to line up in the hallway. I closed my eyes, whispered a little prayer, and pushed the door open to invite the kids inside. One little moment of courage introduced me to an entirely new experience in a job that I loved!

I like to think that the woman who touched Jesus' hem had this same, although much more serious, moment of courage. When she heard about a Savior who could heal her, she went to Him. She had faith. And in one moment of courage, she touched His hem, confident that this would be the answer. **"When she had heard of Jesus, came in the press behind, and touched his garment."**

What seems scary and intimidating to you right now? One moment of courage is all it takes to change the trajectory of your life completely.

If we want that change to be for the better, then we also need to rely on the Savior. We can reach out to Him, utter a prayer in His name, and expect His strength.

– Cali

DAY 77

LUKE 9:62

One August night in 2019, I found myself lying in my niece's bed in Idaho bawling my eyes out. I had just followed the promptings of the Spirit to leave my beloved home in Colorado to move to Idaho where I knew one family: my brother-in-law's. I had left behind some of the best friends I had ever had in my life for what? Fields of potatoes and a town without a Chipotle? It seemed ridiculous.

Through tears, I pulled out my phone and opened a talk from Elder Jeffrey R. Holland that I had never read before. As I listened, his words echoed in my mind and heart, ". . . once there has been genuine illumination, beware the temptation to retreat from a good thing. If it was right when you prayed about it and trusted it and lived for it, it is right now."*

In other words, don't look back. Once God has given revelation about your future, don't spend your time focused on the past. Jesus said something similar to a man who wanted to return home before committing to discipleship. Jesus said, **"No man, having put his hand to the plough, and looking back, is fit for the kingdom of God."**

That night I learned there is no peace or progress in looking back. We can trust in God's revelations that have led us to where we are now, and our best bet for happiness is to keep looking forward.

- Kristen

* Jeffrey R. Holland, "Cast Not Away Therefore Your Confidence," BYU Speeches, 2 March 1999.

DAY 78

MATTHEW 11:28-30

As a teenager, I often felt God's commandments were too burdensome. Honoring the Sabbath, paying tithing, and loving my enemies all felt like rocks in a backpack that made life more difficult instead of easier.

That changed when I saw a dear friend go down a path that led away from the gospel and toward a life of sin and addiction. As I watched this downward spiral, I realized the truth of Jesus' words, "Whosoever committeth sin is the servant of sin" (John 8:34). While my friend's path seemed to be all about freedom, it ultimately led them to a life trapped in addiction and a servant to sin.

That is our choice: we can serve God, or we can serve sin. There is no other option. And the great thing is, when we choose to serve God, we have the promise that He will work side by side with us to help us carry our load. Jesus told His followers, **"Come unto me, all ye that labour and are heavy laden, and I will give you rest. Take my yoke upon you, and learn of me; for I am meek and lowly in heart; and ye shall find rest unto your souls. For my yoke is easy, and my burden is light."**

Sabbath observance, tithing, loving our enemies. . . it all might seem incredibly hard. But when we choose to serve God instead of serving sin, we know we're not carrying our burdens alone.

- Kristen

MATTHEW 12:12

I remember sitting in a Relief Society meeting right after "ministering" replaced the "visiting teaching" program (where we were asked to visit a sister once a month). Questions were flying everywhere! "Well, does it count if I text them one month, as long as I see them in person the next month?" "What if my person only wants to talk on the phone?" "Ugh, I'm so confused on what 'counts' as a visit now!"

Isn't life sometimes easier when someone tells you exactly what to do? Although the strict rules that the Pharisees followed may look like a burden, these rules were likely comforting to them. They just memorized the rules, checked all the boxes, and that was it! But Jesus was trying to teach them a higher and more sincere way of living the gospel. He shared the same message that my sweet Relief Society president was trying to teach the women in our class that Sunday morning.

The Savior, speaking about the Sabbath day as an example, said, **"Wherefore it is lawful to do well on the sabbath days."** My Relief Society president said, "Just do good things! Everything 'counts'!" Whether it's worrying about if an activity is appropriate for the Sabbath day or if something "counts" as service, turning to the Savior's simple advice can help us stay focused on what matters most. Just do good things!

— Cali

BE CAREFUL WITH YOUR WORDS

MATTHEW 12:34

If you didn't know, this book is based on the podcast of the same name: One Minute Scripture Study. I started it back in 2019, and in 2020 I was so glad to be joined by the wonderful Cali Black, the co-author of this book.

After listening to Cali's voice on the podcast for almost a year, my kids finally saw a picture of her, and they were shocked! All of them said, "I thought Cali had black hair!" I assured them that, while her last name is Black, she is indeed a blonde. They expected her to look a certain way from just hearing her say her name over and over again.

That has made me think: what would someone expect of me if all they knew was the sound of my voice and the words that I said? What if someone had no visual reference for me and simply had to judge who I am based on what I said and how I said it?

Jesus said that, **"...out of the abundance of the heart the mouth speaketh,"** or in other words, what you say shows who you really are.

What about you? What would people think of you if they were to judge you based only on what you said and how you said it?

– Kristen

DAY 81

BRING
FORTH GOOD
TIDINGS

MATTHEW 12:35

I recently decided that I wanted to "unfollow" a bunch of people on social media. I could feel that I was following too many accounts and wanted to keep my attention on good things. My criteria for deciding to unfollow certain public accounts were simple: does following this account make me want to become a better person?

I was surprised that many accounts I had followed to make me laugh, actually made me want to complain or judge more. Other accounts I followed because I thought they were interesting, actually made me feel jealous and ungrateful. I narrowed down my list to a much smaller group of people or groups that inspired me to be better. My social media experience has been so much more uplifting ever since!

Jesus taught, **"A good man out of the good treasure of the heart bringeth forth good things: and an evil man out of the evil treasure bringeth forth evil things."**

Good people, causes, or groups will inevitably make good things happen in the world, and I want to be part of anything that is good!

– Cali

DAY 82

GIVE GRATITUDE FOR THE GIFT

LUKE 11:13

Are you a good gift-giver? My grandma has always been the best gift-giver! Ever since I was young, she would pick out the coolest clothes, the latest trendy toys, or the accessories and books I needed for birthdays or Christmas. I didn't realize until I got older that not all grandmas were that spot-on with giving gifts, but it is a talent that mine was blessed with!

I've learned that giving a good gift requires thoughtfulness, good planning, and solid execution! It can be a fun way to express your love for someone, but it also shows a lot of sacrifice on the part of the gift-giver to make it happen.

I think it is so sweet that Jesus makes this connection between giving good gifts and receiving the Spirit. He teaches: **"If ye then, being evil, know how to give good gifts unto your children: how much more shall your heavenly Father give the Holy Spirit to them that ask him?"**

In other words, "You think you are good at giving gifts? Imagine how much better Heavenly Father is at giving you the Holy Ghost!" The Holy Ghost is the ultimate gift, fulfilling whatever role we need Him to fulfill at any time. God gives us this gift at exactly the right times and in exactly the right ways. I am grateful for His powerful ability to know what I need and to make sure it happens!

— Cali

DAY 83

YOU'RE EITHER GROWING OR SHRINKING

LUKE 11:23

I am an inherently lazy person. I love to stay home, read books, and eat chocolate. That, to me, is heaven! Unfortunately, this laziness has led me in the past to try to "coast" spiritually– to let the little things slide.

Scripture study, prayer, and temple attendance would happen sporadically, but I put little effort into them. I would justify my behavior because I wasn't doing anything wrong– I still had a spotless record of not murdering, robbing or taking God's name in vain. But in the back of my mind, I was well aware that I wasn't doing the good things I knew I should.

After several "spiritual coasting" efforts, I learned an important lesson: it doesn't work. You're either growing in the gospel or shrinking– there is no middle ground. During my coasting times, my testimony shrank. My relationship with God suffered. I became more self-centered and less like the Savior. I wasn't being "bad," but I was becoming less "good."

Jesus Christ said, **"He that is not with me is against me: and he that gathereth not with me scattereth."** Did you catch that? If we are not with Jesus, we are against Him. If we are not helping Him to gather, then we are scattering! There is no such thing as standing still in the gospel of Jesus Christ!

– Kristen

DAY 84

LUKE 11:53-54

As Jesus became increasingly popular, the scribes and Pharisees became more upset with Him. Jesus, unlike other spiritual leaders, didn't fear their power or position and would often call them to repentance. This was unacceptable to them!

They tried desperately **". . .to provoke him to speak of many things: Laying wait for him, and seeking to catch something out of his mouth, that they might accuse him."**

Now isn't that interesting? When Jesus called these men to repentance, rather than humble themselves enough to see the truth, they tried to prove that Jesus wasn't perfect either (which, unfortunately for them, was not true).

Do we ever do this when we feel we've been called to repentance? Do we feel "called out" by a church leader, family member, or friend, and then– rather than humbling ourselves– we try to find fault in the one who offered the correction?

I think that we can do better than that! We can do better than the scribes and Pharisees and instead be like the Savior: always humble and teachable!

– Kristen

DAY 85

MATTHEW 13:9

I used to find it very easy to be critical of others giving talks or lessons in church. As someone to whom speaking and teaching come naturally, it was very easy to pick apart what they were doing wrong or make lists of how they could do better.

Jesus taught that He used parables so often because: **"Who hath ears to hear, let him hear."** It was a beautiful turnaround in my church experience when I realized that a speaker or teacher could do their job imperfectly, and yet I could still HEAR what they were trying to say. It had nothing to do with their delivery and everything to do with my ability to hear.

Hearing is a pretty passive and easy thing to do in theory. But I've found it can be surprisingly challenging to do in practice. Do you have someone at General Conference you kind of tune out because you don't connect with their speaking style? Do you have a friend who always wants to "one-up" every story you tell? Do you have a family member where each conversation somehow ends up as an argument?

Hearing is such an important skill, and it puts responsibility on us instead of placing blame on the other person. Jesus invites us to read His scriptures and teachings and do what we can to hear Him.

— Cali

DAY 86

HAVE MORE, GET MORE

MATTHEW 13:12

I'm not going to lie. Matthew 13:12 confused me at first when I read it. Does this seem fair to you: **"For whosoever hath, to him shall be given, and he shall have more abundance: but whosoever hath not, from him shall be taken away even that he hath"**? Those that have more are given more, and those that have less lose what they have? That doesn't seem fair or kind at first!

But as I continued studying it, I realized these are natural consequences. When we "have more" faith, more of the spirit's presence in our lives, more Christlike attributes, or more gospel study, we naturally "get more." We get more out of our study of parables, get more opportunities to serve, get more spiritual promptings, and get more familiar with the scriptures. And the opposite is naturally true too. If we don't have faith, don't have time to study the scriptures, or don't keep the commandments to have the spirit with us, then we naturally lose opportunities to serve, lose spiritual promptings, and lose gospel knowledge.

These blessings and knowledge aren't just being given to us or taken away from us by supreme beings who want to reward and punish us for fun. These blessings and knowledge are naturally given or taken away based on our choices and actions. So really, it makes perfect sense! If you have more, you get more. What are you trying to "have more" of today?

— Cali

DAY 87

MATTHEW 13:19-23

Growing up in Los Angeles, California, I attended early morning seminary and, thanks to my mom, got 100% attendance all four years. Waking up at 5:30 a.m. every school day for four years was not something I wanted to do, so I went to seminary with a less-than-stellar attitude. My teachers were excellent; they worked hard to teach us the gospel and did a good job. Despite my grogginess, I heard and understood what they said. But unfortunately, I didn't do anything about it, which is exactly what Jesus asked us not to do.

In the parable of the sower, Jesus gave a three-part formula for how we can have our lives changed by hearing His words. He said that the people who benefit from receiving His word are those who **". . . heareth the word, and understandeth it; which also beareth fruit. . . ."** Did you catch the three-part formula? We have to hear, understand, and then "bea[r] fruit," or in other words, take positive action.

When I went to seminary, I heard and understood. But whether from exhaustion, laziness, or a bad attitude, I did nothing with what I learned. My lack of action meant that hearing God's word didn't change my life. Today would be a great day to consider: how am I doing at following Christ's three-part formula to hear, understand and act?

– Kristen

DAY 88

MATTHEW 13:22

My husband loves to work out at the gym, and he has for years!

He has always been a great example to me though of making sure that his gym time never comes before family or gospel time. He will skip going to the gym if he needs to be in other places. He knows that his gym habits are good because he still makes time for all the essential things!

Jesus taught this same principle with the parable of the sower. **"He also that received seed among the thorns is he that heareth the word; and the care of this world, and the deceitfulness of riches, choke the word, and he becometh unfruitful."**

What are the thorns in our lives that cause us to become unfruitful? It's tricky because some thorns can look really appealing; they seem good. And to many people, they are good! But if they cause us to become "unfruitful" in the gospel or our families, they are no longer good for us.

This makes me want to reflect: What might be a thorn that I need to cast out so I can produce even better fruits?

— Cali

YOU
HAVE
POTENTIAL

MATTHEW 13:31-32

I recently asked my daughter what she wants to be when she grows up. Her response was, "I want to be an astronaut and a builder and a farmer and a cowboy." She is so excited to become all of those things, and I will be there cheering her on in a spaceship or tractor!

Kids are so good at seeing their future potential. They know that they don't know everything yet, and that's okay! They will learn! But as we get older, it gets a little more difficult for some reason. We have our "fixed mindset" that we are the way we are.

"Oh, I'm just not good at studying the scriptures." "I'm not a natural teacher." "It's really hard for me to want to serve others." We lock down our potential when we say or think these things. Absolutely every skill worth having can be obtained with hard work and practice.

"Another parable put he forth unto them, saying, The kingdom of heaven is like to a grain of mustard seed, which a man took, and sowed in his field: Which indeed is the least of all seeds: but when it is grown, it is the greatest among herbs, and becometh a tree, so that the birds of the air come and lodge in the branches thereof." Do we want to STAY as a mustard seed or GROW into the biggest tree we can be? With Jesus, we can always grow.

– Cali

TURN TO
CHRIST FOR
HEALING

LUKE 8:43

When I realized I had Obsessive Compulsive Disorder (OCD), I immediately ordered a self-help book to "get over" it as soon as possible. After months of effort, I wasn't any better. Finally, completely exhausted, I turned to God and said, "Okay, I get it. What wouldst Thou have me do?" And His answer shocked me, "Go to the temple." It made absolutely no sense to me! But as an act of faith, I began going as often as possible. Though my OCD did not go away, I became more convinced than ever of God's love for me, and I began to see His wisdom in letting me have this trial. Mentally I was not healed. But spiritually, I was. And it was miraculous.

There was a woman in Israel who **". . .having an issue of blood twelve years, which had spent all her living upon physicians, neither could be healed of any, came behind him, and touched the border of his garment: and immediately her issue of blood stanched. "**

She had done what I'd done– she had used all the wisdom of the day to heal herself. Finally, in complete exhaustion, she turned to Jesus, who– in a way that didn't seem practical to most– healed her in a way no one else could. When we find ourselves in the middle of a struggle with no solution in sight, I've learned that it's wise to reach out to Jesus and let Him heal what truly needs healing.

– *Kristen*

DAY 91

LUKE 13:34

When my husband and I got married, his parents told us to choose a piece of Christian art as our wedding present. As we shopped, I was immediately drawn to a painting by Greg Olsen called "O Jerusalem." The painting depicts the Savior sitting on a mountainside looking out over the city of Jerusalem with a sorrowful, contemplative look on His face. As I looked at that painting, I could feel the Savior's love for every person in Jerusalem– even those who rejected Him.

Almost 2,000 years before this painting was made, Christ said these words, **"O Jerusalem, Jerusalem, which killest the prophets, and stonest them that are sent unto thee; how often would I have gathered thy children together, as a hen doth gather her brood under her wings, and ye would not!"**

Isn't that so interesting? Jesus knew who He was trying to save: people who stoned and killed God's prophets. And yet He wanted so badly to gather them to Him. What they had done in the past didn't stop Him. He focused on helping them change and improve to become better in the future.

I love this reminder that no matter how low we feel we have fallen, Christ always wants to help pick us up. There is no distance far enough that the Savior's love cannot reach us!

– Kristen

DAY 92

MATTHEW 14:13-14

Jesus loved His cousin, John the Baptist. Although we don't know too much of their personal relationship, it is clear that they both lifted each other up. I'm guessing they were quite close.

But then Christ got word that His beloved cousin had been killed. **"When Jesus heard of it, he departed thence by ship into a desert place apart: and when the people had heard thereof, they followed him on foot out of the cities. And Jesus went forth, and saw a great multitude, and was moved with compassion toward them, and he healed their sick."**

Jesus did two things after He learned of this devastating news. First, He went by Himself to a separate place. Second, He had compassion on people in need and healed them.

What a powerful example of how to mourn! Christ showed us that it can be helpful to be alone AND to get out and serve others.

We can take time to reflect and focus on our own needs. But we can also find joy in serving the people around us.

— Cali

DAY 93

MATTHEW 14:30

What do we do when we have a crisis of faith?

A few years ago, I faced a big question: Is The Church of Jesus Christ true? I had experienced a faith-shaking moment and had to decide how to handle it as I searched for the answer to my question.

Peter had a seriously faith-shaking moment as he walked on water toward Jesus. The water was choppy, the wind was blowing, and he was far from his friends on the boat he had left. As Peter's gaze left the Savior and turned to the waves, his faith faltered, and he began to sink. What would Peter do next? Would he turn to the boat and call to his friends for help? Would he start to doggy paddle to try to get himself back to the ship? No! As soon as Peter began to fall into the water, **". . .he cried, saying, Lord, save me."**

When we face a crisis of our faith, we have the same options Peter had. But like him, our best choice is not to ask our friends (who probably don't know how to swim) for help. It's not to start doggy paddling in the middle of stormy waters. Our best option is to turn to the Savior immediately for help. As I faced my doubts head-on, I turned to Jesus for help and found that through Him, I was able to find rescue. Answers and peace came as I turned to the only true source of help.

– Kristen

DAY 94

MARK 6:26

The Jane Austen novel <u>Persuasion</u> always drives me crazy when I read it. The heroine, Anne, lives with her ridiculous father and sister who prioritize prestige over everything else. No matter how many debt collectors surround their doors, they still spend money to keep up the appearance of wealth.

Similarly, King Herod loved the prestige of his position and the respect of his followers. And so, when he unwisely promised– in the hearing of many others– to give a beautiful young woman anything she asked for, he dug a hole for himself. When this young woman came to Herod and asked for the head of John the Baptist, he **"...was exceeding sorry; yet for his oath's sake, and for their sakes which sat with him, he would not reject her."** At that moment, Herod placed his prestige above everything else– including his conscience.

Unfortunately, I'm afraid we sometimes do the same thing on a smaller scale. Do we ever follow the crowd, not speak up, or ignore something we know is wrong so that others won't think negatively of us? Do we place the opinions of others above the stirrings of our conscience? Christ is the perfect example of always standing up for what was right– no matter how large the crowd.

– Kristen

SEARCH
THE SCRIPTURES
DILIGENTLY

JOHN 5:39

Have you ever lost a precious possession, or even a person, and gone looking for it? What did you do? How much did you care whether you found what was lost?

When my oldest son was four, I took him shopping at our local Wegman's grocery store. This was a huge store with two floors, a cafe, a sushi bar, and a buffet. My son must have wandered off as I shopped in the bakery area because when I turned to find him, he was gone. I ran frantically through the store looking for him and calling his name, but I could not find him! A concerned employee asked what was wrong and then made an announcement on the PA system for everyone to be on the lookout for a lost child. I was beside myself with worry. Luckily within minutes, someone found my sweet boy and returned him to me. I hugged him and cried in relief. I would have gone to the ends of the earth on my search to find that kid!

Now with that in mind, let's read the words of the Savior who said, **"Search the scriptures; for in them ye think ye have eternal life."** His invitation was not to "read" the scriptures but to "search" them. How much does your current scripture study look like a search? Are you actively and anxiously looking for answers to questions, personal insights, or invitations to change? If not, today would be a GREAT day to go back to Day #1 in this book for a reminder of a quick and easy way you can let the scriptures change your life!

- Kristen

DAY 96

JOHN 6:5-6

After Jesus finished teaching the multitude, everyone looked hungry. Do you know what Jesus could have done? He could have said, "Hey, I'm in charge so let me think. Hmmm. Okay, can you find food anywhere at all? I'll perform a miracle and multiply the food for the group." But instead, here's what happened: **"When Jesus then lifted up his eyes, and saw a great company come unto him, he saith unto Philip, Whence shall we buy bread, that these may eat? And this he said to prove him: for he himself knew what he would do."** Christ asked Philip a question He already knew the answer to. He pointed out the problem to His disciples. He asked them a question about how they could solve it. He listened to Philip's answer. He listened to Andrew point out that someone had brought five loaves and two fishes. And then He asked them to bring the food to Him. He blessed it and told them to pass it to the crowd.

Imagine the apostles' experiences, thinking, and problem-solving through every scenario and finally realizing there was no other way. And then imagine them feeling the miracle as they passed the food around and then collected such a large amount of leftovers. What a great leader Christ is! He included His disciples. He asked them questions. And then He ultimately led and performed a miracle that touched the disciples even more because Jesus had included them in the process.

– Cali

DAY 97

YOU ARE MORE THAN ENOUGH

JOHN 6:13

When I think about everything I'm "supposed" to be doing, I get way too overwhelmed! I've got callings to fulfill in innovative and personal ways. I'm trying to meet all my kids' emotional, physical, and intellectual needs. I'm trying to be a loving spouse who carves out quality time consistently. I'm trying to be a great friend who goes out of her way to cultivate fun memories. There is too much to do!

But I think about Jesus standing there with 5,000 people, five loaves of bread, and two fishes. That was certainly not enough either. And yet, after praying to the Father, it WAS enough.

"Therefore they gathered them together, and filled twelve baskets with the fragments of the five barley loaves, which remained over and above unto them that had eaten." So, not only was it enough, it was MORE than enough! We are enough, too. Heavenly Father has never asked us to knock all our responsibilities out of the ballpark.

We don't have to be perfect for everything to be great. We just have to be enough! We offer what we can to the Lord, look to the Father, and offer sincere prayers. And then we will be even more than enough for what God wants us to do!

— Cali

DAY 98

JOHN 6:39

A few years ago, I volunteered to watch my brother and sister-in-law's kids while they traveled to Europe for a family wedding. I was beyond excited because I love my nieces and nephews, and we ended up having two fantastic weeks together. However, when their parents picked them up, I sighed in relief– no one had been lost or injured on my watch.

It had been a source of constant anxiety the whole time I was watching them. When I would take all five kids (plus my three) out to the park, the grocery store, or on a hike, I found myself counting over and over 1-2-3-4-5-6-7-8-all here, 1-2-3-4-5-6-7-8-all here. I was terrified that I would forget one of them somewhere, and their parents would come home to only four of their five kids.

I would imagine Jesus feels the same loving anxiety for us. He told His disciples, **"And this is the Father's will which hath sent me, that of all which he hath given me I should lose nothing, but should raise it up again at the last day."** But instead of watching over only eight children, Jesus is watching over numberless children. And like me at the park with my eight little charges, He is constantly aware of us, where we are, what we are doing, and how He can keep us safe. Oh, how wonderful it is to have a Brother keeping such careful watch over all of us.

– Kristen

DAY 99

MATTHEW 15:11

Octopus? Unclean. Fish? Clean. Pigs? Unclean. Locusts? Clean.

The Israelites had a long list of clean and unclean foods based on the laws given during the time of Moses. And boy, did the Pharisees love that list of rules! They kept it perfectly and looked down on anyone who didn't.

So they must have been incredibly offended when Jesus said, **"Not that which goeth into the mouth defileth a man; but that which cometh out of the mouth, this defileth a man."** The Pharisees had created an entire church culture based on how they interpreted God's laws– including food laws. Their culture was exclusionary and elitist; they looked down on and rejected anyone who didn't fit into their mold. The Pharisee's culture is the exact opposite of the true culture of Christ's church!

We all create a culture in whatever ward we're in. It's inevitable. Culture is simply our customs, and wherever we are, there are certain customs (or habits) we create.

So what kind of culture are you helping to create in your ward and home? Are you like the Pharisees; do you find yourself excluding or judging others? Or are you making a culture of love, obedience, and hard work? That is the culture Christ created wherever He went.

– Kristen

DAY 100

SEE THE SIGNS EVERYWHERE

MATTHEW 16:2-3

Have you ever gone to the temple with a big question on your mind, hoping to get an answer? I did this a few months ago. I was looking for a sign of what to do about a very big decision. But guess what happened in the temple? After I waited and prayed, the thought came to my mind: "I've already given you all the signs. You just haven't noticed them yet."

Immediately my mind was filled with all the little miracles and answers God had already given me in previous weeks! I was looking for something bigger, so I had unknowingly dismissed the smaller promptings along the way.

The Pharisees and Sadducees came to Christ asking for a sign to show that He was the Savior of the world. Jesus said: **"When it is evening, ye say, It will be fair weather: for the sky is red. . . O ye hypocrites, ye can discern the face of the sky; but can ye not discern the signs of the times?"** Jesus was telling them that they had already been given many signs that He was the Messiah!

But I also love that our Savior is still so loving and kind that He will take the time to point out many of the signs that we have missed and even give us more. When we slow down and reflect, it's humbling to see that the Lord has given us more help than we even realize!

— Cali

MAKE
REVELATION
YOUR ROCK

MATTHEW 16:16-18

When Peter boldly told Jesus, **"Thou art the Christ, the Son of the living God,"** Jesus responded, **". . .flesh and blood hath not revealed it unto thee, but my Father which is in heaven."**

In other words, Peter knew the truth of Christ's divinity through revelation.

Jesus then said some of the most misconstrued words in the entire New Testament. He told Peter, **". . . upon this rock I will build my church."**

Many Christians have interpreted this verse to mean that Peter was the rock on which Christ would build His church. In fact, when my husband and I visited Italy as young college students, we walked through the massive and ornate structure of St. Peter's Basilica-- an entire building devoted to this "rock."

In an effort to follow the words of the Savior, millions have mistakenly worshipped Peter as the cornerstone of Christ's church. But we know that, good as Peter was, our testimonies should not be built on him. Our testimonies are built on the Savior, and the way we come to Him is through the rock of personal and prophetic revelation.

- Kristen

DAY 102

MATTHEW 16:25

Do you want to be like Jesus? I do! But here's the tough question: Is there anything else you want to be MORE than you want to be like Jesus? Maybe you just want to have friends and fit in. Maybe you want your kids to be better behaved. Maybe you want a more prominent job. Maybe you want more money.

These are all fine to want, but when we want them MORE than we want to be like Jesus, we've started focusing on trying to save our own lives rather than turning to Christ to be saved! Jesus even warned, **"For whosoever will save his life shall lose it: and whosoever will lose his life for my sake shall find it."**

Anything that causes us to focus on "saving" our own lives more than turning to Christ is something that should be removed! Anything that causes us to focus on the Savior is something that we should keep. And I have to add that sometimes losing our selfish views of our lives by focusing on the Savior more can actually give us what we originally wanted for ourselves as a by-product! We might become more well-liked BECAUSE we are developing Christlike attributes, or we might earn more money BECAUSE of our righteous desires to bless other people.

But no matter the result, when we really turn to the Savior, we will always find our true purpose in life.

– Cali

MATTHEW 17:5

When you read the following scripture, what scripture story do you think it came from? **"This is my beloved Son, in whom I am well pleased; hear ye him."**

Most people would probably say from Jesus' baptism. But the verse we are studying today actually came from the Mount of Transfiguration! Heavenly Father doesn't reveal very much about Himself through the scriptures. He clearly points us toward His Son time and time again. But there are just a few choice moments that we have recorded when Heavenly Father speaks.

I love the idea that God is so proud of His Son going to the Mount of Transfiguration and ensuring Peter, James, and John receive powerful priesthood keys that Heavenly Father cannot help but tell the world He is pleased with Jesus. Do you know what mountains symbolize in the scriptures? The temple! Do you think God the Father is pleased with you every time you attend the temple or do family history work?

I believe He is so proud and pleased with every effort we make to draw upon real, divine priesthood power and renew our covenants in the temple. And I want to always do the things that will make my Heavenly Father burst with excitement for me!

– Cali

DAY 104

NECESSARY THINGS ARE NEVER IMPOSSIBLE

MATTHEW 17:20

From my early childhood, I tried very hard to make miracles happen. I would harness all my energy and see if I could make a bag of chips fly into my hands; I tried to move mountains, and I'm pretty sure I attempted to speak in tongues once or twice.

I had taken the Savior's words at face value when He said, **"If ye have faith as a grain of mustard seed, ye shall say unto this mountain, Remove hence to yonder place; and it shall remove; and nothing shall be impossible unto you."**

I didn't realize that you have to read between the lines to get the full meaning of those last few words. What the Savior was really saying was that nothing shall be impossible unto you. . . that is necessary and according to God's will.

God didn't need me to move a mountain, speak in tongues, or have a bag of chips fly into my hands. But He has needed me to teach important lessons in church, see a need and immediately know how to help fill it, and anticipate problems coming to our family.

It's true that absolutely nothing will be impossible for us. . . as long as it's something God needs us to do.

– Kristen

JESUS CAN SOLVE
UNSOLVABLE
PROBLEMS

MARK 9:22-24

In the little town of Galilee, there was a family that was exhausted. The mother and father in this family had a child who had been sick for what seemed an eternity. He required constant care because, if left unattended, he would throw himself into the fire and be burnt or into waters where he might drown. His parents had done all they could, and in absolute desperation, the child's father brought him to Jesus' disciples.

Though the disciples tried their best, they could do nothing for the child. And then, seeing Jesus, the father ran to him and begged, **". . . if thou canst do any thing, have compassion on us, and help us."**

"Jesus said unto him, If thou canst believe, all things are possible to him that believeth. And straightway the father of the child cried out, and said with tears, Lord, I believe; help thou mine unbelief."

The example of this father is powerful. Despite the failure of medicine, the disciples, and every effort on his part, he believed the Savior could do what others couldn't. And Jesus did. He healed the child in a matter of moments and returned him whole and healthy to his father. Do you ever feel that your problems are unsolvable? This father probably did. And yet he came to Jesus as we should in total humility and said, "Lord I believe; help thou mine unbelief."

– Kristen

TRUST YOUR HEAVENLY FATHER

MATTHEW 18:3

It's one of the most famous things the Lord has asked us to do: **"Verily I say unto you, Except ye be converted, and become as little children, ye shall not enter into the kingdom of heaven."** We are to become like little children!

But if you've ever spent a lengthy amount of time with little kids, you might think, "Yeah, but not ALL the time, right?!" Yes, kids can be humble, patient, and full of love. Those are great qualities to try to emulate! But I've noticed that kids also have to learn how to listen to their parents, even when it doesn't make sense to them. In the past week, I've had a kid upset because they had to get strapped into their car seat for a long drive, another kid was upset because I wouldn't give them a lollipop for breakfast, and another was upset because a block wasn't fitting into the hole she thought it should go in.

From a parent's perspective, this all makes sense. My kids need to learn how to be safe, they need to learn proper nutrition, and they need to learn that some things just won't work, no matter how hard they try. But kids have a limited perspective which makes this frustrating sometimes for them! I've realized that this is actually an essential part of becoming "like a child"-- learning that we don't know the bigger picture and trusting that SOMEDAY, we will see why the things we had to deal with were necessary.

— Cali

DAY 107

MATTHEW 18:11

My daughter loves to dance, and I recently got her a new purple leotard that she was so excited to wear to her next dance class. It was time to leave for dance class, and we suddenly couldn't find this leotard! We tore apart the house looking, but my daughter was devastated when we had to leave for class without it.

Guess what we did as soon as we got home? We looked for it again! We still couldn't find it. Each morning for the next few days, she would ask about the leotard, and we would keep looking everywhere. Finally, almost a week later, we discovered it had been scrunched up inside a swimsuit at the bottom of a basket. She was so happy that we finally found it, and the search was over!

That purple leotard was important to my daughter, and she was not going to stop looking for it. I think of other times when we've lost a little plastic toy; the amount of effort spent searching for that lost toy has been minimal. And when I've lost car keys, I've put all my efforts into finding them immediately! How much we look for something when it is lost seems to indicate how important it is to us! It is not our Father's will that ANYONE should perish or be lost. **"For the Son of man is come to save that which was lost."** He's not shrugging His shoulders saying we shouldn't have wandered off. He's not casually remembering to look for us every once in a while. He is here to save everyone who is lost.

— Cali

DAY 108

MATTHEW 18:21-22

During my childhood, I had one sibling who would always yell at me whenever she got upset. Inevitably she would later come to apologize and ask for my forgiveness. While I appreciated the gesture, I was frustrated. Did I have to keep forgiving her? Shouldn't she learn to control her temper?! Surely there had to be a limit to how many times I had to forgive her unkindness.

I think Peter might have had a similar problem with one of his siblings because he came to Jesus and said, **"Lord, how oft shall my brother sin against me, and I forgive him? till seven times? Jesus saith unto him, I say not unto thee, Until seven times: but, Until seventy times seven."** In other words: "Peter, there is literally no end to the number of times you are required to forgive." Yes, we should be wise and protect ourselves from people who might harm us (physically, mentally, or emotionally); but there is no excuse NOT to forgive when we have been hurt. After all, God is willing to forgive us, so how can we deny that gift to others?

How blessed we are that God has set no limits on how often He will forgive us. I'm sure I would have used my "seventy times seven" chances by now! On our covenant path to living with and becoming like our Heavenly Father, let's all practice the constant forgiveness He is so willing to offer us.

— Kristen

DAY 109

DON'T BE GREEDY WITH FORGIVENESS

MATTHEW 18:33

Jesus once told a parable about a man who went into an astronomical amount of debt to buy something he felt he desperately needed. When the time came for the man to repay the debt, he couldn't. The consequence? He, his wife, and his children would be sold as bondservants to pay off the debt.

In agony, he begged his lender for mercy which– miraculously and unexpectedly– he received. The debt was erased! And yet shortly afterward, this same man went to someone who owed him a small amount of money, demanding that it be repaid. When the debtor asked for mercy, the man refused him and sent him off to prison.

Just reading that story makes me angry. How could someone who had been forgiven for so much have refused to forgive such a tiny debt? And yet, I do the same. God has forgiven me time and time again, but I find myself holding onto old grudges or judging others for past offenses. I am sure that Heavenly Father looks down at me and thinks, **"Shouldest not thou also have had compassion on thy fellowservant, even as I had pity on thee?"**

Today would be a great day to consider how we are like the unforgiving man and how we can do more to be like our loving and forgiving Father.

– Kristen

GOD'S CHURCH IS ORDERLY

LUKE 10:1

There are many signs of the truth of The Church of Jesus Christ of Latter-day Saints. But one of the signs I think is often ignored is its organization.

There's a need for a temple in Africa? The land is found, the funds are set aside, and local government officials are notified, all before an announcement is made.

A deadly storm happens in a third-world country? Financial and physical aid are organized almost immediately to provide relief.

Too many people in a ward? There is a process and a plan for exactly how to handle it. Order. Order. Order. That is how God's church works, and it always has.

Even during its infant years, Christ's church during His lifetime was organized. In Luke, we're told, **"After these things the Lord appointed other seventy also, and sent them two and two before his face into every city and place, whither he himself would come."**

So, are revelation, temples, the Book of Mormon, tithing, and all of these other things signs of the true church? Absolutely! But so is the order with which it is run!

– Kristen

DAY 111

LUKE 10:25, 29

I noticed that the reason Christ told the Good Samaritan parable is NOT because of an inquisitive disciple, but because of a lawyer who wanted to tempt Him! **"And, behold, a certain lawyer stood up, and tempted him, saying, Master, what shall I do to inherit eternal life?"** And then later, this same lawyer wanted the Savior to clarify, **"And who is my neighbour?"**

At first, these two questions may seem pretty innocent. But Christ saw right through this man's real intent. In actuality, this lawyer was looking for Jesus to limit the good things people need to do here on earth.

He was tempting Jesus to give a reasonable limit to when we could stop loving and serving our neighbors. As Christ gave the powerful story of the Good Samaritan to prove that there are no limits, I can't help but wonder if I sometimes put a limit on my service.

Have I ever thought: They aren't in my ward; that's someone else's calling; they don't deserve help because they got themselves into that mess; or they already have too many other people serving them? Jesus firmly teaches that there are no limits to who we should love and how we should serve!

– Cali

DAY 112

WHAT CAN ONLY YOU DO?

LUKE 10:41-42

One day I was speaking with a friend who, due to health struggles, would sometimes find herself unable to get out of bed, much less complete her to-do list. And so, she began to prioritize her day by asking, "What can only I do?"

She discovered that the local pizza shop could make dinner, a neighborhood teenager could be paid to fold the laundry, and it turned out that no one truly needed to post all those pictures on social media; they could wait for another day. But what only she could do was grow closer to God in prayer, provide a mother's hug to her children, improve her testimony through scripture study, and create an atmosphere of love in her home. And so those were the things she made sure to do— no matter how sick she felt— every single day.

Perhaps this is the lesson that Jesus was trying to teach Martha as she busily bustled around the house cleaning and cooking while her sister sat and listened to the Savior. He said, **"Martha, Martha, thou art careful and troubled about many things: But one thing is needful: and Mary hath chosen that good part, which shall not be taken away from her."** What Martha was doing was good— but anyone could do it. What couldn't be done by anyone was to grow Martha's testimony by hearing the Lord's words spoken directly from His mouth. That was something only Martha could do.

- Kristen

CHOOSE TO GROW TOWARD JESUS

JOHN 7:12

Isn't it mind-blowing that so many people had such dramatically different responses to Jesus living among them? **"And there was much murmuring among the people concerning him: for some said, He is a good man: others said, Nay; but he deceiveth the people."**

People who witnessed the same events came to very different conclusions about who Jesus was. This means they had a choice in how the things they saw would affect their testimonies. I've been asked to serve in several callings that I haven't been very excited about. One time, I accepted a calling but had a terrible attitude about it. I did the bare minimum to get through it and complained the whole time. But the next time I was extended this same calling, I decided to try a different approach. I still wasn't very excited, but I read the handbook to learn all the details and actively reached out for help. Although I still didn't love the calling, I began to see its importance and felt like I drew closer to the Savior in the process.

We may find ourselves in the same situations as others or even the same situations we've been in before. We start with the same situation, even the same attitude, but we can end up with wildly different conclusions and results. EVERYTHING we do either brings us closer to or farther from our Savior! I hope I can make the choice each day to get a little closer to Jesus no matter the circumstances.

— Cali

DAY 114

JOHN 7:17

When the movie, "Napoleon Dynamite," came out, I went to see it in the theater with a friend. We loved it! I came home and laughingly told my husband about it, sharing funny quotes and trying to convey just how great the movie was. He was not convinced.

Over the next couple of weeks, my friend and I would quote the movie all the time; our husbands just rolled their eyes until we convinced them to see it too. When we came out of the theater together, our husbands couldn't stop laughing. They started quoting it with us and finally got what we'd been saying for weeks.

You see, no matter how much we tried to convey the movie's humor, it wasn't until they experienced it for themselves that they really got it. This is why God wants us to experience living the gospel for ourselves. He doesn't just want us to read about prayer; He wants us to pray. He doesn't just want us to hear about service; He wants us to get out and serve. Jesus said, **"If any man will do his will, he shall know of the doctrine, whether it be of God, or whether I speak of myself."**

So do you have a gospel principle you're unsure of? Try living it and find out for yourself! Listening to others talk about it will never be enough. It takes doing it to really "get" it.

— Kristen

DAY 115

JOHN 7:24

I visited a different ward recently where I only knew a few people. The young men sitting up front preparing to pass the sacrament talked and laughed with each other throughout the entire sacrament hymn. Except one! He wasn't talking with the others. He sang the hymn. I was especially impressed because I knew it would have been easy to give in to what his friends were doing around him. They stood up to pass the sacrament, and it was quickly evident that this same young man had on bright purple pants, dirty tennis shoes, and a half-tucked shirt while the rest of the boys looked traditionally presentable.

I couldn't help but think that if someone saw them all walking into church, they might have judged this one young man for his appearance. Maybe they would draw conclusions about how he must not understand the importance of the sacrament if he dresses that way. And yet, he appeared to take the experience more seriously than all his peers: singing the hymns with reverence and abstaining from laughing and joking around! **"Judge not according to the appearance, but judge righteous judgment."** We can never know someone's heart by their appearance. Never! Choosing to be loving and kind to absolutely everyone is the most Christlike thing to do, and it leaves us with more room in our minds to worry about our own relationships with Jesus.

– Cali

DAY 116

JOHN 8:28

If you saw both Heavenly Father and Jesus, who do you think you would run to for a hug? If you said Jesus, you're like 99% of the world.

We tend to see Jesus as a somewhat relatable friend while God seems like a slightly scary, awe-inspiring judge.

But if that's how we see God, then we have missed the point entirely of what Jesus taught us.

Christ Himself said, **"I do nothing of myself; but as my Father hath taught me, I speak these things."**

So, when Jesus healed the sick, spent time with the outcasts, and loved the little children, that was God He was showing us. If Jesus is loving, that means God is loving too. If Jesus seeks out the one, then God does too. If Jesus is patient, forgiving, kind, and gentle, that means God is too.

So, do we need to be afraid of God? Not for one second. As Jesus showed us through His perfect example, God is everything good we could possibly imagine.

- Kristen

DAY 117

JOHN 8:32

I remember the first time I flew a kite on the beach. My dad got kites for my sisters and me, and we spent a windy afternoon getting them into the air. Once my kite was airborne, I felt the strong tension in the string I was holding. I realized I was holding this kite back from being able to fly higher!

In my youthful wisdom, I decided that letting go of the string would be best for the kite because I would allow it to soar higher and higher. But, to my dismay, letting go of the string caused the kite to come crashing down to the sandy beach instead! I thought the string's tension was holding the kite back when in actuality, the string was the only thing allowing the kite to fly.

Many people see the gospel of Jesus Christ in the same way I first saw the string: restrictive, too tight, and too much pressure. But Christ lovingly taught: **"And ye shall know the truth, and the truth shall make you free."**

Knowing the truth of eternal life, our Savior, and the Plan of Salvation doesn't burden us at all! It allows us to be free from guilt, drama, hatred, addiction, and the consequences of sin. Following Jesus doesn't tie us down– He sets us free!

– Cali

YOUR TRIAL CAN ALLOW MIRACLES

JOHN 9:2-3

Jesus' disciples asked Him about a blind man. **"Master, who did sin, this man, or his parents, that he was born blind? Jesus answered, Neither hath this man sinned, nor his parents: but that the works of God should be made manifest in him."**

Do our trials come from our sins? Or even from the sins of family members? Honestly, trials CAN come from our sins or the sins of loved ones! But at the end of the day, when it comes to serving others, does it really matter who caused the trial?

However, in the case of this blind man, Christ clarified that the man was not born blind because of anyone's sins. In fact, this man was born blind so God's works could be made manifest in him! He had to endure this trial to experience the miracle and the change of heart that accompanied it.

What if we looked at our trials and weaknesses with the sole purpose of allowing God's works to be made manifest in us? Isn't that so empowering?! We have our trials for a reason, and that reason can be so that we can see God work a miracle through our eventual change and progression. We can use our heartache, our pain, our silent struggle, our difficult sin, or our frustrating situation to see the grace of God and manifest His good works!

– Cali

DAY 119

JOHN 10:27

Whose voice do you know perfectly?

Think about that– whose voice could you pick out in a crowd or recognize immediately on the other end of the phone?

After twenty years of marriage, I would probably have to say my husband's. Even though it sounds similar to his brother's voice, I can always tell them apart; and I can always follow my husband's voice in a crowd to find him. I think it's simply a matter of having spent time talking with and listening to my husband speak for more than 7,500 days in a row.

This makes me wonder how well you and I know Jesus' voice. Do we talk to Him every day? Do we listen to His voice in the scriptures regularly? He desperately wants us to!

He said, **"My sheep hear my voice, and I know them, and they follow me."**

What do you think you and I would have to do to make Jesus' voice be the one we would recognize best in a crowd? How much more time would we need to spend listening to Him and following Him?

– Kristen

DAY 120

LUKE 15:21

After experiencing a change of heart, the young "prodigal son" realized that his best living situation would be to return to his father's house as a servant. When he finally saw his dad, he said, **"Father, I have sinned against heaven, and in thy sight, and am no more worthy to be called thy son."**

Can you imagine the humility it would take to return to your dad, admit how wrong you were, and request to work as a servant?! I think we can all learn from this powerful example of humility.

When we are repenting on our knees in prayer, humility brings us closer to God. Why? Because humility is what's left when we remove any barriers of pride in our hearts. When we recognize our weakness and God's greatness, there is more room for Him to help us.

Humility is also so important with other people around us! When we make a mistake, do we take the time to acknowledge it? Do we ask for forgiveness without any excuse or explanation?

Humility is NOT weakness. It is pure strength of character to make more room for the good to grow!

— Cali

DAY 121

LUKE 15:31

Picture this: You are doing the best that you can. One day, your righteous brother asks your father for his inheritance early, leaves home, blows through it all, and makes many poor choices. But then he decides to come back home, and your dad throws him a giant party! How could this be fair?

This is the same question the brother of the prodigal son wrestled with. How is it fair that some people can live a life full of sin and pride, but as soon as they repent, they receive the same eternal reward we do?

The father in this parable gives us the answer. He tells this righteous but jealous brother, **"Son, thou art ever with me, and all that I have is thine."** In other words, "You have ALWAYS had everything I have had! You've seen love. You've had access to blessings. You avoided all that extra pain that comes from sin. Your extra reward is that you've been with me the whole time!"

If all that our Father in Heaven wants from us is a broken heart and a contrite spirit, then, in the end, it doesn't really matter how long it took us to get to that point. But if we are doing our best to stay on course, we are already experiencing the real reward every day! It's always worth staying on the path as often as possible.

— Cali

GOD IS THE GREATEST WEALTH

LUKE 16:13

Jesus taught His followers, **"No servant can serve two masters: for either he will hate the one, and love the other; or else he will hold to the one, and despise the other. Ye cannot serve God and mammon."**

But what exactly is mammon? The Greek word that we translate as "mammon" is μαμωνᾶ or mamōnas. Though we often assume the word means "evil," it is better translated as "wealth personified." So, in other words, you can't serve God and money.

Why is that? What's wrong with wanting money?

I want money! I love money! Money makes fun things possible! So is it really so bad to seek after it through hard work? Not at all! The problem comes not when we "seek" money but when we "serve" it.

So for those of us who love money (please tell me it's not just me), it's important to feel deeply in our hearts that the greatest wealth of all is found in God and not in a bank account!

– Kristen

DAY 123

LUKE 17:13-14

The plague of leprosy was a horrible thing during biblical times. According to the Law of Moses, those with leprosy were considered "unclean." They had to live alone (or with other lepers), weren't allowed to enter walled cities, had to change their physical appearance to make their state as a leper evident to all, and if anyone came near them, they had to warn them by shouting, "Unclean! Unclean!"

They were more than outcasts; they were doomed.

It's no surprise that ten lepers called out to Jesus when they saw Him, still standing far enough away not to spread their "uncleanness" to anyone else.

Then the scriptures tell us, **"And they lifted up their voices, and said, Jesus, Master, have mercy on us. And when he saw them, he said unto them, Go shew yourselves unto the priests. And it came to pass, that, as they went, they were cleansed."**

Jesus didn't heal them as they stood there, hoping for a miracle. They were healed "as they went." And that will often be true for us. When looking for miracles, we are much more likely to find them when we are up, working, and doing what we can to help ourselves rather than simply sitting and waiting. As the saying goes, "God helps those who help themselves."

— Kristen

DAY 124

AIM YOUR
GRATITUDE AT
JESUS

LUKE 17:15-16

"I'm grateful for pine cones and glitter!" It was Thanksgiving, and we had the family tradition while growing up of going around the table and saying things we were thankful for during dinner. I was only 4 years old, and when it was my turn, I remembered the craft we had just done in preschool the day before and proudly announced that I was thankful for pine cones and glitter as everyone in my family laughed.

It's so good to be grateful for everything! Research shows time and time again that gratitude leads to a positive shift in our mindset. But where is our gratitude aimed? Is it just a feeling of happiness? Or is the gratitude directed at our Savior and our Father in Heaven? When I read about the ten lepers, I am almost positive that each of them felt "grateful." But only one former leper knew WHERE to place that gratitude. **"And one of them, when he saw that he was healed, turned back, and with a loud voice glorified God, And fell down on his face at his feet, giving him thanks."** He knew to glorify God! He knew to go back to Jesus! We can be grateful for so many good things in our lives, from family members to miracles, to service opportunities, and even to preschool projects. So let's make sure we are grateful TO our Heavenly Father and Jesus Christ for all the beautiful blessings They make possible!

– Cali

JOHN 11:16

Let's play a game of fill-in-the-blank. I want you to say the first word that comes to your mind when you see this phrase and think of a person in the New Testament: "_____ Thomas."

Did you say "doubting Thomas"? If so, you are not alone! I think 99.99% of the Christian world would say the same thing! But today, I want to introduce you to a side of Thomas we don't often see, that of "devoted Thomas."

Jesus had heard that His friend Lazarus was sick. However, to reach Lazarus, Jesus would have to return to Judea where the people had recently attempted to stone Him. Jesus' disciples reminded Him of how dangerous the trip would be, but He insisted on going. Then in response, Thomas turned to the other disciples and said, **"Let us also go, that we may die with him."**

"That we may die with him." Doubting Thomas? Oh, no. This is a man who was willing to lay down his life to protect and be with the Savior! This is Devoted Thomas! Like Thomas, we each have a story full of both ups and downs. Instead of judging others harshly for one negative experience, we should remember that we're just seeing a small part of someone rather than their whole amazing story.

— *Kristen*

DAY 126

JOHN 11:35

The years after my father died were traumatic, to say the least. My mother was learning how to care for my four older sisters and me, and we girls were learning how to live life with just a mom. Life was messy and imperfect and painful for many, many years. But one of the great blessings of that period of my life is that I learned the power of sitting with my worst feelings. I remember my mom sometimes putting all five of us girls in our VW minivan and driving around so that she could talk to us while we were a captive audience. Often these family talking sessions would turn into crying sessions for some of us. We wept. We sorrowed. We felt awful. And it was okay. My mom never told us to buck up. She let us cry, miss our dad, be angry at the world, and feel terrible for as long as we needed.

And Jesus did that too.

Jesus was with His dear friends, Mary and Martha, whose brother, Lazarus, had died. Rather than tell these women to "buck up" because He was about to perform a miracle, the scriptures tell us, **"Jesus wept."** We do not have to be ashamed of tears. We don't have to put on a happy face because that's what "good Christians" do. Even the Savior of the universe, who knew the miracle He was about to perform, wept during a difficult moment.

- Kristen

DAY 127

MATTHEW 19:5

This entry is NOT just for married people, I promise! But if you ARE married, I'm sure you've heard this scripture that encourages spouses to prioritize each other: **"For this cause shall a man leave father and mother, and shall cleave to his wife: and they twain shall be one flesh?"**

Christ often uses marriage as an analogy throughout scripture for how devoted we should be to Him! So, what do you need to "leave" so that you can better "cleave" to Jesus?

Just like we put certain things out of our lives when we get married, we may need to leave behind other things when we want to focus on the Savior. We might need to leave behind working too much, social media, video games, TV shows, sports, old friends who might not be uplifting, selfishness, or laziness. And then, after we know what we need to "leave," what can we do to "cleave" to Jesus even better?

Just like cultivating and maintaining a strong marriage requires time and effort, we can set aside regular time to get to know Jesus in the scriptures, pray with sincerity, study gospel topics, serve others, do hard work, and sacrifice. Good relationships usually require leaving some things behind, but that means there's more room for the good stuff in the future!

– Cali

DAY 128

MATTHEW 19:20

I once wrote a list of everything I needed to do to become "Celestial Kingdom material." When I finished the list, my hand was cramped, and my spirit was depressed. I could never do all of the things on that list! The next day I picked it up again and realized something– I couldn't do everything, but I could do something.

So, I went to God in prayer and asked Him which of all the things on my list He most wanted me to work on. I felt an immediate prompting that regular temple worship mattered most to Him. And so I started working on that. When I got into a good habit of regular temple worship, I went back to my list and asked Heavenly Father, "Which one next?"

I discovered that when we, like the rich young man, come to Jesus and ask, **"What lack I yet?"** He will be generous in leading us to just one or two things. Though He could give us a long list to work on, He knows that our progress will be slow and steady– and He's okay with that.

God does not expect immediate perfection, but He does ask for steady progress. And we should do the same with ourselves. Instead of getting overwhelmed or frustrated because of our imperfections, we can focus on regular improvement.

– Kristen

DAY 129

PRAY FOR THE IMPOSSIBLE

MATTHEW 19:26

Do you want to know what I find super exciting? **"But Jesus beheld them, and said unto them, With men this is impossible; but with God all things are possible."**

Isn't that crazy? With God, ALL things are possible! Hearts can be changed. People can be healed. Circumstances can be altered. We can forgive and be forgiven. It truly is exciting!

What is something you would like that seems pretty impossible right now? Guess what? God COULD make that happen.

Maybe He's waiting for you to ask for it to happen. Maybe it's His will that it won't happen. Maybe He hopes that you'll want something different. Maybe He can use you to start making it happen!

No matter His wise and mighty reasoning, and no matter what is going to happen eventually, prayer is the first step.

Have you asked God for something impossible to happen lately?

– Cali

DAY 130

MATTHEW 20:13

Jesus once told the story of a man who hired workers to help in his vineyard. Some he hired at the beginning of the day, promising them a penny for their work. Others he hired later on, and a few he hired at the very end of the day with absolutely no promise of how much he would pay. Still, these workers were desperate for any wages they could get, so they went to work.

At the end of the day, the man paid all his workers equally– everyone got a penny regardless of how long they worked. Those who had started work early in the day began complaining about how unfair this was. But the employer answered, **"Friend, I do thee no wrong: didst not thou agree with me for a penny?"**

Or, in other words, "Why are you angry because I'm generous with what I have?"

I think sometimes we're guilty of doing the same thing. We seem to believe that God's blessings have a limit; if He gives a gift to one of His children, the rest of us miss out. This is NOT true. God's goodness is endless and limitless. We don't need to feel jealous of what someone else receives from God. Instead, we can use it as a reminder to count the many blessings He has already so generously bestowed on us.

– Kristen

DAY 131

MARK 10:21

The rich young man wanted to know what more he could do to inherit eternal life. Right before Christ answered him, we read this powerful phrase: **"Then Jesus beholding him loved him."** Can you picture Jesus doing that to you?

I can imagine Him looking at me but also seeing the real me, seeing my strengths and the good intentions of my heart. Seeing my weaknesses and the things that I just can't let go of. Seeing who I really am— beholding me.

And then, after seeing all that, He still loves me! It's amazing.

Do you think we could try being this Christlike to the people around us? What if we could, to the best of our human abilities, behold the people we interact with and love them? We can pray and learn to see our friends, our spouses, our kids, our colleagues, or our ward members in a new light and love them.

Why? Because that's what Jesus would do! It brings peace and joy to our souls to behold and love someone. And it helps teach other people that they are worth Christ's love, too!

– Cali

DAY 132

MARK 10:44

I used to think how nice it would be to be exalted someday. I imagined endless days lying on the beaches of the Celestial Kingdom, relaxing for eternity. It sounded truly heavenly!

Have you ever imagined and hoped for the same type of restful eternity?

Then I had my first child. As I changed diaper after diaper, sang the same songs over and over, and played peek-a-boo for the five millionth time, it dawned on me: living life like God isn't about chilling on a beach.

God's life is about raising and shepherding His children along the covenant path. That shepherding involves cleaning up spiritual messes, teaching the same lessons over and over, and having an unbelievable amount of patience. In other words, God's life is all about service.

Jesus taught this when He said, **"And whosoever of you will be the chiefest, shall be servant of all."**

We don't serve here on earth so we can earn a comfy seat on the beaches of heaven. We serve on earth to learn how to live like God.

- Kristen

LUKE 18:43

I gave a talk in church one time and mentioned a small miracle that had happened that week when I received an answer to a complicated question in a surprising way! That next week, I was talking to a co-worker who wasn't a member of the church. I was trying to explain the answer I had received that I had talked about in my church talk. I realized, though, that I kept using the words "coincidence," "luck," and "great timing." The word I wasn't using? Miracle!

But it totally WAS a miracle! When Jesus performed a miracle and gave the blind man sight, we know that the blind man praised Jesus: **"And immediately he received his sight, and followed him, glorifying God."** But guess what happened as a RESULT of this man giving glory to God? **". . . and all the people, when they saw it, gave praise unto God."**

This is a powerful reminder that after we have blessings and miracles and tender mercies in our lives, they should be a natural call to action and platform for sharing our gratitude to God with others. I realized I was censoring myself to make my co-worker "comfortable," when in reality, every miracle should give me a chance to bring others closer to God!

– Cali

MATTHEW 21:9

The last week of Jesus' life began and ended so very differently.

When He entered Jerusalem, **"the multitudes that went before, and that followed, cried, saying, Hosanna to the Son of David: Blessed is he that cometh in the name of the Lord; Hosanna in the highest."**

Jesus was greeted by a multitude– a large number– of people. This great teacher, this miraculous healer, was welcomed by a crowd of adoring people on the last Sunday of His mortal life.

But only five days later, in the crowd that called for Barabas to be released rather than Jesus, where was this multitude? At the foot of the cross where Mary and John stood, where was this multitude?

Do we ever turn our backs on the Savior when things get hard? Where do we stand when the world around us no longer supports Him? Do we support Him only in crowds that honor Him, or do we stand vigil even as others hang Him on a cross?

- Kristen

DAY 135

MATTHEW 21:28-31

Take a quick read of one of the shortest parables that Jesus teaches about two sons: **"A certain man had two sons; and he came to the first, and said, Son, go work to day in my vineyard. He answered and said, I will not: but afterward he repented, and went. And he came to the second, and said likewise. And he answered and said, I go, sir: and went not. Whether of them twain did the will of his father? They say unto him, The first."** So, the first son says that he isn't going to work, but then he repents and gets to work. And the second son says he's going to work but then doesn't.

Have you ever been like the second son? Maybe you've said you'll study your scriptures every day but get too tired. Maybe you've said you'll be a peacemaker in your home, but then you fall back into habits of anger. Maybe you've said you'll help someone, but you get too busy to follow through. We've ALL been the second son time and time again! But we don't have to stay like the second son! Why not be the first son, too?

Let's make commitments, let's make covenants, let's promise to help, let's take on an extra assignment. When we fall short, forget, or run out of time, we can repent and get back to work! Our story doesn't need to end after we fail to keep a commitment. We get a chance to be like the first brother because we can repent. He was the one doing the father's will because he kept going.

— Cali

DAY 136

MATTHEW 22:37-39

How do you know if you are "good enough"? I'm sure everyone has thought about it at one point or another. We know we can't be perfect, and we know we can't be doing incredibly evil things all the time. So how do we know if we are "far enough" over on the spectrum between those two points? Here's my favorite quiz that I like to give myself whenever I start to wonder if I'm actually good enough:

Question 1: Do I love God? Like, do I REALLY love God?
Question 2: Do I show love to everyone else, too?

If my answers are something like, "I'm trying to! I want to!" then I know I'm on the right path! Jesus taught, **"Thou shalt love the Lord thy God with all thy heart, and with all thy soul, and with all thy mind. This is the first and great commandment. And the second is like unto it, Thou shalt love thy neighbour as thyself."** If we have the intent to keep these two great commandments every single day, then we are on the right track. We can pour all our energy into loving God above all else because by turning our hearts, souls, and minds over to Him, we naturally align our wills with His! And when it comes to others, we get to just love. Love everyone, teach the people we have stewardship over, and then worry only about our own standing with God. The amount of love in our hearts reveals a lot about our standing with God!

— Cali

BE YOUR
BEST SELF
INSIDE

MATTHEW 23:27

As a child, I loved to watch the movie "Singing in the Rain." It was about a famous Hollywood couple who made silent movies together. With the introduction of the talking picture, though, they had a huge problem. The starlet of this duo– Lena Lamont– was beautiful, glamorous, and a fabulous silent actress... but she had the voice of a surprised frog! Not only that, but she was spoiled rotten and a nightmare to work with. Though she looked the part of a dream girl, she sounded and acted like a nightmare!

Have you ever found that to be true in real life? Have you ever met someone who had two versions of themselves: the public and private versions?

Jesus warned about this when He said, **"Woe unto you, scribes and Pharisees, hypocrites! for ye are like unto whited sepulchres, which indeed appear beautiful outward, but are within full of dead men's bones, and of all uncleanness."** The scribes and Pharisees considered themselves the pinnacle of righteousness because they kept the Law of Moses exactly. But Jesus– who could see into their hearts– knew the hardness and uncleanness of their hearts. Today would be a good day to consider this question: does my heart match my public appearance? Am I the best version of myself on the inside and the outside?

– Kristen

DAY 138

MARK 11:31-33

During the last week of Jesus' life, a group of chief priests, scribes, and elders approached Him, hoping to trick Jesus into saying something blasphemous or illegal. They questioned Him about the authority with which He performed miracles, taught, and even cleansed the temple. Jesus, being eternally wise, responded with His own question– did they think John the Baptist had the authority of heaven or not?

Well, this really got the scribes, priests, and elders in a pickle! **"And they reasoned with themselves, saying, If we shall say, From heaven; he will say, Why then did ye not believe him? But if we shall say, Of men; they feared the people: for all men counted John, that he was a prophet indeed. And they answered and said unto Jesus, We cannot tell. And Jesus answering saith unto them, Neither do I tell you by what authority I do these things."**

Though these men had their opinions, they didn't dare say them for fear of going against popular opinion.

Do we ever do the same thing? Do we hold back in sharing what we believe because it's unpopular? Do we miss opportunities to share the gospel because we fear what others think about us?

– Kristen

DAY 139

SINCERE IN
WORSHIP

LUKE 19:4

Zacchaeus was the definition of "sincere." He collected taxes for a living and was pretty rich. But he didn't seem to "love" his riches. Instead, he gave HALF of everything he owned to the poor, and if he made a mistake and wronged someone, he would give them fourfold. And then he heard Jesus was coming to town! Zacchaeus went to see the Savior but couldn't because the crowd was too big, and he was a short guy.

So he ran to a tree to see Jesus walking by. **"And he ran before, and climbed up into a sycomore tree to see him: for he was to pass that way."** After that, Christ made eye contact and invited Himself to Zacchaeus' home. Christ knew that others might judge him as a rich publican, but He knew Zacchaeus' heart. I LOVE the sincerity that Zacchaeus had! He wasn't uncertain or unsure. He didn't let obstacles get in his way. He wasn't worried about what others were thinking of him. He just lived a good life and wanted to see the Savior.

How can we all try to be more sincere in how we live the gospel? Are we showing up to every meeting we should be at with good intentions in our hearts? Do we drop everything and "run" when there are good opportunities around us? Are we joyously and eagerly finding ways to grow closer to Jesus? I want to add a little more Zacchaeus to how I live and find more ways to be sincere about my love and devotion to my Savior!

– Cali

FOLLOW JESUS
AT ALL
COSTS

JOHN 12:42-43

What is something you've worked hard for that would be difficult to give up? Is it a good-paying job, a college degree, or a spot on the winning soccer team?

I've worked really hard on this book! I've spent years studying the New Testament. I've also spent the past six months (as Cali has!) pondering and praying over each entry in this book. I've edited the words dozens of times and given up plenty of opportunities for fun to spend time studying and writing.

Now keeping in mind the thing you have worked hard for, here is a difficult question: What would you be willing to give that up for? What would someone have to pay you?

In the time of Jesus, some men had become chief rulers– people with political and spiritual clout– who had worked years to get to that position. These men believed in Jesus and what He said, but they also loved their hard-earned position in society.

These believing chief rulers weighed the cost of following Jesus and realized it would likely cost them all they had worked for. And so, **". . .because of the Pharisees they did not confess [Jesus], lest they should be put out of the synagogue: For they loved the praise of men more than the praise of God."** Would you give up what you've worked hard for to follow Jesus? Something to ponder on today!

- Kristen

MATTHEW 25:3-4

I remember hearing about the parable of the ten virgins as a young kid and thinking how selfish the wise women were! Couldn't they share their oil? **"They that were foolish took their lamps, and took no oil with them: But the wise took oil in their vessels with their lamps."**

I teach my young children how to share all the time. But there are some spiritual things that we just can't share! We can't share our peaceful minds that come from living righteously. We can't share our attitudes. We can't share our obedience to difficult commandments. We can't share our temple privileges. We can't rely on others for spiritual strength! We have to put ourselves in the driver's seat of our spiritual journey and make the sacrifices necessary to reap our own rewards.

This also means that we can't give our oil to others, no matter how much we may want to. We can show them what oil is, talk about how great it is, and share the blessings that have come to us as we've prepared that oil.

But at the end of the day, EVERYONE has to get their own oil! Whether we realize our lamp is a little empty or we desperately want to pour our oil into a loved one's vessel, our spiritual work is all on us.

— Cali

DAY 142

MATTHEW 25:12

Jesus compared the kingdom of heaven to ten virgins waiting for the bridegroom to arrive. Five of them came unprepared and had to run to buy extra oil for their lamps in the middle of the night. The bridegroom came when these women were gone and closed the door of the wedding feast. When they arrived and begged for entrance to the feast, the bridegroom said, **"But he answered and said, Verily I say unto you, I know you not."**

That always seemed rather harsh to me until I read the Joseph Smith Translation of that same phrase. Open up your scriptures and read the real translation of Matthew 25:12.

It's not that the bridegroom (or Jesus) doesn't know those of us who are unprepared for Him; it's that we don't know Him! It's not a matter of knowing about the Savior; it's a matter of knowing Him personally.

And how well can we say we know Him? Do we spend regular amounts of time with Him? Do we listen to Him? Do we follow His example?

If we don't, we need to do better so that when the Savior comes, we can be gathered with those who know Him.

– Kristen

DAY 143

TALENTS

MATTHEW 25:21

"Definitely don't tell the bishop that I know how to play the piano!" It's something many people have heard or even said! But let's talk about what Jesus teaches us to do with our talents and abilities. In the parable of the talents, those who received five and two talents at first ended up doubling their amount. Meanwhile, Mr. I-only-got-one-talent dug a hole and buried it.

What's the difference between these men? Being willing vs. being afraid. Are we willing to share our talents even if they are very underdeveloped, in our opinion? Or are we too afraid to have people judge us? Are we willing to spend time and hard work to improve our talents? Or are we afraid we can't get any better than we are right now? Are we willing to serve where we are needed? Or are we afraid we'll get "stuck" in a calling we don't like? I think that is the most significant difference!

It doesn't matter if your talent is singing, speaking, remembering things, noticing real needs, being calming, staying organized, or being funny. We just need to be willing to see our talents, use them, and grow them! **"His lord said unto him, Well done, thou good and faithful servant: thou hast been faithful over a few things, I will make thee ruler over many things: enter thou into the joy of thy lord."** It's not about quantity. It's not even about quality. It's about our willingness to improve and share.

— Cali

DAY 144

MATTHEW 25:34

The Mansion by Henry van Dyke tells the story of a wealthy man. The gentleman is extremely generous in his donations to worthy causes but always insists that his name be attached to the contributions. He never gives without recognition.

One night, this man has a dream in which he arrives in heaven. He marvels at the beautiful mansions and palaces being given to others– philanthropists like him as well as the poor. However, when he arrives at his house, he finds that it is a simple hut rather than the palace he expected. He is then told that his heavenly home was built using only the materials he sent the angels from his works on earth. Because he received so much praise and recognition on earth, there was very little material left over to build his heavenly home.

The Savior taught, **"Then shall the King say unto them on his right hand, Come, ye blessed of my Father, inherit the kingdom prepared for you from the foundation of the world."** This makes me wonder: what kind of material have I sent to heaven for the angels to build my home? Do I demand so much recognition for my deeds in this life that there will be very little material left in heaven for my mansion in the next life?

– Kristen

DAY 145

MATTHEW 25:40

What do you think most people in your ward need right now? In Christ's time, it was fairly common for people to ask strangers for food, drink, and shelter.

Although there absolutely may be people in your immediate area who need food, drink, or shelter, I would bet that if Jesus were speaking to us now, He would specifically address some other issues.

Maybe He would say that He was lonely at church, and you sat by Him. He needed help, and you stopped by with dinner to ease the burden. He was struggling with His testimony, and you listened and offered support. He was too anxious to voice His problems, and you discerned and served anyway.

We can find godly purpose in serving others in whatever ways they need. When we do these things for others—when we comfort, uplift, and support— we do this to the Savior. **"Inasmuch as ye have done it unto one of the least of these my brethren, ye have done it unto me."**

And while we serve Jesus, we are also performing the service on behalf of our Savior! We become His hands and do as He would. What a blessing it is to serve!

— Cali

DAY 146

MARK 12:44

Why did the widow's "two mites" cause the Savior to teach that she had donated more than anyone else at the treasury? **"For all they did cast in of their abundance; but she of her want did cast in all that she had, even all her living."** The rich men had cast money out of their abundance, and she cast money out of her need for a living!

Sometimes we think we have to wait for abundance to be the people we want to be. We need to have a huge home before we offer to host activities. We need to make a comfortable amount of money before we donate to good causes. We need to have extra time before we really dive into studying our scriptures. But what if we flipped this around? What if we had more of an attitude like this woman who cast in money that she would need to live that week? What if we host and volunteer no matter our current circumstances? What if we donate more and save elsewhere? What if we stay up just a bit later to study the scriptures, no matter how much we need sleep?

I'm reminded again and again that sacrifice is what purifies our hearts and strengthens our love and humility before God. If we wait until it is no longer a sacrifice to do good things, then we miss the point a bit. Let's show faith and humility by sacrificing from the things we think we need and see what miracles the Lord can work with what He has!

— Cali

DAY 147

WITH JESUS NEAR, GOODBYE FEAR!

LUKE 21:26

Jesus warned that in the last days we would see **"Men's hearts failing them for fear, and for looking after those things which are coming on the earth...."**

Do you see that happening around you? Do you see a world filled with fear?

There is fear of financial disasters, terrorism locally and worldwide, wars and rumors of wars, natural disasters, plagues and epidemics, and so much more. It's enough to make anyone's heart fail them!

But for followers of Jesus Christ, we have this hope: we are never alone. The Lord said through the prophet Isaiah, "For I the Lord thy God will hold thy right hand, saying unto thee, Fear not; I will help thee" (Isaiah 41:13).

Through every scary thing happening in the world, we have the Savior by our side, holding our hand. Regardless of the outcome, regardless of the storms, we are never, not for one second, alone. And with the Savior on our side, we have no need to fear!

- Kristen

DAY 148

MATTHEW 26:30

Can you think of a time when a specific song brought the Spirit so powerfully that it was undeniable and testimony-promoting? I have a feeling that you can! There is something powerful about good music! Whether it's a hymn at Girls' Camp, a Primary song in sacrament meeting, an uplifting pop song at a youth camp, or a song with powerful lyrics on a playlist right when you need it; I think everyone has been touched by inspirational music.

Jesus Himself sang a hymn with His disciples: **"And when they had sung an hymn, they went out into the mount of Olives."** Have you ever realized that we sing at least three hymns during each sacrament meeting? Since our hymns and the songs in the Children's Songbook are approved as official "doctrine" for our church, this is like getting three extra sermons of pure doctrine each Sunday! I even had a friend tell me recently that they will sometimes open their hymn book to a random hymn for their weekly family night, read the lyrics, and study the attached scriptures. It's so easy to let our minds race, zone out, or mentally prepare for the lesson we are teaching during second hour as each hymn is played on the organ on Sundays. But no matter our musical abilities, the words we sing in unison are some of the purest learning opportunities we can have! Some hymns teach truths, others help us praise the Lord, and others focus us on important topics. But they can all point us to Jesus if we want them to!

– Cali

DAY 149

MATTHEW 26:39

Right after my son was born, he needed some medical testing done to give us answers regarding his future abilities and development. We were blessed to have many people tell us they were praying for us and for the medical tests to reveal typical results. For some reason, I felt guilty about praying for good test results. I mean, I would love my little baby boy no matter the results, right? I was pondering about this dilemma of what I should be praying for one afternoon when this exact scripture came to my mind so clearly: **"And he went a little further, and fell on his face, and prayed, saying, O my Father, if it be possible, let this cup pass from me: nevertheless not as I will, but as thou wilt."** I've heard that scripture many times, as I'm sure you have, but one sentence jumped out to me this time: "O my Father, if it be possible, let this cup pass from me." What did Jesus do in the Garden of Gethsemane? He asked for what He wanted. He prayed that He wouldn't have to go through a difficult experience. He hoped for an easier way.

It is not un-Christlike to ask for what we want. That's the lesson the Spirit wanted to teach me that afternoon as I thought about my son's procedure. It was completely fine to pray for good test results. Of course, following that up with the understanding that God's will always reigns supreme is essential! Jesus learned that the Father still wanted Him to endure the suffering ahead, and so He humbly submitted to the Father's will. But it isn't un-Christlike to not want to do hard things. — *Cali*

WATCH WITH
HIM ONE
HOUR

MATTHEW 26:40

When the Savior went into Gethsemane, He had to go alone. And yet, likely wanting the comfort of having friends nearby, He asked Peter, James, and John to sit and watch with Him.

After some time in the Garden, Jesus arose and came to His disciples, **". . .and findeth them asleep, and saith unto Peter, What, could ye not watch with me one hour?"**

Have you ever wondered at this– how the disciples could sleep when their Savior suffered so close by? I certainly have!

But then I remember what the Savior has asked of me: to "watch with [Him] one hour" during the sacrament. He has asked that we spend this one hour each week wholly and completely focused on Him and His atoning sacrifice.

How well do you and I do at that? For those of us who aren't busy wrangling small children, do we give Him that one hour of uninterrupted attention and worship? Or do we find ourselves scrolling our phones, falling asleep, or daydreaming?

I wonder if we are more like the sleeping disciples than we might think. Perhaps each week, we could try to do a little better at "watch[ing] with [Him] one hour."

– Kristen

DAY 151

MARK 14:33

Jesus knew what He had volunteered for.

He knew—logically— what would be required in the Garden of Gethsemane.

And yet, as this perfect Man approached the garden where His Atoning sacrifice would be wrought, He **". . .began to be sore amazed, and to be very heavy."**

In the Garden of Gethsemane, Jesus would feel all of your pains. Imagine if you had to experience every stubbed toe, bad day, broken bone, hurt feeling, stomach flu, and dramatic breakup all at once. Put all that pain into a single moment, then multiply it by infinity.

That is what Jesus felt for you. He suffered for an infinite number of people on an infinite number of worlds in just a finite number of hours in Gethsemane. It's no wonder He was amazed at the scope of it all.

But He did it for you. He saw and still sees your potential and who you can become. And He deemed you worthy of that sacrifice and that pain. So live up to that sacrifice! Become the person Jesus sacrificed Himself for you to become!

- Kristen

DAY 152

DON'T LIMIT CHRIST'S ATONING POWER!

JOHN 13:10

When the Savior was washing His disciples' feet, Peter refused. Surely Peter couldn't let his Lord and Savior do the work of a servant for him? When Jesus insisted, Peter– in his typically impetuous manner– told the Savior to wash not only his feet but also his head and his hands. Jesus then gently and reprovingly responded, **"He that is washed needeth not save to wash his feet, but is clean every whit."**

What does it mean to be "clean every whit"? The word "whit" indicates even the smallest imaginable part of something, which is what the Savior's atoning sacrifice offers to all humanity. Through Him, we can all be "clean every whit." Every negative feeling, every sinful habit, and every inclination to sin can be cleansed from us.

Do you believe that is true for you? Often we have faith that others can be cleansed and saved, but what about us?

One of our jobs in using Christ's atonement is to believe that total cleansing is possible for everyone, including ourselves. We need to stop putting limits on what Christ can do for us!

– Kristen

DAY 153

JOHN 13:14-15

Jesus washed His disciples' feet, decidedly one of the dirtiest parts of their body in a world of dusty streets and sandals. **"If I then, your Lord and Master, have washed your feet; ye also ought to wash one another's feet. For I have given you an example, that ye should do as I have done to you."**

Jesus. The Savior of the world! The creator of the world! He never used His position of "power" for special treatment.

He is the ultimate example of humility. Humility comes when we recognize that we are in God's service, while pride often comes from "titles" or allowing the praise of others to enter our egos.

Where do you see pride creeping into your life right now? Whether it's pride in your calling at church, your talents, your home, your kids' accomplishments, or anything else, we need to use Jesus as our example.

He was never "too good" to serve someone else! He was never too busy with administrative responsibilities or cultural traditions to recognize someone in need. I think we can learn a lot about how to be the best leader from Jesus Christ!

– Cali

DAY 154

JOHN 13:18

In college, I attended an audition to join an elite group of singers, dancers, and actors. I was woefully unprepared but still hoped for the best.

The day the results came out, I was crushed to discover I hadn't made the cut. Despite my great enthusiasm and desire, I was deemed "not good enough" for this exclusive group.

Has that ever happened to you? Have you ever not made the cut? If so, I have great news for you: If you want to be on the greatest team of all time, you've made the cut!

It's true!

In the work of our Father and Savior, our desire to be part of the team is enough. Jesus told His disciples, **"I know whom I have chosen."** And who was that? Anyone who chose Him!

As soon as we choose to get on the covenant path, we join God's team, and He will never cut us off as long as we're willing to keep trying and keep going!

– Kristen

DAY 155

OBEY OUT OF LOVE

JOHN 14:15

Recently, I've had some friends ask how you can stay devoted to the gospel when things aren't going well in your life. Have you ever wondered this, too?

My mind always comes back to one of the most famous scriptures in the entire New Testament: **"If ye love me, keep my commandments."** We can't live this gospel because we are expecting certain blessings. Just ask Job, Peter, Joseph Smith, or countless others who had difficult struggles despite their righteousness!

So why would we live the gospel and keep any of the commandments if life might be difficult anyway?

We have to get to the point where we live the gospel and keep the commandments out of love! When we love Heavenly Father and Jesus so much, we naturally want to do anything that will help us become like Them. And that's what the commandments help us to do– become like our Heavenly Father and our Savior!

While it's much easier said than done, we can't feel entitled to receive specific blessings in our lives just because we keep the commandments. Instead, our hearts will be happier when we obey out of pure love!

– Cali

DAY 156

JESUS WILL COMFORT YOU PERFECTLY

JOHN 14:18

I used to be very embarrassed to talk about my anxiety and depression. I thought they made me weird and that, if people knew, I would lose friends.

However, I discovered that when I talked more openly about my mental illness, people began coming to me with their problems. Friend after friend unburdened their hearts to me, sharing deep pains and even sometimes deep secrets. And because I had felt similarly awful pain, I could offer the hug, the listening ear, or the shoulder to cry on that each friend needed.

In a much more perfect way, Jesus does that for each of us. When we are sick, sad, or hurt, we can come to Him to unburden ourselves. We go to Him for a shoulder to cry on or a listening ear because He experienced what we are going through.

Jesus promised His disciples, **"I will not leave you comfortless; I will come to you."** Though He may not physically come to each of us in our difficult moments, we can certainly come to Him spiritually and find rest for our weary souls in One who understands us perfectly.

– Kristen

LET HIM
TEACH AND
REMIND

JOHN 14:26

Ready for my all-time favorite scripture study tip? Always study with a pen or pencil in your hand! I discovered this tip when I wanted to learn how to study the scriptures instead of just reading them. I picked up a pen to write in the margins of my scriptures, and I noticed that two different things started to happen.

First, whenever I would try to write something down in the margins of my scriptures, I could feel the Spirit teaching me something new! Little answers and bits of revelation would come as I wrote things down.

Second, the Spirit would bring quotes, ideas, talks, or doctrines to my mind that I hadn't thought of in a while. The Spirit certainly has a perfect memory, and I was making connections all over the place! The Savior taught about these two important roles, too: **"But the Comforter, which is the Holy Ghost, whom the Father will send in my name, he shall teach you all things, and bring all things to your remembrance, whatsoever I have said unto you."** Give it a try as you read your scriptures this week, and always have a pen or pencil ready to go. You don't need to stress about remembering every detail of what you read or finding all the hidden lessons in the scriptures. Why? Because that is the Spirit's job!

– Cali

DAY 158

LOVE THOSE WHO HATE YOU

JOHN 15:13

What would you be willing to sacrifice to help a friend? What would you be willing to sacrifice to help an enemy?

Though I try my hardest to love everyone, there are certain people that I struggle to feel charity toward. If I was asked to sacrifice a great deal of time, effort, or money to help them I'm not positive I could do it.

In speaking about His atoning sacrifice, Jesus said, **"Greater love hath no man than this, that a man lay down his life for his friends."**

While I believe those words, I think the Savior went beyond that: He laid down His life for those who considered Him their enemy. Jesus died so that those who crucified Him might find forgiveness.

He died so that the crowd that called for Barabas' release instead of His could have mercy on judgment day. He died so those who profane His name can change their hearts and lives and turn to Him someday, hoping for and expecting grace.

Yes, Jesus loved His friends enough to die for them. But He also loved those who hated Him. And so should we.

- Kristen

DAY 159

WE ARE
FRIENDS, NOT
SERVANTS

JOHN 15:15

Take a look at this fascinating teaching from Jesus: **"Henceforth I call you not servants; for the servant knoweth not what his lord doeth: but I have called you friends; for all things that I have heard of my Father I have made known unto you."**

I love that Jesus calls us His friends! But I also find it interesting that He does NOT consider us His servants. He isn't keeping big secrets from us or telling us to do random commands.

Christ promises that He has taught us what the Father has taught Him. When you think about it, we really do know so much! We know the gist of what happened in our premortal existence. We know why we are here on earth. We know right from wrong. We know so many details about our Savior's life so we can emulate it. We know what our rewards can be in the next life. And SO much more!

Even when it seems like we don't know very much, Christ reminds us that what we do know will always be what the Father wants us to know. We are His friends, not His servants, and He wants to help us gain our eternal rewards!

— Cali

DAY 160

THE SPIRIT MAKES US BETTER

JOHN 16:7

The apostles must have been distraught. Their Teacher and Friend was leaving them! What would they do without Him? Go back to their former lives? Impossible! He had changed them. And yet they still needed His help desperately, especially if they were to spread His gospel throughout the world.

But Jesus taught them something powerful. He said, **"It is expedient for you that I go away: for if I go not away, the Comforter will not come unto you; but if I depart, I will send him unto you."**

For reasons we don't fully understand, the Holy Ghost had not been wholly active in the apostles' lives while they had Jesus with them. But once He left, they received that gift in full measure. And boy, did it make a difference!

The apostles who once seemed to struggle with their faith and understanding were now powerful missionaries. They fearlessly shared Christ's gospel– even unto death. They had been good men when Jesus was with them. But now, under the influence of the Spirit, they became great men.

If we want to become truly great we also need to seek out the Spirit. His influence can change us from the inside out.

– Kristen

DAY 161

JOHN 17:3

During a particularly difficult period of my life, I began seeking a relationship with my Heavenly Father and Jesus Christ in a way I never had before. I didn't have any close friends at the time, so I found myself begging and hungering for an eternal friendship with God.

I spent my days reading the scriptures, studying Christian authors, listening to gospel music, and praying like crazy. The gospel became my hobby, and I devoted myself wholeheartedly to it.

What I discovered is this: God is knowable. In fact, God wants to be known! The more I sought Him, the closer I felt to Him until, at times, it was as if there was only the thinnest veil between heaven and me.

Unfortunately, as life has gotten easier, I have lost that closeness to God. I have filled my time with things other than Him. But I can also testify that when the scriptures say, **"...this is life eternal, that they might know thee the only true God, and Jesus Christ, whom thou hast sent,"** it isn't just a nice idea. Knowing God and knowing Jesus – personally and powerfully– is possible. They are ready and willing to be known; it is simply a matter of how much we are willing to work for it!

– Kristen

DAY 162

LUKE 22:26

One of my favorite people in the world is not well known. She hasn't done "big things" in the world. She doesn't laugh the loudest or stand out in a crowd. But what she does better than anyone else I know is show genuine love and kindness. You feel ten feet tall when you are with her because she is so good at seeing the best in others.

And one of my greatest goals is to become just like her!

When the Savior's apostles started fighting about which of them was considered the greatest, Jesus reproved them, saying, **"He that is greatest among you, let him be as the younger; and he that is chief, as he that doth serve."** And it's true!

Think of the most incredible people you know. Are they CEOs and celebrities, or are they people who do small acts of kindness every day?

If we, like the apostles, want to be considered great, our best bet is to stop worrying so much about ourselves and instead start looking for ways to serve others!

– Kristen

BECOME FULLY CONVERTED

LUKE 22:32

Why would Peter, who had seen all sorts of miracles from the Lord and who loved Him, deny the Savior three times? Christ gently reminded Peter before this, **"When thou art converted, strengthen thy brethren."** To me, that crucial word "when" means that Peter's conversion hadn't quite happened yet. Of course, Peter knew that Jesus was the Christ! But when he was suddenly thrown into a stressful situation where people were accusing him, his basic instincts kicked in. And Peter's basic instincts put self-survival above love for the Savior.

I think that's a big test of conversion! We can "know" things and testify about them. But when it comes down to it, when life really gets hard, when we are put in awkward situations with friends, or when we risk offending people, what do we revert to? Do we still find ourselves rooted in Christ?

That shows the difference between simply believing and being truly converted to the Lord. Now, the cool part is that as we keep reading the New Testament, we will learn that Peter does become wholly converted to the gospel of Jesus Christ even when risking his personal safety. So if we aren't truly converted yet, we've always got time to learn about and love Jesus even more!

– Cali

DAY 164

LUKE 22:43

When Jesus suffered in the Garden of Gethsemane, **"...there appeared an angel unto him from heaven, strengthening him."** We don't know who that angel was, but it was probably someone close to Jesus.

In a time of great need, an angel came to minister directly, one-on-one, to Jesus.

Angelic appearances happened frequently in the Old Testament as well. An army of angels protected Elisha. An angel visited Hagar after Sarah had her removed from their home. Lot was rescued from Sodom by angels who dragged him from the place. An angel gave Elijah food to keep him alive.

If angels were so anxiously engaged in people's lives in the Bible, do you think it's possible that they still are now? We know that God has not ceased to be a God of miracles and that He does not change. So it makes sense that angels are still actively and anxiously working in our lives.

Isn't that an empowering thought? Though life may get hard, and we may feel overwhelmed, we, like Jesus, have angels to help us who will come "from heaven, strengthening" us.

– Kristen

DAY 165

LOVE AND BLESS ENEMIES

LUKE 22:51

A mob of angry men was taking Jesus to kill Him. I can't think of many worse situations on this earth. These were "enemies" by every definition of the word! In fact, someone with Christ raised his sword in Christ's defense and cut off the ear of one of the offenders.

And yet what did Christ do? **"And Jesus answered and said, Suffer ye thus far. And he touched his ear, and healed him."** Jesus healed the man's ear.

Did that man really deserve to be healed? Christ didn't ask that question. He didn't just teach about "loving your enemies"-- He lived it.

When other people make poor or terrible decisions, are we stuck a little too much on making sure they get what they deserve? Or can we do better at ignoring that question, just as we hope we never get exactly what we "deserve"?

Showing love to everyone is always an option, no matter what others encourage us to do. Jesus was filled with love and kindness even while being led to His death. We can show love in our hard times, too!

— Cali

DAY 166

LUKE 22:63-64

Jesus was perfect. He never sinned– not once. That means that no matter what happened in His life, He was never unrighteously angry, never wanted personal revenge, and never gave in to the natural man.

I have often been in awe of Jesus' self-control the night before His crucifixion when the chief priests and other church leaders questioned Him. He had just paid the price of the sins these vile, evil men were now committing against Him! **"And the men that held Jesus mocked him, and smote him. And when they had blindfolded him, they struck him on the face, and asked him, saying, Prophesy, who is it that smote thee?"**

Jesus knew He had just suffered for their sins, and He knew what they were planning to do with Him the next day; yet He didn't reply with similar anger or scorn. Not only that, but He didn't even THINK angry or mocking thoughts.

What a beautiful example for us that we get to choose when we respond in anger. No one can make us angry. As Jesus showed, no matter the circumstances, we can choose to have self-control!

– Kristen

DAY 167

FIGHT THE
ETERNAL
BATTLE

JOHN 18:36

The local news channel was on our TV one night. I was baffled by how many controversial news stories there were! By the end of the half-hour broadcast, I was exhausted with how many emotional, legislative, social, or even physical "battles" were occurring, constantly pressuring me to "pick a side"!

Jesus wisely counseled: **"My kingdom is not of this world: if my kingdom were of this world, then would my servants fight, that I should not be delivered to the Jews: but now is my kingdom not from hence."**

I take solace in knowing I don't have to jump into every "battle" I see. Whether in the comment section on social media, with a group of friends, or watching a local TV show; I don't have to be a soldier taking a side in each new controversy.

I can stand firm in knowing what the real battle is! It's to learn about Jesus, be like Jesus, get rid of sin in my life, and proclaim the truths He teaches. His kingdom is not of this world, and I can keep my sights set on eternity to know what matters most.

— Cali

DAY 168

JOHN 18:37

When Pilate was questioning Jesus, the Savior bore witness of His identity, saying, **"To this end was I born, and for this cause came I into the world, that I should bear witness unto the truth."**

Looking at Jesus' life, we can see He worked daily toward the cause He claimed! He taught the truth through word and deed; and especially in His atoning sacrifice, He bore witness to the truth of God's love for His children.

As I consider Jesus' "cause," I wonder what people assume our personal "causes" are. If someone were to look at your life, what would they think your life's cause is? Would it be personal comfort, making money, getting social media followers, or following Jesus?

I'm not sure what the answer for my own life is, but I invite you to ponder this today: What do my daily actions bear witness that my "personal cause" is?

— Kristen

DAY 169

SIN IS NEVER WORTH IT

MATTHEW 27:3-5

If you think about the last time you sinned, there was probably a payoff you were looking for. We lie to avoid getting in trouble. We yell at someone so we can blow off steam. We watch a popular– but inappropriate– movie so we won't stick out among our friends.

But have you ever noticed that the payoffs for sin are always extremely temporary and never as rewarding as you expected?

Judas discovered this in a big way. In payment for betraying Jesus, he received thirty pieces of silver. When he realized the gravity of what he'd done, Judas **"...repented himself, and brought again the thirty pieces of silver to the chief priests and elders, Saying, I have sinned in that I have betrayed the innocent blood. And they said, What is that to us? see thou to that. And he cast down the pieces of silver in the temple, and departed...."**

Judas realized too late that sin is never worth it. No amount of money, pleasure, or fame can outweigh the peace of a pure conscience!

– Kristen

WE CAN'T REQUIRE SPECIFIC MIRACLES

MATTHEW 27:42

Why didn't Christ save Himself from the cross? I think that answer is actually pretty easy and obvious to most of us. Jesus had to sacrifice His physical body for us so that He could then overcome the grave. He knew it had to be done to fulfill the whole plan.

And yet, the priests and others passing by Christ's crucifixion said: **"He saved others; himself he cannot save. If he be the King of Israel, let him now come down from the cross, and we will believe him."** They put specific requirements on the miracle Christ had to perform for them to "believe." Even though He had spent His whole life performing miracles, these onlookers decided that He only was a true Savior if He could get Himself off the cross.

Do we sometimes put our own requirements on the help we feel like we need to get from heaven? We think that because we haven't felt a strong "yes" or "no," we haven't received an answer to our prayer. Or we think that the promptings we follow should always make our lives easier.

With our limited viewpoint, sometimes we think we know exactly what we need. And yet there is someone above who sees the whole big picture! What we or others think the miracle "needs to be" is not always what it is. God's ways are not our ways.

— Cali

DAY 171

JESUS MAKES SPIRITUAL CONFIDENCE POSSIBLE

MATTHEW 27:51

The temple of ancient Israel was much different than modern-day temples. When I was 20 years old I went through the temple to receive my own endowment and be sealed to my husband. Since then I have gone to the temple hundreds of times and personally participated in saving ordinances for my ancestors.

But the average ancient Israelite who obeyed God's laws was not allowed to enter and participate in the holiest areas of the temple. In fact, all of the temple work was done by the Levite priests; and even among them, only the high priest was allowed to pass through the temple veil and enter the Holy of Holies once a year on the Day of Atonement.

But that all changed on the Friday of Jesus' crucifixion. In the moments after Jesus died, **"...the veil of the temple was rent in twain from the top to the bottom...."** Jesus had destroyed the separation between man and God! His atoning sacrifice made it possible for men to enter God's presence once more!

As we attend the temple we can remember that this blessing was not always available. Only through the power of Jesus Christ are we able to enter into God's presence with confidence; not because we are good and worthy, but because Jesus is eternally good and worthy!

- Kristen

DAY 172

LUKE 23:34

One friend told me she was so frustrated right after her first baby was born because everyone wanted to visit her. The visitors brought sicknesses, drained her energy, and didn't allow her to heal as she needed. Another friend told me that she loved having visitors after she had a baby. The visitors would lift her spirits, give her a break from holding her baby, and help break up her monotonous routine.

Isn't that interesting? If someone wanted to visit each mom right after their babies were born, the first mom would think the visitor was inconsiderate; and the second mom would think they were kind and helpful! The Roman soldiers who crucified the Savior did a terrible thing. But they didn't necessarily realize they were crucifying the Savior of the world. They thought they were neutralizing a blasphemous threat.

Once again, we have a perfect example from our Savior of how to forgive others. **"Then said Jesus, Father, forgive them; for they know not what they do."** In our fallen state, we are so good at thinking we know everyone's intentions. We may even think, "They should know better." But we do not know the hearts of the people who offend us! If Christ can forgive and recognize the best intentions of the people who were ending His mortal life, then I think we can do a better job forgiving others in the tricky circumstances we find ourselves in, too!

– Cali

DAY 173

JOHN 19:26-27

I can't begin to imagine Mary's emotions as she watched her son hang on the cross. But I also can't begin to imagine Jesus' emotions as He saw His grieving mother.

With all the power that He holds, I'm sure it was difficult to hold back from helping His mother at that moment.

Instead of reaching out and performing a miracle on His own, He turned to His beloved disciple, John. **"When Jesus therefore saw his mother, and the disciple standing by, whom he loved, he saith unto his mother, Woman, behold thy son! Then saith he to the disciple, Behold thy mother! And from that hour that disciple took her unto his own home."**

We are often told that Heavenly Father answers prayers and meets our needs through the people around us. Have we been given people to look out for? Have we been told, "Behold, thy new friend?"

When we serve and care for each other, we are doing what the Savior would do if He could intervene in all of our lives and serve us personally.

— Cali

JOHN 19:30

This was it. The climax of the story.

For centuries prior, prophets and saints had looked forward to the coming of Christ. For centuries after, prophets and saints have continued to look back at the Savior's life and sacrifice.

"When Jesus therefore had received the vinegar, he said, It is finished: and he bowed his head, and gave up the ghost."

How have you changed so far as you've studied about the Savior's life? How do you feel about Jesus? "Endings" are great natural times to stop and reflect. I challenge you today to take a small personal inventory as we finish studying Christ's mortal life and write down your thoughts about the Savior and what you have learned so far.

And yet, we know that Jesus' story is actually not finished! We know that Christ rises after He dies. We know that prophets for generations to come will continue to teach as the Savior taught. We know that we can continue to grow our testimony of Christ.

So let's celebrate and reflect on "an ending" today. But we can be grateful that we know it's not really "the end" yet.

— Cali

DAY 175

STAND UP FOR JESUS

JOHN 19:38

One scared man is the reason we celebrate Christ's empty tomb on Easter Sunday.

Jesus had died on the cross and needed to be buried before the Sabbath began in just a few short hours. But where could His friends bury Him? The bodies of the other crucified men were to be placed in a public grave for criminals. Was this to be Jesus Christ's final resting place as well?

It might have been if it weren't for a secret disciple. **"And after this Joseph of Arimathœa, being a disciple of Jesus, but secretly for fear of the Jews, besought Pilate that he might take away the body of Jesus: and Pilate gave him leave. He came therefore, and took the body of Jesus."** Joseph, who had been too afraid to openly proclaim Jesus during His life, now publicly asked Pilate for the body of Jesus to provide Him a proper burial in a private tomb. It seems that seeing the death of his Savior had convinced Joseph that he too could risk all– including his social standing– to do what was right.

Perhaps we, too, could consider how we might be bolder, and less scared, in our discipleship. Perhaps we could remember Christ's atoning sacrifice to help us realize that it's worth any risk to stand up for Him.

- Kristen

DAY 176

MATTHEW 28:20

The book of Matthew ends with these comforting words from the Savior to His disciples: "I am with you alway, even unto the end of the world." Don't you love that promise? The phrase "unto the end of the world" can have multiple meanings: it can mean Jesus will be with us until the end of time or that He'll be with us wherever we go. Both of those interpretations are true.

The summer after I graduated from high school, I went on a trip with some friends to Europe. I had worked three jobs over the past year so I could travel to England, France, Switzerland, and Italy. It was an amazing trip with only one negative part: I became incredibly ill.

Because of undiagnosed food allergies, I was limited in what I could eat. I had brought a suitcase full of rice cereal and crackers, but with the rigorous schedule we kept each day and the intense summer heat, my body began to shut down. I remember lying in bed sick while my friends explored Florence, Italy. I felt a lot of self-pity and desperately wanted my mommy! But knowing that was impossible, I turned to my Father and Savior instead. I knew that, though They might physically be far away, They could still minister to me in my time of trouble- and They did!

Distance doesn't matter to Them– time doesn't matter to Them. They are with us always!

- Kristen

DAY 177

LUKE 24:5

Think about these three questions for a minute: Why does it matter that we know that our Savior is still alive today? Why does it matter that we have living prophets and apostles on the earth today? Why does it matter that we receive continued revelation in our lives? I believe the answer is because the gospel is alive and relevant! We have a LIVING Savior with LIVING prophets and REAL-TIME guidance from the Spirit.

Heavenly Father and Jesus Christ care about you right now, living your life. They care about your "modern" problems. The Savior can offer you grace right now! Sometimes when we read about Christ living 2,000 years ago, it's easy to keep Him 2,000 years ago in our mind. Just like the prophets we read about in the scriptures, we keep Him in the time period where we read about His stories. **"And as they were afraid, and bowed down their faces to the earth, they said unto them, Why seek ye the living among the dead?"** Jesus isn't with everyone else we've read about who has since passed on. He is alive! He rose from the dead so He could be on our journey with us as much as He was on the streets in Jerusalem.

I'm grateful for a living Savior, with living prophets, with ever-present personal revelation that can help me in my immediate times of need. So what help, guidance, love, or impressions do you need today? It's all available right now in this living gospel!

— Cali

DAY 178

LUKE 24:29

Two disciples were walking on the road to Emmaus when the resurrected Savior approached them, but their eyes were not allowed to recognize Him! These disciples were sad. They explained to the disguised Christ that their friend, Jesus, had been a mighty prophet; but today had been the third day since His crucifixion, and He hadn't returned yet. After some more conversation, they arrived at their dwelling, and the men pleaded gently with the disguised Jesus: **"Abide with us: for it is toward evening, and the day is far spent. And he went in to tarry with them."**

They didn't exactly know who this man was who had walked with them, but He had read the scriptures to them and invited the Spirit. I can imagine them thinking that if this person did anything to bring them closer to the Spirit, they wanted Him to stick around. What journey have you been walking on recently? Maybe you are learning to love the scriptures more, you want more spiritual experiences, or you are looking to grow your faith.

No matter your path, Jesus is there walking with you, even when you don't realize it! It's tough to see and recognize Him when our lives are filled with all sorts of mortal distractions, sadness, or frustration. But He is with us! And He'll stay with us on our path in the future, too, as we invite the Spirit to abide with us just a little bit longer.

— Cali

DAY 179

LUKE 24:32

How does the Spirit feel to you?

The resurrected Jesus appeared to two of His followers who walked along the road to Emmaus. Though they didn't recognize Him until after He'd left their presence, these followers described how they felt this way, **"Did not our heart burn within us, while he talked with us by the way, and while he opened to us the scriptures?"**

For these disciples, the Spirit felt like a burning fire in their hearts. But that isn't how the Spirit has to feel. In fact, I waited for my entire childhood to feel a burning in my heart that just never came, so I thought I wasn't feeling the Spirit. It wasn't until years later that I realized the Spirit communicates to me most frequently with bursts of ideas or strong nudges in a certain direction. No spiritual heartburn for me!

It's important that we don't miss spiritual promptings because we're waiting for a specific type of impression. The Spirit can speak in strong emotions, burning hearts, nudges, whispers, and so many other ways! It's up to each of us to figure out what the Spirit sounds and feels like!

— Kristen

DAY 180

JOHN 20:1

Mary Magdalene holds a sacred place in history as the first person on earth to see the resurrected Jesus Christ. Why is that? We don't know for sure, but the scriptures give us a good idea.

"The first day of the week cometh Mary Magdalene early, when it was yet dark, unto the sepulchre. . . ."

Mary was so anxious to follow after Jesus that she woke up before the sun and arrived at the sepulchre while everyone else still slept. Mary was likely blessed with this sacred experience because she was an "early" disciple.

Early disciples don't have to be compelled to be righteous. They study the scriptures, serve, repent, and pray without anyone else's influence forcing them to do so.

And because they serve so willingly, they are blessed– not necessarily with the chance to see Jesus in person– but to find Him in their lives earlier and more easily than those who are compelled to do good.

– Kristen

JOHN 20:16

When I was a full-time middle school teacher, I made it a goal to memorize all 90-some kids' names by the end of the third day of school. Now, you have to understand that I am the worst at remembering people's names! But I also think that names are super important. So to meet my goal, I would spend those first three days of school quizzing myself with the students' picture rosters, practicing their names while walking around the room, and honestly praying for help! I was always able to meet my goal.

By the second month of school, I noticed some other teachers would still be asking students in their classes what their names were or repeatedly calling some students by the wrong name. Guess which teacher the kids connected with faster? There is something different, deep, and personal about calling someone by their name!

Jesus Christ, the Savior of all mankind, appeared to Mary first after His resurrection. **"Jesus saith unto her, Mary. She turned herself, and saith unto him, Rabboni; which is to say, Master."**

All He said was her name. Can you imagine the Savior saying your first name? Really imagine it? Learning, remembering, and saying names shows connection and importance. And just like He showed with Mary, Jesus knows your name.

– Cali

DAY 182

FEED BOTH
BODY AND
SPIRIT

JOHN 21:17

At one point, the Old Testament prophet, Elijah, was so depressed He asked the Lord to let Him die. This wasn't part of the Lord's plan, so He prepared to meet Elijah on a mountain for a spiritually uplifting experience.

But before He did that, the Lord did something important: He fed Elijah. After all, life looks a lot better on a full stomach!

Similarly, Jesus asked Peter, **"Simon, son of Jonas, lovest thou me? . . . And he said unto him, Lord, thou knowest all things; thou knowest that I love thee. Jesus saith unto him, Feed my sheep."**

Of course, we know that Jesus was inviting Peter to share the gospel with the world; but, interestingly, Christ used the words "feed my sheep" rather than "guide" or "lead."

It's hard for anyone to appreciate the beauty of the gospel when their stomach is rumbling so loudly they can't hear your message. So while we need to share the gospel with others, we need to share our physical bounties with others as well.

— Kristen

DAY 183

ACTS 1:8

Can you imagine being one of the disciples watching the Savior return to heaven following His resurrection? This wonderful Jesus, who had just spent three years teaching you about the gospel, replacing old traditions with love, performing miracles, and extending forgiveness freely, was now going to His heavenly home. I think it would bring a lot of different emotions, but I'm sure some of the disciples felt scared and alone, unsure how they would be able to keep the pure gospel going that Christ had shared. But Christ taught them just one last thing before He ascended that I'm sure brought them comfort: **"But ye shall receive power, after that the Holy Ghost is come upon you: and ye shall be witnesses unto me both in Jerusalem, and in all Judæa, and in Samaria, and unto the uttermost part of the earth."** The disciples had the power of the Holy Ghost with them! The Holy Ghost was able to sustain these men as they transitioned into their roles as apostles and leaders.

The Holy Ghost prompts us to do the things that Jesus would do if He were physically here with us. The Holy Ghost keeps us connected to the Savior no matter how far apart we are physically. And we can keep this same Holy Ghost consistently in our lives, too! Being away from Jesus was difficult for His apostles, and it can be difficult for us as well! But He has left us with His Spirit so that we can still have direct access to what the Savior would do. What a gift!

– Cali

DAY 184

DON'T
JUST FEEL,
DO!

ACTS 2:37

The story of Alma the Younger is one of the most famous in the Book of Mormon. The wicked young man who fought against the church was called to repent and had a total change of heart.

But rather than simply repenting and going on with his life, Alma felt compelled to go out and undo the wickedness he had spread. He couldn't sit still once he'd felt the power of Jesus; he had to act!

Similarly, after Peter bore his witness to some men in Jerusalem, **"...they were pricked in their heart, and said unto Peter and to the rest of the apostles, Men and brethren, what shall we do?"**

Don't you love that? When the Spirit pricked their hearts, they didn't just go home and feel good; they felt compelled to act! They were so excited about the gospel that they couldn't sit still; they had to change who they were.

So here's a question to ponder today: What do you <u>do</u> because of how you <u>feel</u> about Jesus Christ?

- Kristen

DAY 185

BECAUSE YOU
LOVE

ACTS 2:44

I decided to be a fun mom recently, and I bought my kids a battery-operated bubble machine they could play with in the backyard. It was a great idea until they realized there was only one bubble machine and two of them. They worked together to come up with a plan for how they would take turns holding the bubble machine, but they weren't very good at putting that plan into action. Whenever it was one kid's turn, the other would change their mind and decide they wanted it for longer. There were a lot of arguments and frustration!

Sharing is a tough skill for young kids to learn! But I think it can still be a difficult skill for older people to practice, too. That's why I'm so impressed with how the people that Peter taught and baptized behaved. They had so much love and compassion for each other! **"And all that believed were together, and had all things common."**

They shared because they loved each other.

What do you share right now? Maybe you share your talents, money, home, or time. It's easy to fall into the trap of thinking we share just because we have to. But there is so much Christlike joy and fulfillment to be found when we give and share because we love each other, just like the people Peter baptized did.

— Cali

DAY 186

ACTS 3:12-13

Over twenty years ago, I offended a dear friend by doing something incredibly rude. I went through the repentance process and begged my friend for forgiveness which she gave, but I couldn't seem to forgive myself. I felt like my error had changed my value as a person– that I was somehow more flawed, more filthy than before.

People came running from everywhere when Peter and John healed a lame man. **"And when Peter saw it, he answered unto the people, Ye men of Israel, why marvel ye at this? or why look ye so earnestly on us, as though by our own power or holiness we had made this man to walk? The God of Abraham, and of Isaac, and of Jacob, the God of our fathers, hath glorified his Son Jesus."**

Peter and John immediately turned everyone's attention to Jesus, reminding them that His power is what affected the mighty change. Their invitation was to accept that Jesus could perform impossible miracles. And the same is true for us. We need to accept that Jesus' power to perform miracles can extend even to us and the forgiveness of all our sins. When we refuse to forgive ourselves, it's as if we're saying, "Well, Jesus is powerful, but not THAT powerful." But as Peter and John pointed out, Jesus is great enough that He can perform impossible miracles– including cleansing us of the sins that we struggle to forgive ourselves for.

- Kristen

DAY 187

ACTS 5:2-3

Have you ever wondered why God asks us to pay tithing?

Couldn't God tell the prophet where to find a hidden cave full of diamonds? Or perhaps God could inspire people to donate land and supplies so that temples could be built for free?

The fact is, God could do those things very easily. God would have no trouble providing for His church financially. But He doesn't because that isn't the actual purpose of tithing. The purpose is for you and me.

A husband and wife– Ananias and Sapphira– came to Peter to pay tithing. However, they held some back instead of bringing the full ten percent. Ananias **". . . brought a certain part, and laid it at the apostles' feet. But Peter said, Ananias, why hath Satan filled thine heart to lie to the Holy Ghost, and to keep back part of the price of the land?"**

Peter understood that Ananias and Sapphira didn't deny the church anything they couldn't get in some other way– after all, God is a God of miracles. But they were depriving themselves of blessings that couldn't come in any other way.

- Kristen

DAY 188

ACTS 5:4

Ananias and Sapphira were a couple who conspired together and agreed beforehand that they would lie to God's representatives about how much money they had earned. They thought they could get away with it!

But they got caught. **"Whiles it remained, was it not thine own? and after it was sold, was it not in thine own power? why hast thou conceived this thing in thine heart? thou hast not lied unto men, but unto God."**

Lying is bad. But why was their lie so terrible?

There was no excuse that they had felt pressure to tell a lie during an awkward moment. There was no excuse that they had forgotten to tell the truth. They deliberately decided to lie and thought about it extensively beforehand!

Of course, each of us will make mistakes and sin. When we have good intentions but fall short, repenting and trying again is much easier. But when we have a plan to sin, it is so much more difficult! Heavenly Father always knows our intentions.

Sin happens. There is more than enough of it in our lives without us planning to add more!

— Cali

DAY 189

BE
DESCRIBED LIKE
JESUS

ACTS 5:16

I want you to read this verse as if you don't know any context: **"There came also a multitude out of the cities round about unto Jerusalem, bringing sick folks, and them which were vexed with unclean spirits: and they were healed every one."**

Without any context, who do you think this verse is talking about?

It sounds a lot like Jesus Christ, right? But, surprise, it's Peter! Peter did exactly what the Savior would have done if He was on the earth in that situation.

Food for thought: Wouldn't it be cool if someone described your actions, and others could identify it as being exactly what the Savior would have done in that situation?

I think that's a new goal of mine. I'm not going to always get it right, of course. Some descriptions of my actions will still totally be "me." But I think that as I study the Savior's life more and more, I can have more moments where I'm right in sync with Jesus, just like Peter was.

— Cali

ADD PRIESTHOOD POWER TO FAITH

ACTS 6:6, 8

A few years ago, I was called to be the Ward Choir Director. This is a little embarrassing, but I was annoyed and frustrated with my calling for very selfish reasons. So, in my pride, I thought it didn't matter if I was set apart for this calling. I had a series of experiences that quickly humbled me, but it made me reflect on the question: Why do we get set apart for callings that we receive in our wards, branches, stakes, or missions?

In Acts 6, we learn that the apostles chose Stephen (and a few others) to serve widows in the area. They set him apart: **"...and when they had prayed, they laid their hands on them... And Stephen, full of faith and power, did great wonders and miracles among the people."** Stephen now was equipped with faith AND power! He brought the faith, and the priesthood power was given as he was set apart for his calling. That faith and the priesthood power together allowed him to work incredible miracles!

Priesthood power is available to anyone who is set apart for a calling in the church. It is so sad that I was too prideful to take advantage of priesthood power in my life many years ago, but it's a mistake I don't want to make again. When we claim our priesthood power and add our own faith, we can work miracles, just like Stephen did!

– Cali

DAY 191

INVITE THE SPIRIT TO TEACH

ACTS 6:10

The twelve apostles realized they needed help. Though they were doing their best, they couldn't care for the entire church alone.

And so they called seven other men to help them, one of whom was Stephen. We don't get a complete background on Stephen, but we do know that he was a mighty disciple of Christ who spoke with power and performed miracles.

Stephen's spiritual power bothered some of the synagogue leaders who likely felt threatened by him, and so they began disputing with Stephen, hoping to find a fault in this amazing man.

But the scriptures say that these men who were determined to find fault with Stephen **". . .were not able to resist the wisdom and the spirit by which he spake."**

Don't you love that? Even though they hated Stephen, they simply could not resist the Spirit with which he taught! That is why it's so important when we teach or share the gospel that we invite the Spirit to be the real teacher. His influence is truly irresistible!

— Kristen

DO RIGHT, BE RIGHT

ACTS 7:39

Have you ever wondered why the Israelites in the Old Testament struggled so much with faith and obedience? With a miracle-producing prophet in their midst, they still quickly turned away from God.

The book of Acts provides us with a bit of insight into why faith was so hard for the Israelites. Acts 7:39 says they **". . .thrust [Moses] from them, and in their hearts turned back again into Egypt."**

Isn't that an interesting picture? Though the Israelites' feet were headed forward toward the promised land, their hearts were turned backward toward Egypt. And boy, did it not work out well for them! Though they were doing the "right" things, they did them with the wrong spirit and were ultimately denied entrance into the promised land.

We need to be careful that we don't do the same thing. Do we ever go through gospel actions– doing the "right thing"-- while our hearts are turned in the opposite direction? It's not enough to simply do right; we must be right in our hearts!

– Kristen

DAY 193

HOLY EXPERIENCES CAN HAPPEN ANYWHERE

ACTS 7:55

If I say the phrase "holy places," what locations come to mind? Most people would probably say their home, the temple, meetinghouses, or even nature. Let's look at Stephen. He wasn't an apostle– just a good guy who followed through on promptings and assignments. The local government got a bit nervous about his natural power, set up some false witnesses, and started a trial against Stephen.

In a government building, surrounded by people who were literally out to get him, he delivered a beautiful and powerful sermon. **"But he, being full of the Holy Ghost, looked up steadfastly into heaven, and saw the glory of God, and Jesus standing on the right hand of God."** Did it matter where Stephen was? Nope. All that mattered was that he was filled with the Holy Ghost.

Traditional "holy places" are so important. There are physical locations where it is naturally easier to feel closer to God and heaven. But to have powerful spiritual experiences, we can be anywhere!

Whether you are driving in your car, making sandwiches for your kids, at work, or hanging out with your friend, holy experiences are available to anyone anywhere. When we keep the Spirit with us, we can create holy places all around us.

– Cali

SACRIFICE LOVINGLY

ACTS 7:60

Stephen was the first martyr after Christ's resurrection. He sacrificed his life because he would not move from what he believed. What have you had to sacrifice for this gospel? Friends? A certain lifestyle? Family? Money? Time? Energy? It's a sacrifice to be "all in" with this gospel. Sometimes we get a nice groove going on autopilot, and other times we are painfully aware of what we are sacrificing.

But here's where I think Stephen teaches us a valuable lesson. These are his final words: **"And he kneeled down, and cried with a loud voice, Lord, lay not this sin to their charge. And when he had said this, he fell asleep."**

Stephen sacrificed his own life with a spirit of forgiveness and love to the people who were killing him!

We are all sacrificing, but HOW are we sacrificing? Is it with resentment? Is it longing for things we shouldn't have? Is it self-pitying or self-righteous? Or do we lovingly sacrifice? Stephen taught us that even in the worst situations, we can choose to feel love, grace, and mercy for those around us. We can sacrifice with a compassionate heart!

– Cali

DAY 195

ACTS 8:18

Simon started out as a pretty bad guy, using sorcery and persuasion to gain power. But the great missionary, Philip, came to town, and Simon was wholly converted and then baptized! Simon was now all-in. Then Peter and John came to town hearing of Philip's success, and gave the gift of the Holy Ghost to all the people Philip had just baptized. **"And when Simon saw that through laying on of the apostles' hands the Holy Ghost was given, he offered them money."**

It makes me chuckle a bit that Simon, the sorcerer-turned devout follower, mixed his utter awe for the amazing gift and power of the Holy Ghost with his old ways of using money as a bargaining tool. Of course, money can't buy us the Holy Ghost, and Peter later chastised Simon for thinking that it could, but doesn't this reveal so much of what Simon desired?

Are we living our lives in such a way that we depend on the Holy Ghost for constant nourishment, guidance, and peace? Could someone look at how the Holy Ghost influences your life and want to jump forward, offering money, to have that same gift in theirs? I think it's a beautiful point to consider. Having the Spirit with us at all times is a gift beyond comprehension! And that is the power that Simon, somewhat naively but definitely sincerely, offered money for the chance to have.

— Cali

ACTS 9:6

During the worst of my years with OCD, my life felt entirely overtaken by my compulsive behaviors. I would wash my hands hundreds of times a day and often those hand washings would last up to two and a half minutes. Though my skin was raw and bleeding from being dried out by washing, I still scrubbed and scrubbed and scrubbed.

Then one day, I read a scripture in Acts that changed my life. Saul– who had been actively persecuting the church– was called to repentance by an angel. **"And he trembling and astonished said, Lord, what wilt thou have me to do?"** I realized that in all my hand washing and avoidance behaviors, I did not consider what the Lord wanted me to do. And so, I began to use Saul's question as my own personal mantra. When I would touch something "dirty" like a light switch or a piece of mail and found myself at the sink, I would ask, "Lord, what wilt thou have me to do?"* Though it seems silly, I found so much power in seeking the Lord's will instead of following through with what the OCD had trained my brain to do.

Could you do the same? When you find yourself going through your day somewhat mindlessly or in a routine rut, could you pause a moment and ask, "Lord, what wilt thou have me to do?" I think you'll find, as I did, that the Lord wants to be in the details of our lives if we'll let Him.

– Kristen

*For anyone with Obsessive Compulsive Disorder, this practice can make some OCD behaviors worse and lead to scrupulosity and religiosity. This entry does not contain therapeutic or medical advice. Please consult your doctor and/or therapist for help!

DAY 197

ACTS 10:17

A few years ago, my husband and I made a big purchase– a house! I was having a hard time committing to a home, but then I had a beautiful experience in the temple where it was clear this house was it. But then the anxiety started. "Well, what if it's not right? There are so many things that could go wrong with this purchase!" We ended up purchasing the house, and it turned out to be exactly what we needed in so many ways!

Have you ever wondered: "Is this my anxiety, or is this the Spirit?" Here's what I learned with our house purchase: I had a strong confirming spiritual experience, and then I DOUBTED that I had interpreted the message correctly.

"Peter doubted in himself what this vision which he had seen should mean." Peter saw a marvelous vision and then afterward doubted what he had learned. It's normal to not fully understand a prompting or revelation when it is first given to us, just as Peter experienced. Just like when I started being concerned about buying the house, doubts happen.

But when those doubts come, we must remember to trust what the Spirit told us the first time! We can trust our past spiritual experiences and stay anchored in peace instead of anxiety. The Spirit can help get rid of our doubts!

– Cali

DAY 198

ACTS 10:20

I was at a leadership conference for work a couple of years ago and was introduced to the concept of different planning styles people have. Most people fall into one of two categories: Some want to see the forest before they can see the individual trees. (In other words, they need to see the big picture before they can start going through the little details.) Others want to see all of the individual trees before they can see the forest. (In other words, they need to know how all the details will work before they can see the big picture.)

I am part of the first group, 100%. But I love Peter's example! Peter has a big, kind of confusing vision. While pondering, he gets the inspiration that three men are there to meet him. **"Arise therefore, and get thee down, and go with them, doubting nothing: for I have sent them."** In other words, Peter gets some very small tree details with no big vision of the whole forest! But Peter goes. His faith is unshakeable. He is slowly able to piece together that his new purpose will be teaching and converting the first group of non-Jews.

What an example! I certainly prefer to see the big picture in my life before getting the details, but I'm learning that I can always trust the Lord to be the best leader, even when He only gives me the details. The "big picture" might come much later, but I've got the best master planner in charge!

— Cali

BEFRIEND EVERYONE

ACTS 10:34-35

The Israelites had a long history of religious exclusionism. Their familial connection to the great prophets Abraham, Isaac, Jacob, and Moses was a point of pride for them and gave them a feeling of elitism.

In fact, it was against Jewish custom and law for an Israelite to even enter the home of a non-Israelite! Yet, as Peter preached the gospel, he had a vision that taught him the gospel was meant to go to all the world– Israelite and non-Israelite alike.

So, led by the Spirit, Peter entered the home of Cornelius, a centurion, and said, **"Of a truth I perceive that God is no respecter of persons: But in every nation he that feareth him, and worketh righteousness, is accepted with him."**

This was earth-shattering! Peter had entered the home of a non-Israelite and began to preach the gospel to him! I love Peter's example of speaking to and befriending someone despite his personal feelings or discomfort.

Do we go out of our way to befriend those outside our usual circles? Do we seek out those who God points us toward, or do we spend our time only with those "like us"? Something to ponder on today!

– Kristen

DAY 200

RESIST GOD'S
PROMPTINGS

ACTS 11:17

Peter's dinner party with the non-Israelite, Cornelius, did not go unnoticed among his fellow disciples and friends.

When he returned home, they questioned him about his behavior. Entering the home of a Gentile was unexpected and– in fact– illegal! Peter had gone against hundreds of years of Israelite tradition. What was he thinking?

Peter patiently explained his vision and experience in detail. He told his friends what he had learned and how he'd felt. Then he asked these men, **"...what was I, that I could withstand God?"**

Preaching to Cornelius and breaking Jewish custom probably wasn't what Peter had wanted to do; it had not been part of his plans. And yet he knew the prompting to do so came from God, and he refused to resist that prompting.

Have you been trying to resist a spiritual nudge from God? Have you felt pushed to start or compelled to stop something but haven't? Let's all be a bit more like Peter and stop trying to withstand the promptings of God!

— Kristen

DAY 201

ACTS 12:15

The whole church was praying for their beloved prophet, Peter, who was in jail. A group of saints gathered at Mary's house to pray. There was a knock on the door, and a young girl named Rhoda went to see who it was. Guess who she heard at the door? Peter! She was so excited that she ran back to the others and told them Peter was there! But all the saints who were gathered together, intently praying that Peter would be set free, told Rhoda that she was crazy. **"And they said unto her, Thou art mad. But she constantly affirmed that it was even so."**

Dear, excited, sweet Rhoda stood her ground. She didn't second guess what she had just experienced. She didn't defer to the older people in the room. But she also didn't argue or make a scene. Instead, she constantly affirmed that it was Peter. Personal spiritual experiences and personal revelation are so interesting because they are just that: personal. Nobody else experiences exactly what you experience!
Do you have enough spiritual confidence to trust your promptings and constantly affirm them in kind ways to others?

When Rhoda constantly affirmed what she heard, the people's hearts were finally softened enough to check the door themselves and receive that same witness. We can soften hearts and invite others to come hear what we have heard, too!

— Cali

DAY 202

ACTS 13:22

This book was inspired by the One Minute Scripture Study podcast that Cali and I host together. But the podcast didn't start with both of us!

I began podcasting as a solo project and wasn't introduced to Cali until I interviewed her for the podcast. As we video chatted, I kept thinking, "I love this girl! She's a scripture nerd just like me!" She was a girl after my own heart! A week later, I asked her to co-host the podcast with me; the rest is history.

Who is someone you would say is a "person after your own heart"? Why would you say they are?

The Lord described David as **"a man after mine own heart, which shall fulfil all my will."** God knew He could trust David because he aligned his will with God's!

I love that description and wonder if God could describe me similarly. Are my will and desires so aligned with God's that He feels like I'm someone He can trust?

Could He say that about you?

– Kristen

DAY 203

WORTH IT

ACTS 14:15, 22

Last year I made a goal to compete in a triathlon for the first time. I've wanted to do this for years, and I decided this was the year it would happen.

I've spent the past eleven months running, lifting, biking, swimming, and learning as much as possible to prepare for the big event. It has been a huge effort and the hardest thing I've done physically in my life. But the vision of crossing that finish line has kept me going through all the sweat and tears . . . and yes, even some blood!

This experience has also taught me something important: the things most worth having are usually hard to get. Paul taught, **"We also are men of like passions with you, and preach unto you that ye should turn from these vanities unto the living God. . . we must through much tribulation enter into the kingdom of God."**

As much as we want life to be easy, the price of getting back to God is high and will take a lot of work.

But if we can keep our eye on the finish line– on the moment when we get to enter God's glorious presence– we will realize and remember that it is more than worth the price!

– Kristen

DAY 204

LISTEN
TO THE
"NO"

ACTS 16:7

Have you ever received the answer of "no" to a prayer? We like to come up with really good plans. Maybe it's an idea for your calling at church, plans for your next career move, or a plan for how to help your child. But sometimes, God says "no."

Did you know that Paul experienced this, too? Paul really wanted to travel to certain areas to share the gospel. **"After they were come to Mysia, they assayed to go into Bithynia: but the Spirit suffered them not."**

Paul's desire was perfectly righteous! And it probably made sense for them to preach to the people in Bithynia, too. Maybe Paul had travel arrangements or contacts there. But he prayed, and the Spirit told him, "no."

For me, "no" answers usually come with stupors of thought. I feel like the next step is not available to me. Or I feel "off" as I pray about it.

It takes a lot of faith to NOT go through with something we want to do. And usually the promptings for what we should do instead do not come until we have shown the faith not to go down the first path. We can all work on having the faith to set our pride and ideas aside in order to truly improve on aligning our wills with God's!

– Cali

DAY 205

ACTS 16:25

Paul and Silas were doing the right thing. They were preaching the gospel and anxiously engaged in God's work. And yet, they were stripped, beaten, and thrown into prison.

If there was ever a time to be depressed, this was it! But in the middle of the night– in the middle of their afflictions– **"Paul and Silas prayed, and sang praises unto God: and the prisoners heard them."**

These men didn't know how their trial would end. They didn't know if they would be imprisoned for the rest of their lives. They didn't know if they would be starved, continuously beaten, or killed. And still, they prayed and sang praises to God.

How well do you and I do the same?

Do we express gratitude in the middle of our trials, or do we wait for them to end? We can learn from the example of these men that gratitude and praise are possible in any circumstances!

– Kristen

DAY 206

ACTS 17:11

What are your scripture study strengths? What are you fantastic at? What are your scripture study weaknesses? What is more difficult for you? I love taking inventory of my scripture study habits from time to time! Isn't it so easy to recognize our weaknesses? It can be a lot more challenging to give ourselves credit for the things we are doing right.

But scripture study is so important! It's worth any effort to repent, change, and improve. Look at what we learn about a particular group of saints: **"These were more noble than those in Thessalonica, in that they received the word with all readiness of mind, and searched the scriptures daily, whether those things were so."**

Searching the scriptures every single day brings the Spirit into our lives. That is so powerful! I've heard it said that no one can lose their testimony of Jesus if they truly study the scriptures every day. I'm not sure if that's true, but I know that when I spend time in my scriptures every day, I know more about the gospel. I can teach better, receive inspiration more easily, and I feel like I'm showing my Savior that I'm willing to put in the work to learn.

Whether it's for hours or only one minute a day, studying my scriptures is always worth the effort!

— Cali

DAY 207

SPEND TIME DOING IMPORTANT THINGS

ACTS 17:21

What do you do when you have free time?

Recently I was hanging out with my mom and sister who live 1,500 miles away from me, and I kept picking up my phone.

I was checking news websites, email, and social media instead of talking with the people I'd traveled all this distance to be with!

Paul discovered the same problem in Greece. He said, **"For all the Athenians and strangers which were there spent their time in nothing else, but either to tell, or to hear some new thing."** They were constantly caught up in the thick of thin things.

Instead of spending their time having essential conversations, focusing on building relationships, or drawing closer to God, the Athenians were busy finding new ways to entertain themselves.

Perhaps you and I could work on spending our time caught up in important things instead of turning to our phones or the internet "to hear some new thing."

- Kristen

DAY 208

ACTS 17:27

Has it ever bothered you that the Holy Ghost speaks in a still, small voice? Do you ever wish He would talk in a shaking, loud voice that you couldn't ignore?

I sure have!

During my dating years, I desperately pled with Heavenly Father to know if my (now) husband was "the one." I prayed, fasted, and attended the temple hoping for God to send me a big sign (preferably a billboard-sized one) to point me in the right direction. But a big sign or even a hard push in the right direction never came.

Instead, I felt a simple sense of peace, happiness, and excitement about my future.

Paul explained that there's a reason we hear the Spirit and the voice of our Savior as a still, small voice. He said, **"That they should seek the Lord, if haply they might feel after him, and find him, though he be not far from every one of us."**

The voices of the Lord and the Spirit are quiet because They are close by. They don't have to yell from across a celestial distance because They are right next to us!

- Kristen

DAY 209

ACTS 18:23

Why do we go to church each week? Maybe you've asked yourself this question during a time of spiritual struggle, when you've had to deal with a toddler, or when you feel like you don't have any friends in your ward.

Besides partaking of the infinitely important sacrament, Luke (the author of the Acts) gives important commentary on Paul's travels: **"And after he had spent some time there, he departed, and went over all the country of Galatia and Phrygia in order, strengthening all the disciples."** He went around strengthening all the disciples! What a fantastic reason to go to church!

Instead of focusing on teaching a lesson, conducting music, or listening to a teacher, we can turn outward! We can focus on finding ways to strengthen the people around us. I've been strengthened by people who had conversations with me, shared meaningful comments in lessons, or even those who just smiled at me. And we certainly don't need to be perfect to strengthen others! Your strengths are probably someone else's weaknesses and vice versa. We all get to be strengthened, and we all get to strengthen others as we share what's worked for us and how we've gotten closer to Jesus. Try it out! The next time you go to church, think of one way that you could use your particular gifts to strengthen someone else. And you might just find you have strengthened yourself!

— Cali

DAY 210

ACTS 21:13

Paul's friends were worried for him. They thought that if Paul went to Jerusalem to preach the gospel, he would likely be imprisoned.

They begged him not to go. **"Then Paul answered, What mean ye to weep and to break mine heart? for I am ready not to be bound only, but also to die at Jerusalem for the name of the Lord Jesus."**

In other words, "You're worried about me being imprisoned? That's no big deal! I'm willing to die for Jesus Christ!"

I love this example of valiant discipleship, and it makes me wonder what you and I would be willing to sacrifice for our testimony of Jesus.

Would we give up our favorite TV show that always has inappropriate scenes in it? Would we give up sleeping in one Saturday a month so we can go to the temple?

Jesus doesn't ask us to give up our lives, so what part of our lives can we give to Him instead?

— Kristen

DAY 211

ACTS 22:10

Who enjoys being told what they are doing wrong in their life? Not me! But at the same time, I also am fully aware that I am not perfect. One role righteous leaders have, whether it's general church leaders, local organization presidents, or parents in their own homes, is to invite people to repent and change.

When Paul was called to repentance by a heavenly appearance from the Savior, guess how Paul responded? **"And I said, What shall I do, Lord?"** Can you imagine if that was our response to every lesson, every talk, every family council?

Instead of feeling anger because someone dared tell us we were doing something wrong, annoyance because they aren't perfect either, or even apathy because we think we couldn't learn from anyone like that, the Lord invites us to always change! He wants our hearts to be willing to be molded and refined.

A boring seminary lesson? "What shall I do, Lord?" A long stake conference talk? "What shall I do, Lord?" A book of scripture we don't understand? "What shall I do, Lord?"

There's always something we can learn and improve, and the Lord will always lead us in the right direction if we ask.

– Cali

DAY 212

ACTS 22:15

A few years ago, a dear friend asked me for my thoughts on a very serious personal problem she was facing. I realized that I'd had a powerful spiritual experience that related to her question and went searching in my journals for a record of it.

I was shocked to discover that I had never written it down. This had been one of the most important spiritual experiences of my life, and there was absolutely no record of it ever happening! As I counseled with my friend about her concerns I had to rely on my memory of this amazing experience. There were gaps in what I remembered, and much of the feeling was lost. I had missed out on a great opportunity to record a powerful spiritual moment and to share what I'd learned with my struggling friend.

What about you? Have you had powerful spiritual experiences? Have you recorded them as a witness to what happened?

Paul taught, **"...thou shalt be his witness unto all men of what thou hast seen and heard."** It's hard to be a witness of something we have forgotten!

Today would be a great day to consider what spiritual experiences we have yet to write down and then start writing so we can be ready witnesses when called upon!

- Kristen

DAY 213

YOU CAN CHANGE!

ACTS 22:19

When Saul (later known as Paul) was called to repentance and to preach the gospel, he felt unworthy. He said, **"Lord, they know that I imprisoned and beat in every synagogue them that believed on thee."**

Saul's unworthiness wasn't a small problem! Saul had caused physical harm to those who believed, and now he was supposed to work side by side with these same men? Luckily for Saul and us, the Lord doesn't focus on who we were. He focuses on who we can be, and He knows we can change!

A prison warden, well-known for his work rehabilitating his prisoners, was once asked why he went to such great lengths to help convicted criminals. He was reminded that "a leopard can't change its spots."

The warden replied that he didn't work with leopards; he worked with men. And unlike leopards with their spots, men change every single day.

That warden was right, and God is right! You and I can change! We are not stuck forever being who we are today. We can become better and wiser every day.

– Kristen

DAY 214

BE OF GOOD CHEER

ACTS 23:11

"And the night following the Lord stood by him, and said, Be of good cheer, Paul." Can you put your name in that sentence? Imagine the Lord appearing to you, calling you by name, and saying, "Be of good cheer!"

Paul, as usual, was in dire circumstances with people plotting against his life from every angle. But Paul, as usual, was still preaching of Christ and doing what he thought was right.

And that's why the Savior told him he could be of good cheer. Not because of Paul's circumstances but because of his actions and choices!

No matter the circumstances in your life right now, whether they are dire, confusing, boring, joyous, frustrating, or nerve-wracking, the Lord knows you can choose to do what is right. There is always room for service, love, personal gospel study, and keeping the commandments!

Our Savior invites us to be of good cheer because He knows we can use our agency to do something good and righteous despite our circumstances.

— Cali

DON'T WAIT FOR CONVENIENT SEASONS

Paul was in prison. . . again.

Felix, who was a Roman leader in Judea, investigated Paul's case and even listened to Paul speak in his defense. Despite Felix being married to an Israelite, he seemed to have never heard about the gospel of Jesus Christ. As Paul spoke to him and **". . . reasoned of righteousness, temperance, and judgment to come, Felix trembled, and answered, go thy way for this time; when I have a convenient season, I will call for thee."**

Whether this referred simply to Paul's case or perhaps Felix's awareness that God was calling him to repent, that "convenient season" seems to have never come.

How often do we put off good things, waiting for a "convenient season"? We think we'll finally study the scriptures, pray sincerely, attend the temple, or do service when life calms down. But as it was for Felix, convenient seasons always seem to be in the future and not right now.

Let's determine today that we'll do what's right no matter how busy or inconvenient the season may be!

- Kristen

DAY 216

ACTS 26:28

I attended a high school volleyball training camp the summer before ninth grade. I participated in every practice, worked hard, and practiced at home until I was quite good! But when the time came for tryouts, I chickened out and didn't go.

You could say I "almost" played volleyball in high school. That word "almost" means I missed out on a lot of opportunities. Games. Practices. Friendships. I was close to playing but lacked the follow-through to benefit from being on the team.

Thousands of years before my volleyball failure, Paul stood before King Agrippa and bore a powerful testimony. The king was moved by Paul's words and believed in the prophets. This was great news!

"Then Agrippa said unto Paul, Almost thou persuadest me to be a Christian."

That one little word, "almost," kept the king from a lifetime (perhaps an eternity) of blessings. Almost following Jesus, almost bearing your testimony, almost getting married in the temple means almost getting the blessings that come with these actions. We need to make sure we don't waste our lives in a string of "almost" actions and instead commit to doing the things God asks us to do!

– Kristen

DAY 217

ACTS 28:5

Paul was bitten by a venomous snake. This was going to be it! It would surely kill him!

But instead: **"And he shook off the beast into the fire, and felt no harm."** Paul felt no harm from this snake bite that should have killed him. No harm! This miracle had to have taken great faith in God and mighty priesthood power.

What if we looked at this from a spiritual perspective? There are some brutal, emotional, heartbreaking, "venomous" situations God asks us to endure.

Do we believe we can call upon God to lessen the "harm" we feel to our spirits? I'm not talking about sadness. But when that sadness turns into bitterness, regret, hatred, anger, or resentment, we've started to let some of that venom enter our hearts.

God can help us keep that venom out. We need to ask for help! We also need to have faith that His help is available.

Once we do this, we'll still feel the sting of the snake bite, but it won't make us bitter toward our Heavenly Father. In fact, it will turn into a miracle that allows us to grow closer to our God.

– Cali

DAY 218

ROMANS 1:12

It was a Sunday morning in college, and I did not feel like attending church. Life had dealt me a couple of rough blows recently, and I felt like I just wanted to stay in bed. My roommates kindly encouraged me to get up and go to church. Even though people surrounded me, I felt alone that Sunday. I thought that no one could really understand what I was going through.

But as I sat in Relief Society, the teacher started to share some struggles she was currently dealing with which were almost exactly the same as mine! Tears welled in my eyes as she shared how she was turning to God and having some incredible spiritual experiences despite her trials.

That was the message I needed to hear! I had been so frustrated and overwhelmed that I wasn't turning to God like I knew I should. On that Sunday morning, I needed to be comforted by someone else's faith so that I could grow my own faith.

When Paul wrote his letter to the Roman saints, he told them that he couldn't wait until they were reunited again. Why? **"That is, that I may be comforted together with you by the mutual faith both of you and me."** When we meet together with friends, family, or ward members during tough times, we can help comfort each other by sharing our experiences and our mutual faith in Christ!

– Cali

DAY 219

ROMANS 2:1

The other day I was sitting at a professional baseball game that was– to be honest– quite dull. The local team was playing terribly, and I was tired of watching them lose, so I turned my attention to the other spectators.

I quickly became engrossed in watching a young mother whose tiny toddler was crawling and walking around without her notice. The little boy looked barely old enough to be walking, yet his mother was paying him no attention as he crawled up on the bleachers and almost fell over repeatedly.

I became increasingly upset as the mother stared at her phone or talked with her friends instead of paying attention to her child. He kept standing up on the bleachers and almost falling backward! How irresponsible of his mother!

Oddly enough, as I sat there judging this distracted mother, I lost track of my own children and had no idea what they were doing. They could have run onto the field naked for all I knew! How often do we do that? We judge others for doing the same things we sometimes do ourselves! Paul taught that **". . . wherein thou judgest another, thou condemnest thyself; for thou that judgest doest the same things."** The next time we start judging others, we can remember it might be a call to repentance for ourselves!

- Kristen

DAY 220

ROMANS 3:10-11

In the scriptures, we frequently read about "righteous" people and "unrighteous" people. But what actually makes someone righteous or unrighteous? If none of us are perfect, how can we possibly know whether or not we are at least on the right track to being considered "righteous"?

Paul gives us a great clue! **"As it is written, There is none righteous, no, not one: There is none that understandeth, there is none that seeketh after God."**

If a group of people doesn't have any righteousness in them, it's because they aren't seeking after God!

So, are you seeking after God? If I lose my cell phone during the day, I'm proactively going to get up and look everywhere until I find it. That's how I picture "seeking after God." It's someone looking for the Spirit, service opportunites, personal growth, and prayer with God.

Don't forget, we still don't have to be perfect at this! We just need to take some sort of action each day to seek after God, even if it's just a silent prayer in our hearts that we are on the right track. Small but proactive actions like that are all it takes to be righteous!

— Cali

DAY 221

ROMANS 3:23

Have you ever felt overwhelmed by your Celestial Kingdom "to do" list? To "make it" spiritually, you need to be sure to:

- ☐ Study the scriptures
- ☐ Pray sincerely
- ☐ Attend the temple regularly
- ☐ Serve others willingly
- ☐ Overcome your sins
- ☐ Think pure thoughts
- ☐ Keep all of the commandments

And on, and on, and on. This imaginary list can make discipleship and eventual celestial glory seem impossible! That is until we remember that we were never supposed to make it on our own. Paul taught that **". . .all have sinned, and come short of the glory of God."**

In other words, no one makes it back to God without help. No one can do "the list" perfectly. Every single person needs Jesus Christ's help to make it, and that is part of the plan. It's not a backup! It's not Plan B! "Trust in and rely on Jesus" is a part of that Celestial Kingdom "to do" list.

- Kristen

BELIEVE WHAT JESUS SAYS!

ROMANS 4:20-21

I remember reading the book <u>Believing Christ</u> by Stephen Robinson as a teenager. In the book, Brother Robinson taught that there is a distinct difference between believing in Jesus and actually believing Jesus.

Many Saints believe in Jesus. They believe He lived, died, and was resurrected. What they struggle to believe is Jesus' promise that He can redeem them. Sure Jesus can redeem their bishop, their ministering brothers, and their mom. . . but themselves? No way. They're just too far gone.

Paul taught, though, that the Savior has power to perform miracles within each of us.

Speaking of Abraham, who was promised a son in his old age, Paul said, **"He staggered not at the promise of God through unbelief; but was strong in faith, giving glory to God; And being fully persuaded that, what he had promised, he was able also to perform."**

Abraham believed despite all the evidence to the contrary. And we need to do the same! Though we know our weaknesses intimately, we need to believe that as long as we're trying, Jesus can and will redeem us!

— Kristen

DAY 223

ROMANS 5:3-4

Someone I admire very much recently talked with her daughter about a difficulty she was having in school. Most parents would want to swoop in and make things easier for their kid! But this person wisely asked her daughter, "Would you rather your life be easy or hard?"

Even more credit goes to her daughter, who bravely responded that she would rather have life be hard. She said that if life were easy, she would never feel triumph, learn to trust, or love others as much.

I want you to think about that for a minute. Would you honestly rather have life always be easy or always be hard?

"And not only so, but we glory in tribulations also: knowing that tribulation worketh patience; And patience, experience; and experience, hope."

The biggest blessings I've seen from my trials are that they give me empathy and a greater capacity to love. They've brought me closer to my friends, family, and spouse. And most of all, these difficult times have brought me closer to my Savior.

And I wouldn't give that up for all the ease in the world.

— Cali

DAY 224

ROMANS 6:16

A few months ago, I realized I was getting into a bad habit. I went to bed every night scrolling on my phone then woke up every morning and checked my phone first thing. My daughter would even bring me my phone if I left it in a different room– it was my constant companion, and I always looked at it.

Though I was using my phone to feel "free"– to be entertained or connect with peers– it quickly became a crutch I relied on.

Paul taught, **"Know ye not, that to whom ye yield yourselves servants to obey, his servants ye are to whom ye obey; whether of sin unto death, or of obedience unto righteousness?"**

Though I bought my phone to serve me, I quickly found myself serving its siren call!

What about you? Do you have anything that has become a master over you? Is it the call of the TV at night, the glow of your phone, or an addiction to any substance? Though these things may have signaled freedom when we first started using them, we need to remember to keep them in check so that they don't become our masters!

– Kristen

DAY 225

ROMANS 8:16-17

Why does God require so much of us? Why does He ask us to go through so many trials, keep so many commandments, and work so hard to avoid sin?

It wouldn't make sense if all we were trying to do in this life was stay out of an eternal hell. That would simply require us not being bad. No murder, no stealing, no worshipping idols: done!

So why does God require us to do and be so good?

Because God is not just saving us from hell, He is preparing us for glory in heaven. **"The Spirit itself beareth witness with our spirit, that we are the children of God: And if children, then heirs; heirs of God, and joint-heirs with Christ; if so be that we suffer with him, that we may be also glorified together."**

While many Christians believe they will spend eternity singing praises to God, this scripture from Paul clarifies that God is actually preparing us for life with and like Him!

So does that require work? Yes! But God is not just preparing us for life outside of hell; He is preparing us for life with Him in celestial glory!

- Kristen

DAY 226

LEARN WHAT
TO PRAY
FOR

ROMANS 8:26

Right out of college, I prayed really hard to get what I thought was my dream job. And I didn't get it. I was devastated! Have you ever prayed for something, and it didn't happen? It's not a fun experience. But, if we take a step back, it actually makes sense. We may have righteous desires, but we never see the whole picture as Heavenly Father does! He knew I needed to find a different job that would be perfect for my family and me and lead me to lifelong friends.

Paul teaches us how the Spirit can help us know what to pray for! **"Likewise the Spirit also helpeth our infirmities: for we know not what we should pray for as we ought: but the Spirit itself maketh intercession for us with groanings which cannot be uttered."**

It's okay to pray for what we want. But the Spirit can also help nudge our hearts toward what our Heavenly Father desires for us! Our desperate prayers for a particular job all of a sudden start ending with "if it be Thy will." And then we feel prompted to start praying for new job opportunities to pop up. And then we are praying for acceptance at a new job!

One of the roles of the Spirit is that He can teach us what to pray for. When we start changing our prayers into beautiful experiences where we listen to inspiration and follow the Spirit, we end up aligning our wills with God's.

— Cali

IT'S ALL
FOR YOUR
GOOD

ROMANS 8:28

I've always loved the phrase "hindsight is 20/20." It's so fun to look back at how I met my husband and realize that there were so many things that "just happened" to work out or conversations I "randomly" had that led us to each other. Looking back, it all worked out perfectly and for our good!

But I also remember what it was like to be in the dating phase of life. It certainly didn't always seem like things were working together for my good! There were plenty of frustrating, heartbreaking, and weird moments along the way.

"And we know that all things work together for good to them that love God, to them who are the called according to his purpose."

So, what if we could enjoy the joy and peace of "hindsight" right now? What if, when trials and hard times come, we trust that we will be looking back one day fully understanding why we needed to travel that path?

I want to try really trusting that all things are working together for my good, without having to wait until they actually do to believe it.

— Cali

DAY 228

GOD LOVES YOU ENDLESSLY

ROMANS 8:35, 38-39

Have you entered into a covenant with God? If so, then God has something called "chesed" for you!

Now don't get confused. That word "chesed" has nothing to do with cheese, much to my young daughter's chagrin. The word "chesed" is often translated in the scriptures as "lovingkindness" and explains God's special love for His children who make covenants. Though God loves all His children, those who enter into covenants with Him create a special relationship with Him. And in response to this covenant relationship, God promises to have "chesed" for these children– a patient love that will never, ever end.

Paul spoke about this "chesed" type of love saying, **"Who shall separate us from the love of Christ?. . . I am persuaded, that neither death, nor life, nor angels, nor principalities, nor powers. . . shall be able to separate us from the love of God, which is in Christ Jesus our Lord."**

No matter how much you and I mess up, no matter how far we feel we have fallen, we can never fall beyond the love God has for us. We are always wanted and loved by God and Jesus Christ; They have "chesed" for you!

– Kristen

DAY 229

ROMANS 11:33-34

If God gave you a chance to write a plan for your life, what would it include? Would you have added the trials you've gone through– the sicknesses, the deaths of friends and family, and personal struggles?

Most of us don't want life to be hard. We want sunshine and rainbows rather than storms and sorrow. But luckily for us, God sees what we can't– that life's difficulties can make us more like Him.

"O the depth of the riches both of the wisdom and knowledge of God! how unsearchable are his judgments, and his ways past finding out! For who hath known the mind of the Lord? or who hath been his counsellor?"

While we are focused on today, God sees the whole picture. He sees the gaps that need to be filled and the rough places that need to be smoothed. When we turn to God in prayer, rather than trying to counsel Him about how our lives should be going, perhaps we can remember that He sees what we don't and understands what we can't.

Though it might be painful, God is using your trials to make your life into a beautiful masterpiece.

- Kristen

DAY 230

DON'T CONFORM! TRANSFORM OTHERS!

ROMANS 12:2

When I entered middle school, I had no close friends. I had a lot of acquaintances from elementary school but no one to hang out with. I was desperate to not be alone, so I quickly found a group of established friends who would take me in.

I didn't know any of these girls before and quickly found that we had nothing in common though they were kind enough to befriend me. And so, I promptly began to conform. I wore similar clothes, listened to the music they liked, and joined in their activities whether or not I enjoyed them. I quickly became someone I was not, hoping to be accepted and loved.

Do you ever find yourself doing the same thing on a smaller scale: changing your topics of conversation, the types of words you say, or the outfits you wear depending on who you're with?

The scriptures warn that this is the opposite of what we— as followers of Christ— should be doing. **"And be not conformed to this world: but be ye transformed by the renewing of your mind, that ye may prove what is that good, and acceptable, and perfect, will of God."** Instead of being conformed by the world, we should be working to transform the world!

– Kristen

DAY 231

ROMANS 12:5-6

When I drive my car, my body coordinates pretty seamlessly. My hands and arms turn the steering wheel, my foot adjusts on the gas pedal, my eyes move around, and my neck turns to check for blind spots. Each body part is doing something different, but that is the only way that the car will actually drive!

Paul taught about the diversity and unity we find in the body of Christ: **"So we, being many, are one body in Christ, and every one members one of another. Having then gifts differing according to the grace that is given to us, whether prophecy, let us prophesy according to the proportion of faith."**

To build that connected body of Christ as saints, we recognize the variety of talents, life experiences, testimony stages, and education we each have. And we celebrate it! We use it to uplift each other and connect with each other! Driving a car means a lot of different things happening at once. So we need people with all sorts of different strengths working together toward the same goal of becoming a Christlike people.

This means we have to truly get to know people instead of assuming and judging. Connection is the real way to become unified in Christ, working toward the same purpose! So how might you reach out to someone today and build that authentic connection together?

— Cali

1 CORINTHIANS 2:4

Paul said, **"And my speech and my preaching was not with enticing words of man's wisdom, but in demonstration of the Spirit and of power."** I participated in a speech contest when I was in high school, and I ended up going pretty far! I learned the best structure for captivating speeches from interesting hooks, switching your tone of voice often, and balancing lighter anecdotes with heavy, straightforward points.

So, when I get asked to give a talk in sacrament meeting or when I teach a lesson, you could say that I know how to use the "enticing words of man's wisdom."

But I've learned that even if people say, "Wow, great talk! I paid attention the whole time!" it doesn't actually have a spiritual impact if I don't teach "in demonstration of the Spirit and of power."

Isn't it cool that people from prophets to members of our congregation don't need any formal "speech" training to change lives through the Spirit? We don't pick our local bishop based on who gives the best sermons because we don't need someone who is entertaining or well-educated. It honestly doesn't matter if we can use "enticing words" or not; we can still make an impact if we teach and preach while keeping the Spirit with us!

– Cali

DAY 233

1 CORINTHIANS 2:9

As young college students, my husband and I had the chance to visit Ireland. Having lived in Europe for the past year, we'd been able to travel to amazing places: France, Italy, Spain, Germany, Austria, and more. But as we drove along the Irish countryside, we were shocked. It was the most gorgeous country we had ever seen!

Every turn in the road brought another unbelievably green pasture, the ruins of an ancient castle, or a breathtaking shoreline. We spent the entire trip gasping in awe at the country's beauty, stopping to take pictures that couldn't possibly capture the magic of seeing it in real life.

As I think of that experience, I can't help but wonder what life with God will be like. Paul declared, **"Eye hath not seen, nor ear heard, neither have entered into the heart of man, the things which God hath prepared for them that love him."**

I imagine the Celestial Kingdom will be overwhelming to us– that we'll continually find ourselves gasping in awe at the glory of all God has given us.

It's essential to keep this in mind as we go through the trials of life. Yes, life might be hard. Yes, we will struggle. But will it really matter in the end if we get to spend eternity living with God in awe-inspiring glory?

– Kristen

DAY 234

1 CORINTHIANS 2:14

I've heard it said that if you think someone hasn't thought you were foolish for believing in the gospel, then you probably just aren't aware of it! I mean, if you look at everything in our scriptures and our church today, there are certainly things that seem completely foolish from the outside looking in. **"But the natural man receiveth not the things of the Spirit of God: for they are foolishness unto him."**

So why are some of the smartest and most well-educated people I know members of this church and believers of this gospel? Because the Spirit HAS to be involved when seeking gospel truths, hearing revelations, listening to prophets, and reading scriptures. The Spirit has to whisper those confirming messages. The Spirit has to give us that feeling of warmth. The Spirit has to appeal to our logical mind and show how it actually all makes perfect sense.

Are we just believing the foolish traditions of our fathers? Not when the Spirit is involved! Are we just exercising blind obedience and following whatever some authority figure tells us to do? Not when the Spirit is involved! When we have the Spirit with us, we shake off the bands of "foolishness" and begin to see what truth is! And at the end of the day, we can only get that heavenly perspective by keeping the Spirit with us.

– Cali

1 CORINTHIANS 3:2

My daughter drank only milk for the first few months of her life. And guess what? That was all that she needed! But then she got a little older and needed nutrition from a variety of foods, so we added solid foods along with the milk. She needed to practice and learn how to deal with different textures and tastes. Sometimes she loved the new things she tried; other times, she would spit them back out. Then she got even older, to the point that she didn't want us to feed her, and she needed to learn how to feed herself.

Do we see the parallels in our own gospel growth? We have to start with the basics of going to church, reading our scriptures, and praying. And then we start taking bites of the heartier meat of the gospel. We learn how to truly study the scriptures, how to communicate better in prayer, and how to serve in the temple.

Some of these new bites are hard to handle at first. But the "milk" concepts are no longer quite enough on their own. We recognize that we need something more to continue our spiritual growth. We move step by step along our spiritual progression!

"I have fed you with milk, and not with meat: for hitherto ye were not able to bear it, neither yet now are ye able." What spiritual steps are you ready for next?

– Cali

NO SHAME, JUST CHANGE

1 CORINTHIANS 4:14

Shame = you are bad because you did something wrong.

Have you ever felt shame? Have you ever realized you have shamed someone?

Well, that's precisely what Paul said he was NOT doing! **"I write not these things to shame you, but as my beloved sons I warn you."** He was trying to correct some pretty serious sins that the Corinthians were committing, but he made it clear that he was not shaming them. He was warning them, teaching them, and rebuking them.

What's the difference?

We believe that there are "rights" and "wrongs." But when we choose the wrong, we are not bad people! We are loved beyond belief. We have infinite worth. We are spiritual sons and daughters of Heavenly Parents.

We all make bad decisions. But we can correct ourselves and repent. And we will make bad decisions again. And we can correct ourselves and repent again. That's the whole purpose of this gospel! Shaming ourselves or others will never lead to the best results. We can always choose love and constantly improve by turning to our Savior! No shame necessary.

— Cali

DAY 237

1 CORINTHIANS 6:19-20

As a teenager, I would often buck against the strict rules my mother had set. My curfew was too early, my clothes had to be too modest, and there were always so many chores to complete. I thought to myself, "This is MY life! I should be able to do what I want!"

But the fact is, this isn't really my life. As Paul said, **"What? know ye not that. . . ye are not your own? For ye are bought with a price: therefore glorify God in your body, and in your spirit, which are God's."**

Our mortal experience and the bodies we live in are gifts from God; they are not our own. We did not create them or earn them! God and Christ created everything. They are the authors of our salvation.

The older I've gotten the more I've realized that I actually own nothing: not my life, my body, or anything else! And, in fact, not only do I own nothing, but I owe everything to God and Jesus Christ!

When we get upset about the rules and commandments that surround us, we can remember that they are part of the price of our mortal experience; a price that we happily agreed to pay in the premortal world!

— Kristen

DAY 238

1 CORINTHIANS 7:3

During the early years of my marriage, I found myself picking fights with my husband a lot. I chalk it up to immaturity, but there was no excuse. I would get upset with him over ridiculous things like toothpaste, being late to church, and which TV show we would watch at night.

I discovered a disturbing trend when I would fight with him. While I was being a rude and obnoxious grump to my eternal companion, as soon as an acquaintance would call on the phone or we would show up at church, I would be happy and kind to everyone around me. My husband was getting the cold shoulder while I gave friends and acquaintances warm hugs. That is not how a marriage or any family relationship should be!

Paul taught, **"Let the husband render unto the wife due benevolence: and likewise also the wife unto the husband."** Or in other words, be kind to the people who matter most in your life!

We need to be careful that the people we're connected to eternally aren't getting the worst of us while the world gets the best of us!

- Kristen

DAY 239

1 CORINTHIANS 9:24

Last year I ran a 5k for the first time. I got set up at the start line and immediately saw that there was no way I could win. There were extremely fit and well-trained runners who were obviously going to go much faster than I was.

I gave up any hope of winning and decided to just try to finish.

Paul taught, **"Know ye not that they which run in a race run all, but one receiveth the prize? So run, that ye may obtain."**

In this life there are winners and losers. If you win a race, I lose. If I win a raffle, you don't. But in God's marvelous plan, everyone can win the race. Limitless "first place" prizes are available, and no one has to lose.

So even if you look around and see that others might be able to spiritually "run" faster or better than you, remember that this life is not a contest. You can win the same race going at your own spiritual pace!

– Kristen

YOU'RE STRONGER THAN ANY TEMPTATION

1 CORINTHIANS 10:13

We are all tempted to sin every single day. You get tempted, I get tempted, even the prophet gets tempted!

Do you ever face a temptation that feels impossible to overcome? Maybe someone upsets you, and all you want to do is scream at them. Or something inappropriate pops up on your phone, and you know it's wrong, but you really want to click on it.

Our temptations can feel completely insurmountable during these moments, like there's no way out! But the fact is, there isn't a single temptation that you don't have the power to overcome.

Paul taught, **"There hath no temptation taken you but such as is common to man: but God is faithful, who will not suffer you to be tempted above that ye are able; but will with the temptation also make a way to escape, that ye may be able to bear it."**

Did you catch that? Your temptations are not unique, brand new, or impossible to overcome. God has already prepared a way for you to overcome it because others have also had to overcome it. Your job and mine when we face temptation is to discover the "emergency hatch" God has already prepared for us.

– Kristen

GIFTS COME FROM THE SPIRIT

1 CORINTHIANS 12:4

I once visited a beautiful tulip festival. I was blown away by how gorgeous the flowers were! The bright, vibrant colors were breathtaking, and I took very amateur pictures all afternoon.

Some of the tulips were easily visible, planted right along the path. Other tulips were meant to be viewed from across a pond with a beautiful water feature. Some tulips were planted in diverse patterns. Other tulips were planted in areas where they all looked the same. Despite their different locations, colors, purposes, and surroundings, every single flower was still a tulip.

Paul wrote to the saints in Corinth and talked about the diversity of spiritual gifts that are available. But he started by talking about how all the gifts come from the same Spirit. **"Now there are diversities of gifts, but the same Spirit."**

Each spiritual gift has a different purpose, just like the various tulips I saw while walking through the festival. But at the end of the day, each gift comes from the Spirit! No matter what your spiritual gifts may be, staying close to the Spirit is the way to help them flourish.

— Cali

1 CORINTHIANS 12:10

The "gift of tongues" has always seemed like a cool gift to me. Learning a new language seems so difficult!

But have you ever realized which other spiritual gift is ALWAYS listed with the gift of tongues? "**. . . to another divers kinds of tongues; to another the interpretation of tongues.**"

Speaking with tongues and interpreting tongues always go together because often they need to work hand in hand! The purpose of spiritual gifts is not just to easily speak a new language because it would be cool. Spiritual gifts are all about working together and edifying each other!

There is no point in a missionary miraculously knowing how to teach a lesson after just arriving in a new country if there is no one prepared to hear that lesson.

All our gifts can and should only be used when we need to edify someone! What a beautiful, circular relationship Heavenly Father has allowed us to create through His gifts. We help others when they are ready to receive, and we can be ready to receive blessings at the hand of others' gifts. How can you edify someone with your spiritual gifts today?

— Cali

EACH GIFT IS NEEDED

1 CORINTHIANS 12:21

I've noticed that when I judge other people, I'm usually comparing my strengths to their weaknesses. "Ugh, his meetings are so unorganized!" "Why can't she just do her ministering assignment? It's not that hard!"

And on the flip side, when I'm sinking into self-pity, I'm usually comparing my weaknesses to other people's strengths. "Why can't I be that kind of creative mom?" "I'll never catch up on everything I need to do!"

It sounds a lot like the situation Paul describes: **"And the eye cannot say unto the hand, I have no need of thee: nor again the head to the feet, I have no need of you."**

We all have been given different spiritual gifts and talents.

There is no need to compare our gifts and talents with each other, no matter how tempting it may be to do so! We need everyone in the kingdom of God at every skill level and with every kind of gift imaginable. You are needed exactly as you are!

– Cali

SHOW YOURSELF
CHARITY

1 CORINTHIANS 13:8

Have you ever tried to change something about your life by bullying yourself into it?

I know people who put pictures of someone with the "perfect body" inside their refrigerator to shame themselves into eating healthier. My husband struggles to wake up in the morning and once set an alarm on his phone which he named, "Wake up lazy bones."

Have you ever done something like that?

Not surprisingly, these efforts to bully ourselves into change rarely work. Why? Because they speak to our lowest selves, to our "natural man" who doesn't want to change.

So how do we change permanently? By speaking to ourselves the way God does: with kindness and a visionary focus on our amazing potential.

As Paul taught, **"Charity never faileth. . . ."** Why does it never fail? Because charity speaks to our eternal nature, to our spirits that long to be like our Father. Though it might take some time, loving ourselves and others through change is the only way to make lasting transformations in our lives.

— Kristen

GOD
SEES YOU
CLEARLY

1 CORINTHIANS 13:12

I'm not an expert in Greek, but I love to study the original language from which the scriptures were translated. For example, when Paul says, **"For now we see through a glass, darkly. . ."** there are two important differences found in the Greek version of the verse. When I first read that scripture, I understood it to mean that I can't clearly see God's plans for my life and the lives of others because it's like I'm looking through a darkened glass. That pesky veil of forgetfulness makes it hard to understand God's designs!

However, the word "glass" in that verse is translated from the Greek word ἔσοπτρον (pronounced esoptron), which is better translated as "mirror." And the word "darkly" is actually the simple Greek word ἐν (pronounced en) which indicates a fixed position. So that verse can also be translated to say, "In this life, I only see myself in a fixed mirror," or in other words, "I can't see myself the way God sees me." And how true that is!

We look at ourselves and see our weaknesses, failures, and faults. But God sees us for our strengths, successes, and potential! Perhaps we could each work on moving that "fixed" mirror so that it angles up to point at God. Then as we focus on Him, He can help us see ourselves as He does.

– Kristen

DAY 246

1 CORINTHIANS 14:5

Growing up, I was always jealous of my sister, who seemed perfect. She got straight A's, was student council president, and captain of the soccer and volleyball teams. It was so annoying to be her younger sister because I was just so. . . not perfect.

I envied her gifts and felt inferior for years. But recently, we were having a conversation in which she admitted that she had felt envious of me during those same years. "Why?!" I asked her incredulously, to which she replied that I had always had so much fun with friends while she was busy with school and extracurricular activities. While I envied her ability to accomplish so much, she envied my ability to balance friendships with school work.

I think we often do the same thing with our spiritual gifts. We see someone who can teach publicly, or understand various languages, or has the power to heal; and we want the same gift!

But Paul said, **"I would that ye all spake with tongues, but rather that ye prophesied: for greater is he that prophesieth than he that speaketh with tongues. . . ."** Or in other words, the flashy, fancy, "perfect" spiritual gifts aren't necessarily the ones we need. Each gift is needed, and your gift is no less important than the more publicly obvious ones.

– Kristen

DAY 247

1 CORINTHIANS 14:33

Change is always a little bit uncomfortable. I've been experiencing lots of change in my personal life recently, and most of it has been pretty good. But it's still challenging to go through any change, good or bad.

I feel like God is refining me right now with all of this change. I've been picturing the Savior waiting for me at the other end, ready to embrace me once I've become more Christlike.

One morning, I was listening to music and heard an arrangement of the hymn, "Be Still, My Soul." I love that hymn, but one phrase in particular stood out to me this time: "The Lord is on thy side."

What a beautiful reminder! I don't have to "get through" these changes to find my Lord on the other side. He's with me right now! He wants me to conquer and smash and totally rock every challenge and change coming my way!

"For God is not the author of confusion, but of peace, as in all churches of the saints."
God is not the author of confusion. He's not trying to trip me up by throwing things my way. He's not waiting to see if I make it or not. He is the author of peace. And He is on my side.

— Cali

IT'S ALL POSSIBLE
THROUGH
CHRIST

1 CORINTHIANS 15:14

Quick quiz: What do these phrases have in common? "The atonement," "The enabling power of the atonement," "Applying the atonement," and "Being strengthened by the atonement."

They are all phrases that President Nelson has asked us to STOP using. Why? Because they completely take Christ out of the picture! He has encouraged us to use terms like "the Savior's atoning sacrifice" that keep our focus on Jesus.

I used to attend church and learn about service, church history, families, spiritual gifts, or my Savior. But I remember it clicking in my mind one day that everything is actually tied back to Christ! **"And if Christ be not risen, then is our preaching vain, and your faith is also vain."**

We go to church to partake of the sacrament as a reminder of Christ's sacrifice. We learn about service to become more charitable like Christ. We study church history to see how others turned to Christ during their trials. Everything is connected to and possible only because of Jesus! Give it a try– the next church lesson, class, or talk that you sit through, make an effort to see how it is all possible only because of Jesus Christ, and share that testimony with others!

– Cali

TEMPLE SERVICE IS CHRISTLIKE

1 CORINTHIANS 15:29

What's one of the doctrines that completely sets The Church of Jesus Christ of Latter-day Saints apart from other Christian churches?

"Else what shall they do which are baptized for the dead, if the dead rise not at all? why are they then baptized for the dead?"

In our church, we baptize people on behalf of those who have passed away. We also know that all temple ordinances are made available by proxy for people who have died. Have you ever wondered why faithful, busy church members would spend time researching their ancestors' names and attending the temple to do temple work?

Church members spend time, effort, and even money to attend the temple, performing service for people who have died. And these people might not even accept the ordinances that are performed on their behalf!

I think the answer is because of Christlike love and compassion! Isn't vicarious temple work actually in similitude of what Jesus has done for us? He made the ultimate sacrifice to offer everyone a gift they may or may not even accept. Performing baptisms and other temple work for people who have passed on is one of the most Christlike sacrifices we can make!

— Cali

DAY 250

1 CORINTHIANS 15:51-52

Sometimes those who have grown up believing in Jesus Christ don't recognize how good the "good news of the gospel" really is. We are so used to reading about, and singing about, and teaching about the atoning power of Jesus Christ that we don't stop to think how miraculous it is.

But Paul taught the Greeks in Corinth what he referred to as a "mystery," saying, **"We shall not all sleep, but we shall all be changed, In a moment, in the twinkling of an eye, at the last trump: for the trumpet shall sound, and the dead shall be raised incorruptible, and we shall be changed."**

Can you imagine their surprise? We take this information about the resurrection for granted, but it would have been amazing news to the Greeks! They would get to see their dead fathers, mothers, brothers, sisters, and children again in the flesh! How they must have rejoiced and praised God for the revelation of this "mystery" that brought them so much hope.

Today, let's each take a moment to think about the many gospel "mysteries" and miracles we have gotten so used to that we forget to be in awe of them!

- Kristen

DAY 251

DEATH'S
STING IS NOT
ETERNAL

1 CORINTHIANS 15:55, 57

Losing someone you love hurts—a lot.

I lost my dad when I was seven. I lost a baby when I was pregnant. I lost my mother-in-law just a few years ago. Each one of these losses has been unbelievably painful.

This is why I've always been confused by Paul's words to the Corinthians when he said, **"O death, where is thy sting?"** If someone you love has died, you know that it stings intensely. The grief is immense and hurts more than you can explain!

It's important to understand that a sting in the ancient desert region where Paul lived wasn't just an inconvenience. A sting from a bee or even a scorpion could mean death! So Paul wasn't saying death doesn't hurt– he was saying it wasn't permanent!

As Paul said, **". . .thanks be to God, which giveth us the victory through our Lord Jesus Christ."**

Because of Jesus Christ, the death of a loved one might sting for a while– sometimes a long while– but that sting will go away and eventually be swallowed up in eternal joy.

– Kristen

DAY 252

1 CORINTHIANS 15:58

I made a goal to do some form of physical movement for an hour a few days a week. I was really good at first! I met my goal perfectly and wouldn't let any excuses get in my way. But one day, I had a super busy day, and I only had 15 minutes left to work out. I decided it wasn't worth it, so I watched a show instead. I quickly lost the momentum I had been building for my goal and stopped working out completely for a while.

Paul was a great motivator! He taught: **"Therefore, my beloved brethren, be ye steadfast, unmovable, always abounding in the work of the Lord."** Steadfast and unmovable! What an amazing goal. But what happens when we aren't quite steadfast? What happens when we move from the path we were hoping to stay on? It's tempting to throw the whole goal away when we fall short! It's tempting to think that if we can't do the full hour workout, we shouldn't even try. Or that if we are too tired to read a whole chapter of the scriptures, we shouldn't even bother studying for that day.

But any sort of progress is always worth it! Becoming steadfast and unmovable isn't a goal we can meet perfectly every day. But we can always work out for 15 minutes or read just one verse of scripture– any step forward is a reason to cheer!

– Cali

DAY 253

2 CORINTHIANS 1:3-4

Whenever I used to hear women complain about being sick while pregnant, I would say something like, "Oh, sorry," and that was it. It's not that I didn't care; it just didn't seem like a big deal to me. And then I got pregnant with my first child. And I got super sick. After surviving that pregnancy, anytime someone shared how sick they were while pregnant, I would empathize with every little detail! I would let them vent endlessly. I would check in on them often.

What hard things have you gone through? Have you noticed how you begin to empathize with and love other people who are going through similar trials? There seems to be a special connection that forms. And it all stems from God. **"Blessed be God, even the Father of our Lord Jesus Christ, the Father of mercies, and the God of all comfort; Who comforteth us in all our tribulation, that we may be able to comfort them which are in any trouble, by the comfort wherewith we ourselves are comforted of God."** God knows how to comfort us when we need it. So when we have to go through our own trials, we gain the ability to comfort others with that specific need. It's almost like a unique spiritual gift that we develop!

We can be the hands of God and comfort in the ways He would. Considering the trials you've had to navigate in your life so far, what are your "comforting" superpowers that you can use to reach out and help the people around you?

– Cali

DAY 254

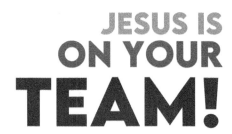
JESUS IS ON YOUR TEAM!

2 CORINTHIANS 3:5

Did you ever have to do a group project in school?

I was lucky that all my school friends were very, very smart. I, unfortunately, was not great at certain subjects like science, math, and geography.

When my friends and I would do a group project, I would try my hardest and contribute my best work; but I knew that if we got an A, it would be because of my friends, not because of me.

We're incredibly blessed that in the "group project" of seeking exaltation, our partner is Jesus Christ. We're expected to try our hardest and contribute our best work, but when we make it to heaven, it will be because of Jesus' perfection, not our own power.

Paul taught this to the Corinthians saying, **"Not that we are sufficient of ourselves. . . but our sufficiency is of God. . . ."**

So, if you ever get down on yourself thinking that you just can't make it, remember that you're not doing this project alone! You've got Jesus on your team, and with Him, you're destined to get an A+!

– Kristen

FOCUS ON THE ETERNAL

2 CORINTHIANS 4:18

When I got married, I was given the advice that if I had an issue involving my husband and the problem wouldn't matter in five years, then I shouldn't worry about it. But if the problem would be an issue in five years, then it would be worth bringing up and solving together.

I like the gist of this advice and use it in basically all of my relationships. It has helped me let the little things slide and focus on what matters most! It doesn't really matter if the dishes aren't all done tonight. But it does matter if we establish the habit of family prayer because that absolutely will have repercussions five years down the road.

Paul taught about this similar distinction: **"While we look not at the things which are seen, but at the things which are not seen: for the things which are seen are temporal; but the things which are not seen are eternal."** Some issues are temporal, and some issues are spiritual. Temporal issues like losing a job, not getting accepted into a school, or establishing a chore schedule are still big issues worth trying to solve in the best ways we can. But it's also important to give our top priority to solving issues that have the greatest impact on our spirit! Figuring out how to pray, study the scriptures, and cast sin out of our lives are worth our best efforts. When we focus on the things that will matter in the eternities, our focus can become much more clear!

— Cali

DAY 256

2 CORINTHIANS 5:7

Think about Paul's life. He was constantly all over the place– in and out of prisons, preaching to anyone and everyone, and traveling long distances.

If anyone can give us this advice, it would be Paul: **"For we walk by faith, not by sight."**

I'm sure Paul walked "by sight" to the best of his ability, using his own logic to plan, prepare, and seek appropriate food and shelter. But he relied on walking "by faith" time and time again when roadblocks would come up. He would rely on his faith when he didn't know who to teach or what to say. He would rely on his faith when he didn't know where he would get his next meal.

Planning out our lives "by sight" is great to start with as we use all the knowledge available. But when the roadblocks inevitably pop up, do we trust the Lord enough to walk "by faith" for a bit? To listen for any inspiration, "gut instinct," or prompting? I'm grateful for Paul's outstanding example of walking by faith!

– Cali

DAY 257

2 CORINTHIANS 5:20

When my husband and I lived in Belgium, I often felt like we were representatives of America.

As we mingled with local Belgians, we tried our best to be polite, to use the local language when possible, not to be obnoxious (locals often told us that Americans are too loud), and to be good citizens of the country we were visiting.

We wanted people to think well of Americans based on their interactions with us. It was almost like we were ambassadors for America!

Paul once said, **"Now then we are ambassadors for Christ. . ."** which you and I are! As members of Christ's church, we represent Him to others. And we should be careful of how we behave so that we are constantly showing others how Christ would act!

What would others think of Christ based on how you act at church? Or the way you behave at school or work? Or especially the way you act at home?

Today might be a good day to consider how well you are doing as an ambassador for Christ!

- Kristen

DAY 258

2 CORINTHIANS 6:14

The words of Paul are sometimes easily misconstrued. For example, he told the Corinthians, **"Be ye not unequally yoked together with unbelievers."**

It's easy to read that and think he's teaching that we shouldn't spend time with those outside our belief system, which is incredibly unhealthy and untrue! Some of the most wonderful people I've ever met are members of other faiths or don't belong to any religion at all.

The second half of Paul's statement clarifies what he actually meant. He warned, **"... for what fellowship hath righteousness with unrighteousness? and what communion hath light with darkness?"**

Paul wasn't talking about distancing ourselves from those who simply don't believe; he was talking about distancing ourselves from evil. So is it okay to make friends with neighbors who don't attend church? Heavens, yes, you absolutely should! But should you go to a movie filled with vulgar language, actions, and music? Absolutely not!

Those who are filled with light should only spend time with people and in places where they can maintain and spread that light– whether with those who believe or those who don't!

– Kristen

CREATE
IN YOUR
TRIBULATIONS

2 CORINTHIANS 7:4

When I was dealing with a pretty big emotional trial, the local missionaries stopped by our home. One of the sisters asked me, "What really brings you joy?"

It took me off-guard more than I expected. I couldn't quite narrow it down to just one answer, plus I wasn't feeling much joy at the moment. **"Great is my boldness of speech toward you, great is my glorying of you: I am filled with comfort, I am exceeding joyful in all our tribulation."** I wasn't finding a lot of joy in my tribulation.

But we ended up having a beautiful conversation about the connection between joy and creation. Something totally clicked in my mind! I have joy when I create a life for myself where I can feel the spirit and become more Christlike. I have joy in my life when I create a marriage and home where we keep the commandments, show love, and have fun! I have joy when I create breathtaking music that transcends any emotions words can capture. I have joy when I create beautiful, strong friendships.

And ultimately, I have joy when I am going through difficult trials, and yet I still create moments of happiness and peace with my Savior. So, what brings you joy? What are you able to create? When we create, I believe we find joy because we partner with Heavenly Father to bring goodness into existence.

– Cali

2 CORINTHIANS 8:14

When my husband and I bought our first home, I quickly realized that owning a home means constantly going back and forth between feelings of "abundance" and "want"!

At first, the home seemed perfect, and I felt abundant living in it. But then I wanted the walls painted. When they got painted, I felt abundant again! But then we wanted to redo our backyard. When our yard was finished, I felt overwhelmingly abundant and wanted to throw all the parties! The cycle has continued on and on. I think we go through similar cycles in almost every area of our lives! Paul acknowledged this, too: **"But by an equality, that now at this time your abundance may be a supply for their want, that their abundance also may be a supply for your want: that there may be equality."**

Isn't that such a cool balance that we've been asked to help with? Whether in our wards, our neighborhoods, or the walls of our own homes, we can help use our abundance to fill others' wants while our wants are assisted by other people's abundance. We will always have wants, whether it's emotional needs like good friendships and authentic connection or spiritual needs like a testimony or a desire to read the scriptures. And we can find a sweet equality when other people have an abundance to share with us! What do you feel like you currently are "abundant" with? How can you find someone with a "want" to share with?

— Cali

SERVE OTHERS CHEERFULLY

2 CORINTHIANS 9:7

Getting my kids to do chores can be challenging. They're like every other kid in the history of the world and don't love when I ask them to do dishes, clean the kitty litter, or tidy their rooms.

That is why it is such a joyful shock when occasionally, one of my kids will happily do their chores without being asked. It makes my day!

I imagine that is how God feels when He sees His children willingly serving each other. He must love it when we sit next to someone who is alone, care for the poor, or invite the missionaries into our homes.

The scriptures teach us that, **"Every man according as he purposeth in his heart, so let him give; not grudgingly, or of necessity: for God loveth a cheerful giver."**

Of course, serving is good, but how joyful it is for God when we serve willingly and happily! It must make His day!

So let's go out and ruin Satan's day (while making Heavenly Father's day) by serving others joyfully and willingly!

- Kristen

DAY 262

2 CORINTHIANS 11:3

As a teenager, I thought belonging to The Church of Jesus Christ of Latter-day Saints was pretty complicated. When my friends of other faiths would ask me about movies I watched, the language I used, or clothes I wore, it seemed like I was always reciting endless lists of rules I had to follow.

But as I've matured in age and spiritual understanding, I've discovered that the gospel is actually pretty simple. It's all about Jesus! When I focus on Jesus, all the "extra" things seem much more simple, too, because I'm adjusting my language, media use, and clothing to become more Christlike.

Paul taught, **"But I fear, lest by any means, as the serpent beguiled Eve through his subtilty, so your minds should be corrupted from the simplicity that is in Christ."**

Sure, membership in this church may look complicated from the outside looking in. And when we focus on the little elements of tithing, Sabbath day observance, temple attendance, and more, we can get caught up in the long to-do list, too!

There is so much peace to be found when we focus on "the simplicity that is in Christ." He is the goal, and everything else just helps us get to Him!

— Cali

RECOGNIZE GOD'S MIRACLES

2 CORINTHIANS 11:33

I have long loved the quote, "Opportunity is missed by most people because it is dressed in overalls and looks like work." I think it's equally true to say the following about how God works in our lives: "Miracles are missed by most people because they're dressed in overalls and look like helping yourself."

God is certainly a God of miracles, but He's also a God who helps those who help themselves! This was the case for Paul while he traveled through the land of Syria. Paul became aware that the governor of Damascus wanted to find him and hold him prisoner. But rather than wait for an angelic rescue, Paul said, **". . .through a window in a basket was I let down by the wall, and escaped his hands."**

There were likely guards, soldiers, and citizens all on the lookout for Paul. But the Lord provided a miracle for him to be able to escape in a basket. Did it require work on Paul's part? Absolutely! But it was still a miraculous occurrence.

How often do we say that something was just good luck, a happy coincidence, or that our hard work paid off? Perhaps we could practice recognizing that the experiences that just happen to come together for our good are miracles dressed up as work!

– Kristen

DAY 264

WEAKNESS CAN BRING CHRIST CLOSER

2 CORINTHIANS 12:9

Commas and quotation marks can make a big difference. I love the t-shirts that teach this by showing the two sentences "Let's eat grandma" versus "Let's eat, grandma." Punctuation is important!

In 2 Corinthians, Paul and the Lord both say some powerful things, but the lack of punctuation (in the form of quotation marks) can make it hard to understand who is saying what. You see, Paul was dealing with a huge trial. The scriptures never tell us what this trial was, but we know that on three separate occasions, Paul begged the Lord to remove it from him.

But the Lord said to him (and this is where I'm going to add some important quotation marks), **"My grace is sufficient for thee: for my strength is made perfect in weakness."** In other words, the weaker you are, the more My strength is made clear!

Then Paul said (quotation marks added again), **"Most gladly therefore will I rather glory in my infirmities, that the power of Christ may rest upon me."**

I love the message these words teach (and the punctuation clarifies): that we can rejoice in our weakness and trials because they are what can bring us closer to Christ than ever!

– Kristen

2 CORINTHIANS 12:10

I don't know about you, but I do not feel strong when I am weak! Why would Paul say something like this? **"Therefore I take pleasure in infirmities, in reproaches, in necessities, in persecutions, in distresses for Christ's sake: for when I am weak, then am I strong."**

When I looked at the footnotes, I noticed "weak" is linked to "humility." So Paul is really saying that when I am humble, then I am strong. This seems to make much more sense!

When I am humble, I am teachable, obedient, and repentant. But when I am prideful, I am stubborn, incapable, and sinful.

That's what I feel the gospel teaches me so well! I always have more to learn. I always have things to repent of. There will always be opportunities to be obedient.

My real Christlike strength comes from being humble!

— Cali

DOCTRINES ARE TAUGHT REPEATEDLY

2 CORINTHIANS 13:1

Have you ever realized how many sources of doctrine and religious teachings we have? It's overwhelmingly awesome! We've got the Bible, General Conference talks, the Book of Mormon, hymns, official proclamations, and countless more good content from church leaders constantly available to us.

But how do we know what is actually doctrine and what we should focus on the most? Paul taught, **"In the mouth of two or three witnesses shall every word be established."**

We can recognize doctrine by looking for the patterns! When we have multiple prophets and apostles agreeing and speaking out on certain topics, even across generations, we can know this is gospel truth!

We would not just hear one prophet say an important and essential thing to know, only to have it never mentioned or expounded upon again by others.

So what patterns have you noticed in General Conference recently? What topics have you seen pop up over and over in the New Testament? What doctrines have been reiterated time and time again? That's probably a big clue that these are the places our focus should be!

— Cali

DAY 267

GALATIANS 1:10

Most people don't enjoy conflict– I know I certainly don't! We want to fit in, make others happy, and not rock the boat!

But Paul taught that Christ's gospel isn't designed to fit in and keep the boat steady– it is a boat-rocking gospel! Paul asked, **". . . do I seek to please men? For if I yet pleased men, I should not be the servant of Christ."**

Seeing God's church and His leaders being criticized in the news can be disheartening. It can be difficult to feel like your religious beliefs are in direct conflict with what is currently popular.

I've had many awkward conversations with friends and family members who don't agree with the positions of the Church, and sometimes I think it would be nice if Christ's gospel rocked the boat just a little bit less.

But isn't it interesting that one of the identifying characteristics of the true gospel is that it won't be pleasing to the world? We can take great comfort in that as the world moves further and further from the standards of The Church of Jesus Christ!

– Kristen

SERVE PEOPLE AROUND YOU

GALATIANS 2:2

Every time I've asked someone in my ward why they moved into their current home, they have a long story involving many "coincidences" or answered prayers. They feel like God led them to be where they are. And I've got a similar story for why we are in the place we live right now! I've realized that most people I'm surrounded by are here because of some form of personal revelation.

Paul went on his journeys with the same guidance in mind: **"And I went up by revelation, and communicated unto them that gospel which I preach among the Gentiles. . . . "**

I like thinking that everyone has been guided to where they are right now for a purpose, no matter how long they'll be there! If this is true, what do you think your purpose might be?

Who can you reach out to and serve in a totally unique way? What new friends are waiting to be discovered? Who can you love? When we allow our lives to be led by personal revelation, God can lead us to the people who need our specific help the most!

— Cali

GALATIANS 2:16

I recently read an article by a pastor from a different church who read the entire Book of Mormon. He wrote about some of the good things he had learned from those scriptures in much the same tone I would write about learning new information from an encyclopedia. I was shocked by how casual the article was! The Book of Mormon has been so transformational in my life that it's hard for me to imagine someone else reading it and not also being transformed.

But it's true– religious scholars and curious critics have read the Book of Mormon and not been converted. This means that it's not just reading our scriptures that strengthens our testimonies and brings us closer to the Savior. There has to be something else!

Paul taught: **"Knowing that a man is not justified by the works of the law, but by the faith of Jesus Christ, even we have believed in Jesus Christ, that we might be justified by the faith of Christ, and not by the works of the law: for by the works of the law shall no flesh be justified."** We aren't saved or "justified" by the act of reading our scriptures. Instead, we need to open our scriptures with faith in Jesus Christ! We need to have the intent to grow our testimonies and the confidence that the Spirit will testify what we need to do. Our faith in Jesus Christ is what makes all the difference, and it's what turns the scriptures from books filled with ancient stories to living, powerful words straight from God!

– Cali

THE LAW POINTS TO JESUS

GALATIANS 3:24

A friend once told me of an unfortunate experience that happened to her at church. She struggled with being active as a youth but decided to attend all three hours of church one Sunday. When she arrived at Young Women, one of the leaders took issue with the skirt my friend was wearing. She measured this girl's skirt in front of all the other girls and told her it was too short for church. My friend was mortified and never returned to church again.

This story is sad for so many reasons. Although I'm sure everyone in this situation was doing what they thought was best, this Young Women leader was misguided in thinking that my friend's dress standards were what mattered most. In this situation, what mattered most was that a girl came to church looking for belonging. She should have been welcomed with open arms regardless of what she wore.

The point of the gospel is not the rules! As Paul taught, **"Wherefore the law was our schoolmaster to bring us unto Christ, that we might be justified by faith."** In other words, the rules, standards, and commandments are there to help bring us to Jesus! So when we find ourselves judging someone because they aren't keeping the commandments perfectly, we should remember that our job probably isn't to enforce the rules. Our most important job is to simply love others and help them find their way to Jesus.

– Kristen

DAY 271

GALATIANS 5:1

Thousands of years ago, you lived with Heavenly Father and had to make a choice. Would you follow Heavenly Father's plan or Satan's alternative?

Your Father's plan came with some risks but also the opportunity for tremendous blessings. Satan's alternative came with the promise of no risk but also a loss of freedom.

Your presence here on earth is a sign that you fought for freedom! You stood for God's plan– risks and all– because you wanted the ability to choose!

So, why would we ever want to give up the freedom we fought so hard for? Paul advised the early saints to **"Stand fast therefore in the liberty wherewith Christ hath made us free, and be not entangled again with the yoke of bondage."**

The choice to sin is the choice to lose the freedom we once fought for. It is the choice to have Satan be our master and to become enslaved by our bad habits and sins.

We need to make sure that every day we make the same choice we made premortally: God's plan of freedom over Satan's plan of bondage!

- Kristen

GALATIANS 5:22-23

I've had the chance to work with teenagers in the Church for almost twenty years (wow, I feel old)! From seminary to EFY, the question I hear more than any other is, "How do I know if I've felt the Spirit?"

I think we get the wrong impression from scripture stories that the Spirit should feel or sound a certain way. We expect our hearts to burn. We expect to hear a voice. But the fact is that you and I are feeling the Spirit all of the time without realizing it!

In Galatians, we're given a simple list of the ways the Spirit prompts us throughout the day: **". . . the fruit of the Spirit is love, joy, peace, longsuffering, gentleness, goodness, faith, meekness, temperance. . . ."**

In other words, when you have good and pure feelings, you are feeling the Spirit!

When was the last time you felt love? That was the Spirit! When was the last time you felt joy, peace, patience, a desire to do good, or had faith? That was the Spirit!

We are surrounded by the Spirit all of the time! It's not so much a matter of figuring out what the Spirit feels like; it's learning to recognize how we're already feeling it every single day!

– Kristen

DAY 273

WEARY NOT!

GALATIANS 6:9

William H. Flaville wrote the words to an older hymn that is no longer in our current hymn book called "Weary Not." Here are just a few lines from his hymn: "If the way be full of sorrow, weary not! Happier will be the morrow, weary not! Here we suffer tribulation, Here we must endure temptation, But there'll come a great salvation, weary not!"*

What lines would you add to this hymn? At different points in my life, I would have added lines like: "If it's a Monday morning, weary not!" "If my kid needs another snack, weary not!" "If I'm not getting an answer that I'm hoping for, weary not!"

Life is tiring! Having mortal bodies and dealing with mortal problems can make us weary. But William H. Flaville took inspiration from the encouragement of Paul, who taught: **"And let us not be weary in well doing: for in due season we shall reap, if we faint not."**

If you are tired right now, it's okay. Keep doing the good, small things that you can. The big reward will come in the future, but Christ can still help lift us up today.

– Cali

*"If the Way be Full of Trial, Weary Not", Lyrics by W. H. Flaville, <u>The Songs of Zion</u>, 1918.

YOU'RE FOREORDAINED TO FOLLOW CHRIST

EPHESIANS 1:4-5

"What were you foreordained to do here on the earth?" A teacher at church asked our class this question once, and everyone squirmed in their seats. Because when we think of being foreordained for something, it's usually for something big and important.

We know prophets were foreordained for their roles. But what about regular old me?

In my life, there have been some big and important moments where friends have shown up at my door at just the right moment or when a speaker in church said a sentence that answered a prayer. We are most likely doing big and important things already, even if we don't realize it!

Paul also offers a different perspective: **"According as he hath chosen us in him before the foundation of the world, that we should be holy and without blame before him in love: Having predestinated us unto the adoption of children by Jesus Christ to himself, according to the good pleasure of his will."**

We've also been foreordained to be disciples of Christ. And I can't think of anything bigger and more important than that! So how can we fulfill our destiny today?

— Cali

DAY 275

GOD CREATED YOU PERFECTLY

EPHESIANS 2:10

Every time I'm out in nature, I am in awe of God's creations!

The variety of plants and animals makes the world absolutely beautiful, and I can't help but give a small prayer of gratitude for how wonderful the world is.

If asked what my favorite parts of nature are, I would say I love quaking aspen trees, lilac bushes, and river otters; but I am so grateful that that isn't all there is in the world. I'm thankful for maple trees, oak trees, and fir trees! I'm grateful for toucans with their colorful beaks and for jaguars that run so majestically. Each of these creations is magnificent and perfect and so are we.

The scriptures teach that **". . . we are his workmanship, created in Christ Jesus. . . ."** We are part of God's creations! The fact that we don't all have the same body shape, eye color, or facial features is a sign of the Creator's mark on each of us.

Just like we wouldn't want a river otter to have a toucan's beak or a fir tree to lose its leaves like a quaking aspen, we shouldn't wish to be different than we naturally are. The bodies we've been given are the works of a perfect Creator, and God does not make mistakes!

– Kristen

DAY 276

WELCOME THE STRANGER

EPHESIANS 2:11

The book of Ephesians has a lot of things: encouragement, advice, and doctrine. But in all my searching of this book, I've only found one of something most books of scripture are full of: a command.

Only once in this entire book of scripture are we emphatically told that we must do something. And what is it we're told we must do?

Paul told the Ephesians to, **". . .remember, that ye being in time past Gentiles in the flesh. . . ."**

That might sound a little confusing, but it means that it's important to remember what it felt like to be a stranger– in Paul's words, a Gentile.

Do you remember when you were new in your ward, school, or work? What did it feel like to be a stranger? I distinctly remember how lonely it was to be in a new ward! I felt nervous and wondered if I would find friends. I wasn't sure where my classes were and hoped someone would help me find my way around.

Is there something you could do to reach out to those who are new in your ward (or school or work) to help them feel less like a stranger?

– Kristen

DAY 277

EPHESIANS 2:20

Did you know that all 15 living apostles and prophets today are set apart as "special witnesses of Jesus Christ"? They have unique permission and ability to testify of Jesus Christ anywhere in the world with that special priesthood power.

The next time you listen to General Conference talks, give this a try: Listen to each talk the apostles give and see if you notice them bear witness of Jesus Christ at some point during their message.

Paul was a perfect example of always bearing witness of Jesus Christ! In every letter he wrote, he testified of Christ, taught of Christ's abilities, and then gave correction or specific direction as needed. Listen to Paul's words: **"And are built upon the foundation of the apostles and prophets, Jesus Christ himself being the chief corner stone."**

While we may not have the title of "special witness of Jesus Christ," are we still His witness? Do we mention Christ in our prayers, talks, and lessons? Do we speak of Christ openly with those around us, including our family members? Jesus Christ can be our chief cornerstone, too!

— Cali

DAY 278

EPHESIANS 4:3

Last summer my family spent two weeks in Texas. We drove from Dallas to Austin to San Antonio and everywhere in between in a small car that just barely fit our family. It was hot, and everyone was a bit done with traveling, so the car rides became a chance to push each other's buttons.

Have you ever had a similar experience with your family?

To stop the fighting, I spent most of our car rides encouraging my kids to focus on a common goal. We played "car rainbow" and "solve that riddle." We listened to audiobooks and Hank Smith talks. And, to my surprise, it worked like magic! The more everyone focused on the same goal, the kinder we were to each other!

Paul taught the Ephesians that they should **"Endeavour. . . to keep the unity of the Spirit in the bond of peace."** Note that he said "unity" comes first, and then what comes? Peace!

So when you find yourself in a personal struggle with someone, judging someone, or feeling left out, what can you do? My experience taught me to look for ways to create a common goal, because unity can also lead to greater understanding, peace, and kindness.

– Kristen

DAY 279

EPHESIANS 4:32

Would you say it seems easier to be angry or kind to someone who has hurt you?

I have to be honest, when someone hurts or offends me it feels completely natural to let anger take over. I become defensive and sometimes even want to lash out at the person who has wronged me.

It often feels like anger is the easiest option– overcoming it can seem impossible. Does it feel that way for you? If so, it might surprise you that psychological studies have shown that anger actually takes way more energy than happiness!

Those who are angry feel compelled to protect their territory, are constantly on the defensive and create damage in relationships that takes time and energy to repair. So, might the initial decision to give into anger be easier? Sure, but it ends up leading to a lot of extra work.

Paul encouraged the Ephesians to, **"...be ye kind one to another, tenderhearted, forgiving one another, even as God for Christ's sake hath forgiven you."** Just like God and Christ choose to be kind to us every single day, we can choose kindness in every circumstance. After all, in the long run, it's the easiest option!

– Kristen

DAY 280

EPHESIANS 5:20

"I know I have a lot of things to be grateful for! I'll think about it later when I'm not so busy." I caught myself thinking this recently as my husband, my kids, and I all had our schedules filled to the brim. I call this the trap of "future gratitude." It's when I know that I have things to be grateful for, but I don't want to focus on them yet.

I have found the antidote to thinking that I'll wait to be grateful in the future! It's learning to live with a constant "attitude of gratitude." Paul put it this way: **"Giving thanks always for all things unto God and the Father in the name of our Lord Jesus Christ."**

Giving thanks always can be tough when we are looking for specific things to be grateful for! I don't feel very grateful when I've got busy days or heartbreaking trials. But when I can shift to an "attitude of gratitude," I can focus on God. I can zoom out and see the bigger picture. I feel gratitude for being alive, for having a mortal experience, and for my Savior's atoning sacrifice. It's a constant baseline of gratitude, no matter what else is happening in my life!

If you've been stuck in a rut of waiting for "future gratitude," try turning to Heavenly Father and Jesus Christ more and more often and see what attitude of gratitude is possible!

— Cali

DAY 281

SHARE
OUT OF
LOVE

PHILIPPIANS 1:20

When I was in third grade, my class was learning about sign language. I raised my hand to tell my teacher that I knew how to do some sign language thanks to a class I was taking in church. She invited me to the front of the room, where I proudly signed the alphabet for my class. I then told my teacher I knew how to sign an entire song. I stood in front of my entire class and sang and signed the words to "I Am a Child of God." Talk about being a brave missionary!

Paul was even more brave in sharing the gospel– not because he didn't care what anyone else thought, but because he loved Jesus so much he couldn't help but talk about Him. Paul said, **"According to my earnest expectation and my hope, that in nothing I shall be ashamed, but that with all boldness, as always, so now also Christ shall be magnified in my body, whether it be by life, or by death."**

What a fantastic reminder that love is the secret ingredient to sharing the gospel boldly. Whether it's love for our neighbors or love for Jesus, that pure love can motivate us to speak when the Spirit prompts.

Perhaps the next time we want to share the gospel but feel awkward or ashamed, we can focus less on ourselves and more on our love for others and the Savior!

- Kristen

DAY 282

PHILIPPIANS 3:8

During my teenage years, I made a difficult decision: to throw out all of the CDs I owned that had profanity or inappropriate messages.

Into the trash went hundreds of dollars worth of music that I honestly enjoyed but knew was keeping me from being as close to the Spirit as I wanted.

On a much larger scale, Paul did the same thing. He gave his whole life to preaching the gospel of Jesus Christ and proudly declared, **". . . I count all things but loss for the excellency of the knowledge of Christ Jesus my Lord: for whom I have suffered the loss of all things, and do count them but dung, that I may win Christ. . . ."**

In the end, nothing else will be as important as our relationship with our Father and our Savior. Paul considered everything he had to sacrifice as if it were dung compared to what he gained spiritually. In other words, nothing else mattered at all!

What "dung" could we give up to gain a closer relationship with Jesus? Is it inappropriate media, an unhealthy friendship, or a specific sin? If so, we can be like Paul and happily give it up for the blessing of being closer to Christ!

– Kristen

DAY 283

PHILIPPIANS 3:15

Imagine an apostle (pick any one!) coming to live with you for one week. He wouldn't do anything special; he'd just watch what normal life looks like for you and your family over the course of a week. He would then return home and write you and your family a personalized letter. What would that letter say?

I asked this question to a group of 11 and 12-year-olds, whose answers ranged from, "He would tell me to not fight with my brother so much" to "He would give me tips on how to be a kinder sister." We talked about the positive things the apostle might praise as well, and I got responses such as, "He would tell my family we are doing a good job at trying to read the scriptures each day."

Wouldn't that be cool to have your own personal epistle from an apostle? Well, I honestly think we don't have to wonder about this hypothetical situation because of the Holy Ghost! **"Let us therefore, as many as be perfect, be thus minded: and if in any thing ye be otherwise minded, God shall reveal even this unto you."** God will reveal to us what we can change and improve through the Holy Ghost! What can I improve? What am I doing well? The Holy Spirit can give us those specific answers when we ask with sincere intent to act on the counsel we receive. And we then can discover our own personalized epistle, straight from the Savior.

— Cali

DAY 284

PHILIPPIANS 4:8

What are the things that you spend your time thinking about?

I spend a lot of time figuring out my family's weekly schedule, planning my next podcast episode, or pondering "whodunit" in my current mystery book.

Perhaps you spend a lot of time thinking about work, school, your favorite hobby, or the latest political scandal you read about in the news.

But Paul taught us what our thoughts should be focused on. I'm going to take some license and switch the end of this verse to the beginning: **"Think on these things. . . whatsoever things are true, whatsoever things are honest, whatsoever things are just, whatsoever things are pure, whatsoever things are lovely, whatsoever things are of good report."**

Is my "whodunit" pure?

Is the latest political scandal "lovely"?

If not, perhaps we could spend more time thinking about things that are truly of "good report."

- Kristen

BE CONTENT IN ALL SITUATIONS

PHILIPPIANS 4:11

Paul taught: **"Not that I speak in respect of want: for I have learned, in whatsoever state I am, therewith to be content."** Paul learned how to be content in any situation!

Do you know what I think of as one of the biggest opposites of feeling "content"? Feeling stressed! Can you think of anyone who could rewrite this scripture as "I am able to be stressed in all circumstances"? (Don't worry, I'm raising my hand, too!)

We all have a lot of things to do. And I'm a professional at feeling stressed whenever my plate starts getting too full! But if Paul, the guy who dealt with everything from shipwrecks to jail, said that he could be content in any circumstance, then I've probably got something to learn from him.

What if we could live a busy, everyday life without feeling stressed? What if we could feel "content" with whatever we've got on our plate right now, and if the plate is getting too full, we take something off?

Jesus is the one who can help us feel content in all the situations we find ourselves in. When we turn to Him in constant prayer, He is the one who can send us inspiration and guidance on how to find peace at all times, as long as we ask.

— Cali

DAY 286

PHILIPPIANS 4:13

I've flown a lot with little kids since my extended family lives in different states than I do. One particular time, I was flying with my daughter, who wasn't even two years old yet. It was a late-night flight that got delayed a few times. The flight experience was brutal! She freaked out during the safety demonstration and wouldn't calm down. She kept kicking the seat in front of us and got bored with every distraction I had packed in our bag. I kept praying that she would either calm down or fall asleep! But she did neither of those things.

As the flight ended, the person sitting directly in front of us (whose seat I kept trying to protect from my daughter's crazy kicking) turned around and said, "She did so well for such a little person! And you did an amazing job with her." The Spirit poured comfort into my heart. I had wanted the hard time on the plane to stop. That's what I prayed for. And yet, as trivial of a situation as this may have been, Christ was there, strengthening me to endure and learn from the experience. **"I can do all things through Christ which strengtheneth me."** I just couldn't see this until a stranger pointed it out to me, and the Spirit quietly confirmed it.

Christ often doesn't take away the tough time, no matter how big or small it is, probably because He's really good at strengthening us to endure, learn, and find moments of peace in the meantime.

— Cali

DAY 287

JESUS RECONCILES YOU TO GOD

COLOSSIANS 1:21

I've often heard it said that we are spirit beings having a mortal experience. Our true nature is to be in perfect alignment with God; our spirits naturally desire to follow the will of our Father!

And yet, each of us has sinned. We've each given in to temptation at least once, and because of that sin, we've become estranged from God.

You see, God is perfect, so nothing unclean can dwell with Him. That means that even if you and I only ever committed one tiny sin, we would be separated from Heavenly Father forever!

Luckily, as Paul taught, **"And you, that were sometime alienated and enemies in your mind by wicked works, yet now hath he reconciled. . . ."**

Without Jesus, we would spend a miserable eternity out of alignment with God; but because of Him, we have the chance to be reconciled with God so we can have an eternity not just with God but like Him as well!

— Kristen

DAY 288

OFFER
THOUGHTS AND
PRAYERS

1 THESSALONIANS 1:2

The phrase "thoughts and prayers" has recently gotten a lot of pushback from the public. When faced with a tragedy, most people say that the traditional offering of "thoughts and prayers" doesn't do anything; only actions will change things or offer any real help.

I always think, why not both? Thoughts and prayers AND action! We should always accompany our prayers with sincere effort to try and help support our family members, ward members, or even our nation.

But what do we do when "action" isn't an option? What do we do in those impossibly difficult moments when someone is enduring a trial that we wish we could take away but can't? I have learned that prayer works. God is powerful. There are some blessings that God wants to give to us, but He needs us to ask Him in prayer. That's the only condition for the blessing! We have to ask. **"We give thanks to God always for you all, making mention of you in our prayers."** We can plead for those around us in our prayers.

We should absolutely accompany our sincere prayers with actions and service if possible. But our Heavenly Father recognizes the form of "work" that offering a prayer is and is willing to give us and others blessings from that action!

— Cali

LIVE
WHAT YOU
BELIEVE

1 THESSALONIANS 1:5

My friend once told me a harrowing story from her childhood. She was the youngest child and had four older brothers. One of those brothers promised that if she washed the dinner dishes for him, he would give her five dollars.

Even though they didn't have a dishwasher, and she knew it would take over an hour, my friend felt that five dollars would be worth it. And so, she did the dinner dishes, scrubbing and working for more than the anticipated sixty minutes.

When my friend finally finished, she went to her brother and demanded her five dollars. He immediately handed over five doll hairs, which he insisted was what he'd promised her in the first place.

My friend said it took her years to trust her brother's word again. And that is how it often is in life. No matter what people say, we learn much more about them by watching what they do!

Paul pointed out the difference between words and actions, saying, **"For our gospel came not unto you in word only, but also in power. . . ."** Paul and the other missionaries didn't just preach the gospel; they lived it! And by living it, they did some of their best missionary work!

— Kristen

1 THESSALONIANS 3:12-13

How do we become "more holy"? It's a vague question that probably has many different answers.

But Paul gives one possible answer to this question: **"And the Lord make you to increase and abound in love one toward another, and toward all men, even as we do toward you: To the end he may stablish your hearts unblameable in holiness before God. . . ."**

Did you catch that? More love towards ALL = more holiness!

How would our interactions at church be if we went with the purpose of showing love to everyone we met? How would our ministering change if we felt pure love? How would our home life change if we just loved our children or our siblings? How would our marriages change if we just loved our spouses? How would we change if we just loved ourselves?

Christ was the perfect example of showing love to everyone around Him, and He was the perfect definition of holiness. When we show more love, that is one way to become more holy.

– Cali

DAY 291

1 THESSALONIANS 5:17

I recently started reading a series of mystery books that I adore! The storylines are intriguing, the mysteries are impossible to solve in advance, and best of all, I'm learning a lot about how to pray!

The heroine of the series is a woman named Sarah who can't help but pray all day long; it just comes naturally to her.

Sarah prays in her heart for help when her children are struggling. She prays as an expression of gratitude when things go right. She says a prayer in her heart when she's confused and unsure what to do. It often seems like Sarah talks more to God than to any of the characters in the book!

As someone who struggles with prayer, it is a powerful (albeit fictional) example of truly communing with God! All day long throughout each book, Sarah keeps up a constant internal dialogue with Heavenly Father. Her prayers aren't separate events in the morning and evening; they are an ongoing conversation that never ends.

I think this is what Paul meant when he commanded the Thessalonians to **"...pray without ceasing."** Even without ever bowing our heads or folding our arms, we can talk to God all day long!

- Kristen

DAY 292

DON'T QUENCH THE SPIRIT

1 THESSALONIANS 5:19

I've had a goal for the past few years to improve my response time when it comes to spiritual promptings! It will probably be a goal I have for the rest of my life because it can be a lot of work.

One time, I had a thought to check in on a friend. But then I thought, "Eh, not right now; it's a weird time. Plus, I think she's fine. Plus, what would I even say? Plus, I don't want to seem weird." And so I didn't check in on her. Looking back, I realized that I had suppressed a prompting! And when I suppress a prompting, I'm probably missing out on more and more promptings in the future.

The next time I thought about checking in on a different friend, I texted her immediately. I wanted to show the Spirit that I was willing to act on any good thoughts that came my way! I was surprised when even more friends' names came to my mind, and I spent the next little bit catching up with lots of amazing people.

Look at Paul's simple warning: **"Quench not the Spirit."** "Quench" means to suppress, extinguish, or hinder. It's pretty straightforward, even if it's trickier to always follow in real life. But I know that if I want to continue becoming as Christlike as I can be, I can't quench the Spirit.

– Cali

DAY 293

2 THESSALONIANS 3:3

During my childhood, I had a friend who turned out to be a "frenemy"-- someone who acted like a friend to my face but acted like an enemy when I wasn't around.

We would play together at school and even formed a club, but I found out that when I wasn't around, she would talk about how much she hated me and how annoying I was. I was crushed and struggled for years to believe that anyone who was my friend truly liked me. Actually, I still struggle with that!

Have you ever been affected by the unfaithfulness of someone else? If so, it can be hard to trust others. But the scriptures give us the good news that there is One we can trust implicitly.

Paul taught that, **"...the Lord is faithful, who shall stablish you, and keep you from evil."**

Jesus will never, for any reason, be an unfaithful friend. He will always speak kindly of us, keep His promises, and be our greatest defender. His loyalty and love are perfect. So even if we struggle to trust the faithfulness of those around us, we can always trust our Brother, Jesus Christ!

– Kristen

DAY 294

2 THESSALONIANS 3:13

I worked as a counselor for the Especially For Youth program one summer, and let me tell you: There ain't no tired like Saturday-morning-EFY-counselor tired. The counselors had spent from early Monday morning until early Saturday morning with a group of teenagers, staying up too late, teaching gospel lessons, sharing testimonies, and creating fun. So on Saturday morning, after all the youth were picked up, you felt utterly exhausted. But it was a GOOD tired. Your body was craving 40 hours of sleep while also totally floating on a spiritual high. It's one of the most extreme times I've ever felt energized by doing good things. Paul taught, **"But ye, brethren, be not weary in well doing."**

I love looking at the "opposites" of scriptures for a fresh perspective. To me, Paul is teaching us to be spiritually energized by the good things we choose to do! I know I feel much more satisfied at the end of the day when I've spent my energy in service, creating fun memories with my family, or sharing my talents. And maybe part of this is realizing all the "good" that I'm already doing each day and trying to draw more spiritual momentum from those efforts! A quick prayer in the morning leads to more peaceful interactions with my kids, which leads to studying my scriptures, and so on. We are going to feel tired, just like the morning after EFY ends, but we can also be spiritually energized to stay engaged in the good stuff!

– Cali

1 TIMOTHY 1:9

Have you ever thought that keeping the commandments feels impossible?

For me, certain commandments feel like I'm climbing a spiritual Mount Everest. These commandments take so much effort and leave me feeling like I will never make it. I try over and over again, but I keep messing up and falling short! Is there a commandment like that for you?

Well, here is a great piece of news: the commandments were intended for everyone to be able to keep them!

Paul taught, **". . .that the law is not made for a righteous man, but for the lawless and disobedient, for the ungodly and for sinners, for unholy and profane. . . ."**

God didn't make the commandments so difficult to keep that only the elect could possibly obey them. He made them for the disobedient, for the sinners, and for the profane.

So, if you wouldn't consider yourself lawless, ungodly, and profane, then know that you are more than capable of keeping the commandments. (Yes, even the ones that feel like a personal Mount Everest!)

— Kristen

DAY 296

BE DIFFERENT! BE A BELIEVER!

1 TIMOTHY 4:12

Why does it matter if we are a good example to other people? Why can't we just do our own thing and worry about our personal salvation?

I think it's important to be good examples in order to attract others to the gospel. We want to prove that being a follower of Christ actually changes who we are for the better!

But I also think it's important to learn how to be comfortable being different! Paul taught: **". . . Be thou an example of the believers, in word, in conversation, in charity, in spirit, in faith, in purity."**

If we are going to choose to be different in the words we say, our topics of conversation, the way we serve, the sensitivity of our spirits, the faith we develop, and the purity of our minds, then we are choosing to stick out amongst the rest of the world. Are we okay being different and peculiar?

Jesus sure was different when He walked on the earth. He stood out. He was peculiar and unique in the things He said and the way He acted. So, if we stick out a bit by being a believer of Christ, we are in good company!

– Cali

DAY 297

AVOID EVIL; SEEK GOOD

1 TIMOTHY 6:11

After exhorting us not to get caught up in our love of money, Paul taught that we should **". . .flee these things; and follow after righteousness. . . ."**

I love this teaching because it points out the two things we need to do to be truly righteous. First, we have to flee from temptation! When we see Satan coming, we need to run the other way.

But just as importantly, we need to "follow after" good things. It's not enough just to not be bad. We also have to seek after good things and become the kind of people God wants us to be.

I've found this to be true time and again. When a bad thought fills my mind, I can't simply push it out. I have to fill my mind with something good to replace the bad. Often it's something as simple as a hymn; but if I don't bring in a righteous thought, the evil ones are much more likely to return.

So the next time you're tempted to sin, use it as a reminder of Paul's two-part formula: run away from evil, but also run after things that are good!

— Kristen

DAY 298

GOD DOESN'T SPEAK WITH FEAR

2 TIMOTHY 1:7

There were a few years when my anxiety was so intense that I couldn't recognize the Spirit. I told my husband that he would have to make all the important decisions for our family because I just couldn't rely on my ability to feel or hear promptings.

When I felt like we shouldn't get on a plane, I wondered if it was my own fear or the Spirit talking. When I felt compelled to start going to the temple weekly, I wasn't sure if it was fear of not getting blessings or a spiritual nudge.

But luckily, I discovered the words of Paul that provide a formula for how to tell the difference between anxiety and the Spirit. Paul taught that **"God hath not given us the spirit of fear; but of power, and of love, and of a sound mind."**

Did you catch that? God does not give us a spirit of fear, which means that the Spirit doesn't speak with fear!

I quickly realized that my fear-based nudges weren't the Spirit talking to me, they were my anxiety. So as you feel promptings, you can ask yourself, "Is the motivation for this action fear?" And if it is, you can be sure that it isn't God talking!

– Kristen

DAY 299

FOCUS ON THE BEST INFORMATION

2 TIMOTHY 3:7

Every day 720,000 hours of new videos are uploaded to YouTube.

The average news outlet (pick your favorite one!) publishes an average of 200 to 300 stories every single day.

Almost 5,000 new books are published on a daily basis.

There is no end to the information available to us. And yet, what good does this information do if it isn't leading us to the most important knowledge– how to return to God?

Have you ever found yourself scrolling through the internet or TV, learning new things but not actually becoming better because of it? I have wasted so many hours of my time being entertained but not enlightened!

Paul taught that people are **"Ever learning, and never able to come to the knowledge of the truth."** We need to be careful that in this sea of information, we are paying attention to the words that matter most: those found in the scriptures, the words of living prophets, and in our personal revelation!

– Kristen

DAY 300

2 TIMOTHY 3:15

When I was a little kid, I wanted to be that person who knew the scriptures really well. I would hear people give talks in church and casually throw in references to "Elijah and Elisha" or "the sons of Mosiah." I was so impressed because I would always forget who these scripture heroes were!

How did people learn the scriptures so well? Was it from their missions? Was it a single religion class at BYU? Was it from a really good lesson that someone taught them?

Well, I think I've figured out the answer. It's consistency! People who know the scriptures really well have been reading and studying the scriptures day after day and year after year. Paul taught, **"And that from a child thou hast known the holy scriptures, which are able to make thee wise unto salvation through faith which is in Christ Jesus."**

We, too can become "wise unto salvation" by being in the holy scriptures as often as we can be– day after day, week after week, and even year after year. But don't let that sound intimidating if you didn't start as a child! You can start right now! There is always time to start, even if you need to start over and over again throughout your life. Wisdom comes through consistency, and knowledge of Jesus Christ comes through reading His words over and over!

– Cali

DAY 301

LEARN FROM PAUL'S EXAMPLE

2 TIMOTHY 4:7

2 Timothy chapter 4 contains the last words, chronologically, that we ever hear from Paul; written from jail close to right before his martyrdom. In honor of his final words, here are the top three lessons I've learned from Paul's life:

1. It doesn't matter what we've done in the past. We can be better. Saul became Paul!

2. How well or poorly we think our life is going right now has NOTHING to do with our relationship with God. Paul was thrown in jail multiple times, shipwrecked, hated, banned, and ultimately killed because he was following the Lord.

3. Attitude makes all the difference. Paul is one of the happiest prophets I have ever read teachings from. He was always so positive and kind, corresponding with saints from all over.

What have you learned from Paul? I invite you to reflect on that today! And I'll end with the very last words we have recorded from this amazing, Christlike man: **"I have fought a good fight, I have finished my course, I have kept the faith."**

— Cali

DAY 302

CHRIST MAKES HAPPY ENDINGS POSSIBLE

HEBREWS 2:10 AND 5:9

Imagine that you've scheduled a boat tour of an unknown island, but the captain isn't there when the time comes.

Or imagine you're anxiously anticipating the final release in your favorite book series, but the author has gone missing and left no hint of a manuscript behind.

In the case of the boat, the tour would have to be canceled. In the case of the author, you'd be left with no book to read. Without a captain, boats can't sail; without authors, books can't be written.

Let's keep that in mind as we read these verses that explain Christ's starring role in our salvation: **"For it became him. . . to make the captain of their salvation perfect through sufferings. . . And being made perfect, he became the author of eternal salvation unto all them that obey him."**

Christ is both the captain and author of our salvation. In other words, our salvation wouldn't happen without Him: no one-way trip to the eternal promised land, no happily ever after in our book!

How grateful we should be to our perfect Captain and Author!

– Kristen

DAY 303

HEBREWS 2:17-18

I have often felt like Jesus couldn't possibly understand my temptations. He lived His life so perfectly and appeared to be so far above every sin that it seems He couldn't relate to me when I struggle against temptation.

But Paul taught us that Jesus understands temptation perfectly because **". . . in all things it behoved him to be made like unto his brethren, that he might be a merciful and faithful high priest. . . For in that he himself hath suffered being tempted, he is able to succour them that are tempted. For we have not an high priest which cannot be touched with the feeling of our infirmities; but was in all points tempted like as we are, yet without sin."**

Jesus understands temptation perfectly because He felt it and fought it perfectly. If you have faced a temptation, Jesus has faced it too. And He understands exactly the way out of it because He followed that path and remained sinless!

So when we face temptation, rather than feeling alone or out of options, we can turn to Jesus and ask Him to help us see the way He created out of sin!

– Kristen

HEBREWS 4:2

"Wow, what an amazing lesson! Couldn't you feel the Spirit in that room?"

My roommate asked this question as we left Relief Society one Sunday. I was embarrassed because I hadn't felt or noticed the Spirit at all! In fact, I had kind of zoned out the entire lesson.

Has something like this ever happened to you? Maybe you felt the Spirit during a talk, but the person sitting next to you didn't. How can this happen?

Paul teaches us the answer: **"For unto us was the gospel preached, as well as unto them: but the word preached did not profit them, not being mixed with faith in them that heard it."**

We need to be engaged with sincere faith to feel the Spirit! If we aren't "spiritually engaged" with our faith, we can't learn what others learn, even when we listen to the same lessons, podcasts, or talks. Think of some ways that you can use your faith to "profit" more from your temple worship, scripture study, or your next Sunday meeting!

– Cali

JESUS HELPS WITH TEMPTATIONS

HEBREWS 4:15

It's a lot easier for me to talk about mistakes I've made in the past, than it is to talk about current temptations. I think it's because talking about my present temptations means I'm admitting that I still get swayed from the straight and narrow path! It's not fun to admit that we don't want to read our scriptures, that we'd rather not attend church, that we enjoy getting angry, or whatever your current temptation might be. But we all will constantly face temptations! Satan won't stop tempting us once we are "good enough."

Guess who knows what it is like to be tempted? Paul teaches: **"For we have not an high priest which cannot be touched with the feeling of our infirmities; but was in all points tempted like as we are, yet without sin."** We don't have to hide our temptations from the Lord because He knows exactly what it's like to be tempted Himself! Jesus wants us to tell Him about our temptations and ask for help, rather than thinking that He will only help us once we "get through" them.

So, try telling Him! Tell Jesus that you don't like reading your scriptures but want to get better. Tell Him you have a tough time attending sacrament meetings but want to get your desire back. Tell Him that it's so easy to yell at your kids but that you want to try to improve. Tell Jesus about your temptations, and let Him help you now!

– Cali

COME BOLDLY TO GOD

HEBREWS 4:16

Awkward. I don't know about you, but that's how I feel when I have to ask someone for help or forgiveness. I hate admitting that I'm not capable of doing something on my own, or worse, admitting that I was wrong.

My middle son is fantastic at this though! He is quick to ask for help when a problem arises. He'll happily come to me with Legos he can't separate or difficult words he wants to make sure he's pronouncing correctly. And if he makes a mistake he'll admit it freely. He is unashamed to admit that he is still learning and growing.

Paul taught that we should **"...come boldly unto the throne of grace, that we may obtain mercy, and find grace to help in time of need."** It might seem impossible to some of us to boldly request God's help and mercy. It can become easier, though, as we remember an eternal truth: sin and the Atonement of Jesus Christ aren't the backup plan; they are the plan! God knows that we are weak. He knows we can't make it on our own.

So when we come to Him asking for help or forgiveness, it simply means God's plan is unfolding perfectly! We are seeking to improve and become like Him; no awkwardness there!

— Kristen

DAY 307

HEBREWS 5:8

"You learn obedience during the hardest times in your life." Do you agree with this statement?

I can think of a time when my husband and I were struggling financially, and I couldn't find a job anywhere. That time of suffering refined me! I immersed myself in the gospel and learned how to obey with exactness.

But I can also think of another time when I was dealing with some tough emotional trials, and I let go of all my good, spiritual habits. I felt that I had too much going on and didn't spend time growing closer to the Lord.

Paul taught: **"Though he were a Son, yet learned he obedience by the things which he suffered."**

Obedience can be learned through suffering! But it comes down to a choice: Will we let suffering push us to cling to our obedience and the Lord, or will we let it be an excuse to turn away from obedience? I've done it both ways, and the light that came into my life when I continued to turn to obedience during tough times was so, so powerful! Suffering can bring us closer to the Lord if we let it.

– Cali

DAY 308

HEBREWS 6:12

Someone gave me a book recently that I really wanted to read. But anytime I tried to sit down and read, I felt a bit guilty. Isn't it lazy to sit here and just read a book? There are so many other productive things that I could be doing! I've battled for a long time with the difference between being "slothful" and slowing down to enjoy life. If I'm not productive 100% of the time, I'm tempted to feel like I'm wasting time! But certainly, this is not true. Paul taught: **"That ye be not slothful, but followers of them who through faith and patience inherit the promises."**

Like many things in life, I've found that the difference between being "slothful" or "lazy," and taking a well-deserved break is my intent! Stopping my busy schedule to sit and cuddle with my kid for a while, looking at fun content on social media, or doing small things that bring me joy are all worthwhile endeavors. We aren't here on the earth just to be productive human beings. We are meant to find joy!

So when does this cross into slothfulness? I've found that I don't even need to ask myself that question! I know when I've hit the "next episode" button one too many times or scrolled my social media feed for way too long. I know when I'm wasting time and not getting anything meaningful or joyful in return. Take a moment today to reflect on how you can add more joyful "non-productive" times into your life while also avoiding slothfulness!

– Cali

DAY 309

HEBREWS 9:11

Have you ever noticed how negative the news is? Every time I check a news website, I'm inundated with headlines that declare "catastrophe," "scandal," "doom," and dozens of other negative words. But have you noticed that those words are rare during General Conference? We get to hear from the most spiritually well-informed people on earth, and they tend to use words like "hope," "light," "love," and "goodness."

Some people might call this naïve, but I don't believe that. I think these wise men and women are instead focused on things of eternal importance. They know what is wrong in the world, but they focus on the hope of Jesus Christ instead.

If we choose to, we can become overwhelmed and depressed about how things are. But if we focus on Christ, whom Paul described as **"...an high priest of good things to come,"** we will see that life is full of glorious potential for eternal growth.

Trials are an opportunity to learn and draw closer to God. Conflict is a chance to understand others. Disasters are an opportunity to serve.

And at the end of this life, we will find an eternal reward full of "good things" beyond our earthly imagination!

- Kristen

DAY 310

HEBREWS 10:24

I recently had a rough Sunday where my baby seemed to cry all during church. It was a pretty loud and public struggle that I was dealing with, so everyone in my ward definitely noticed! After church, someone I don't know very well showed up at our doorstep with cupcakes and a sweet, supportive message.

I was overwhelmed with gratitude, and I totally felt her love! But I was also immediately inspired to check in on a friend I had also seen having a rough time at church that day. I texted her, and we had a nice conversation filled with sympathy and connection.

Paul wrote: **"And let us consider one another to provoke unto love and to good works."**

How do we provoke each other to love more? The answer to that is pretty easy when I think about what other people have done that helped inspire me to do good works: They've loved ME and done good works for ME! We can start a chain reaction of goodness and love when we choose to act as the Savior did!

– Cali

DAY 311

HEBREWS 10:35

A couple of years ago, I had a somewhat unsettling spiritual experience. I was preparing for a podcast interview which forced me to study a part of Church history I had previously avoided. It was a bit of a surprise that the more I learned, the more uneasy I became. I was using good resources that I knew were correct, but the information in them wasn't leading to the happy conclusions I had hoped for.

I realized that what I needed was some spiritual reassurance. I prayed intently, asking for peace to know that-- while this part of history might not make sense-- the Church was still true. I immediately felt an overwhelming sense of peace. I was reminded of the hundreds, if not thousands, of times in my life I have felt the Spirit testify to me of the truth of the gospel, Joseph Smith's role in the Restoration, and the reality of God and Jesus Christ.

That night I was able to use past spiritual experiences to help in the face of a current faith crisis. Paul counseled us to **"Cast not away therefore [our] confidence. . . ."**

Even though a spiritual question might make us unsure of what's true, we should not throw out all of the other marvelous spiritual experiences that have led us to the testimonies we have today! Though questions will arise and doubts will come, we can find spiritual power in remembering what we once felt!

- Kristen

DAY 312

HAVE PATIENCE FOR FUTURE BLESSINGS

HEBREWS 10:36

Did you know that you could do whatever you wanted to do today? Really! Anything!

But, of course, every choice you make has consequences! Choosing not to go to work, choosing to eat ice cream all day, or choosing to buy a new car all have consequences that we would need to deal with.

I've always thought of the commandments in a similar way. Sure, I can watch whatever media I want or say whatever I want to say! But there will be spiritual consequences, for better or worse, for whatever I choose. This is where patience comes in!

As followers of Christ, we've just got to be patient. We put off so many immediate pleasures in search of future blessings. And that sure takes a lot of spiritual maturity to do. So this is a cheer-you-on devotional! You've got this! You are not alone in putting off the natural man for the promise of a greater reward in the future!

"For ye have need of patience, that, after ye have done the will of God, ye might receive the promise." The promises are there. God will fulfill His covenants! We might just need to exercise some patience to get there.

– Cali

WHAT'S YOUR FAITH STORY?

HEBREWS 11:7

What's your "faith story"?

I love Hebrews chapter 11 because Paul lists what many righteous people have done "by faith." One that he mentions is Noah: **"By faith Noah, being warned of God of things not seen as yet, moved with fear, prepared an ark to the saving of his house; by the which he condemned the world, and became heir of the righteousness which is by faith."**

He also tells the stories of what Abel, Enoch, Sarah, Abraham, Moses, Rahab, and many more did "by faith."

So what would your personal verse be in Hebrews 11? What big thing have you needed to do in your life "by faith"? What small things have you needed to do "by faith"?

When we build our faith in Jesus Christ day by day with small intentional actions, we lay the foundation for our own "faith story"! We'll each have different details and different paths, but we can still be united with other believers through our mutual faith.

– Cali

DAY 314

HEBREWS 12:1

My nephew played basketball in high school, and one of his training exercises sounded just torturous to me.

Instead of simply dribbling the basketball down the court to warm up, the coach would first tie a long resistance band around my nephew's waist. That simple run down the court became a heart-pounding, muscle-burning exercise in frustration.

It sounds miserable, but I think we do the same thing to ourselves when we choose to run the race of life carrying the weight of sin on our backs. What could be a simple and joyful experience becomes heavy and laborious.

That's why Paul counseled, **"...let us lay aside every weight, and the sin which doth so easily beset us, and let us run with patience the race that is set before us...."**

Have you ever carried the weight of sin longer than necessary? In the past I've hauled around spiritual burdens for weeks, months, or even years at a time. It was such a relief to finally repent and let that unnecessary burden go!

No matter what, we will all run the race of life. But it's up to us whether we have the pull of sin holding us back or if we run free of that weight!

– Kristen

DAY 315

LOVING PARENTS CHASTEN OFTEN

HEBREWS 12:6

One nice day at the park, my young daughter ripped a shovel out of her friend's hands and said, "No, mine!" I pulled her aside and gave her a little talk about sharing and kindness.

Do you think I will need to talk to my daughter about sharing and kindness again? Absolutely. But I love her. And I want her to learn how to be kind. I want her to make good friends and keep them. I want her to learn how to be selfless.

So I'll keep teaching her about kindness every time she chooses another way.

Imagine how our Father in Heaven must feel watching us! He puts the perfect service opportunity in front of us, but we choose selfish pursuits instead. He knows a scripture verse will give us the answer to our prayer, but we don't open the pages.

Thank goodness that He'll never say, "Well, I'm done with this one. There's no hope."

"For whom the Lord loveth he chasteneth. . . ." Chastening and correction are signs of God's never-ending love for us!

– Cali

DAY 316

JAMES 1:5

One of the most freeing things I've learned is that my Heavenly Father cares about all the little details of my life. He cares about me trying to potty train a toddler! He cares about me wanting to make new friends. He cares about me trying to plan a party.

We don't ONLY need to talk to our Father in prayer about "spiritual" matters or deep life questions; we can also pray and ask for advice on anything! **"If any of you lack wisdom, let him ask of God, that giveth to all men liberally, and upbraideth not; and it shall be given him."**

I love the empowerment that comes from knowing that I can ask for help any time I lack wisdom in any aspect of my life.

Asking for help doesn't make me want to just wait around for Him to tell me what outfit to wear and make all my decisions for me. Instead, it empowers me to ask for help in every little thing because I know that if He wants to give me wisdom, He certainly can.

– Cali

DAY 317

JAMES 1:12

Have you ever felt guilty simply for being tempted to sin?

I remember when, years ago, an inappropriate ad popped up on my computer, and I felt a strong urge to click on it. I didn't, but all day I felt terrible that I had even wanted to.

Looking back, I can see that what was happening wasn't godly guilt; it was Satan's shame. While God's guilt encourages us to do better, I felt Satan's shame which makes us want to give up. And that's exactly how I felt! I felt defeated, as though I'd already sinned by being tempted, so I might as well commit the sin itself!

But the fact is, Satan is a liar, as he's always been. It is not a sin to be tempted! In fact, the scriptures teach, **"Blessed is the man that endureth temptation: for when he is tried, he shall receive the crown of life, which the Lord hath promised to them that love him."**

This verse didn't say, "blessed is the man who is never tempted." It says, "blessed is the man who endureth temptation." Being tempted is part of the plan and is not a sin, so don't let Satan get you down and convince you to actually go through with the temptation! You're too smart and too strong for that!

- Kristen

DAY 318

JAMES 1:19

When I taught middle school, I sometimes got frustrated emails from parents. When I first started teaching, I would try to write a response immediately. The parents had usually written their email in an emotional state, and then I was responding in an emotional state. It led to a lot of misunderstandings and problems that could have been solved faster if I had just waited a bit to respond.

I quickly learned the practical nature of this advice from James: **"Wherefore, my beloved brethren, let every man be swift to hear, slow to speak, slow to wrath."** Did you catch those three essential elements? Swift to hear, slow to speak, AND slow to wrath!

While this advice helped me practically in the classroom, it also has brought more peace to my life and removed anger. It's helped me as a parent, as a wife, as a leader, and as a partner. The Savior was a fantastic listener to both what was said aloud and what people silently pleaded for in their hearts. He took time to gather His thoughts before responding. And He was so slow to wrath, always avoiding escalating His tone just because someone else got angry.

What a perfect recipe for peace! Which part could you use some practice with the most?

– Cali

DAY 319

JAMES 1:22

I once had a teacher who said there was very little difference between the devils in hell and the saints in heaven. At first, I thought this must be impossible! The difference was a lifetime of good works, resisting temptation, and following the Savior! That difference is huge.

But it turns out that one choice differentiates the people in these two groups: action.

Both the devils in hell and the angels in heaven know God's plan of redemption. Both know that Jesus is the Christ. It sounds strange, but Satan and his devils know these things to be true!

So what is the difference? It seems small, but the difference is that the saints in heaven don't just know these truths; they've done something about them!

James counseled us to **". . .be ye doers of the word, and not hearers only. . . ."** You see, knowledge is not enough. We can hear beautiful sermons and scriptures our whole lives and not become any better because of them. We have to be changed by what we know. Taking action and becoming better are the tiny differences between devils and angels!

- Kristen

USE YOUR
WORDS TO
UPLIFT

JAMES 3:5

Have you ever noticed that characters in TV shows are always perfectly themselves? These people are funny at the right times, speak their minds in dramatic and eloquent fashions, and every conversation is meaningful. Misunderstandings only happen if they have a purpose, and they always get joyfully resolved in the end.

But real-life speaking without a team of paid writers scripting our every word is messy! We have complex emotions. We are awkward. We think of great "comebacks" in the shower two days later. We say things that sound good to us but make no sense to others. We offend people when we don't mean to.

James points out that only a perfect person would be able to actually control their tongue to the point that no one would ever take offense. **"Even so the tongue is a little member, and boasteth great things. Behold, how great a matter a little fire kindleth!"**

But how am I trying to use my awkward and unrefined words? Am I lifting my family members and loved ones? Am I criticizing and nagging? Those are the decisions I can control. I always want the scale to be fully tipped towards positive and uplifting words because they can make a huge difference in the lives of the people I love.

– Cali

DAY 321

JAMES 3:10

Robert Louis Stevenson wrote a book you've probably heard of called <u>The Strange Case of Dr. Jekyll and Mr. Hyde</u>.

In the story, the kind and gentle Dr. Jekyll would occasionally transform into Mr. Hyde, a violent and self-indulgent man. The well-respected Dr. Jekyll had a side to him that others feared, and in the end, it led to his ruin.

It's a sad story but also a commentary on human nature. Are we ever a bit like Dr. Jekyll and Mr. Hyde, with two sides to our behavior?

Do different versions of our personality show up at school, church, work, and home? Do we use different language, have different media standards, or treat those around us differently depending on where we are?

If so, such behavior does not please God! James warned, **"Out of the same mouth proceedeth blessing and cursing. My brethren, these things ought not so to be."**

Our "Sunday best" behavior should not be limited to Sundays. We need to be one person at all times: the very best version of ourselves!

– Kristen

DAY 322

SEEK GOD'S WILL IN PRAYER

JAMES 4:3

"According to Thy will" might just be the four hardest words to say.

Over the years, I've said many heartfelt prayers. I've begged God to heal people I loved. During pregnancy, I begged Him for the health of my unborn babies. I've begged for a job offer to come through.

As I said these prayers, they should all have ended with the words "according to Thy will," but— to be honest— I didn't want to give God an "out." I wanted things done my way or no way at all.

And yet James warned, **"Ye ask, and receive not, because ye ask amiss, that ye may consume it upon your lusts."**

Our prayers are often not answered because we aren't seeking God's will at all but our own. We're not trying to align our will to His, but His to ours— and it simply doesn't work that way!

Perhaps the next time our prayers aren't answered the way we want, we could consider if we were praying for God's will to be done or our own.

— Kristen

SPEND
MORE TIME
REJOICING

1 PETER 1:3

At Girls' Camp this summer, our Young Women President put me in charge of the music. Every time our ward was hanging out by our tents, I would turn on happy music the girls could sing along to.

One song was new to them, though, and required some training.

It's a Christian song about how we so often get bogged down in who we should be that we forget to rejoice in Christ's salvation. During the chorus, the music would really pick up, and I encouraged the girls to do their happiest dance to show their joy in Jesus. Well, they thought I was ridiculous, but they danced along with me and rejoiced in the hope of Christ's atonement.

It was a silly thing— dancing out of joy for Jesus— but it's something I think we should do more of! Peter declared, **"Blessed be the God and Father of our Lord Jesus Christ, which according to his abundant mercy hath begotten us again unto a lively hope. . . ."**

Instead of getting bogged down in our spiritual to-do lists, let's spend more time rejoicing in the lively hope that fills our lives because of Jesus!

— Kristen

DAY 324

1 PETER 3:8

What things keep you from feeling compassion toward everyone that you meet?

Here are some things that have stopped me: Being judgmental. Feeling pride that I'm better than they are. Feeling pride that they are better than I am. Feeling pity but not wanting to actually help them.

What things would you add to the list? Peter teaches: **"Finally, be ye all of one mind, having compassion one of another, love as brethren. . . ."**

Christ asks us to have compassion on one another, and one way to do that is by removing all the "stumbling blocks" that keep us from feeling that compassion. The first step to removing stumbling blocks is to recognize that they are even there!

When I eliminate judgment, pride, and pity piece by piece, step by step, I make more room for pure compassion toward others!

– Cali

DAY 325

1 PETER 3:10

I absolutely love getting together with a big group of friends to hang out! But isn't it so tempting to start talking about other people when you are with friends? Sometimes it starts as telling true stories, but it often ends up in some sort of judgmental comments or "I just think. . . ."

Here's what I've found, though. It is much more uplifting to make new, fun memories with friends instead! To share our real current joys and struggles, to bond together, to create strong, positive memories. Or, as Peter put it, **"For he that will love life, and see good days, let him refrain his tongue from evil, and his lips that they speak no guile."** ("Guile" means dishonesty.)

It may feel good to make judgmental comments or gossip in the moment.

But I want to "love life, and see good days"! Life is so much happier and lighter when we stay far away from negative stories and gossip.

— Cali

TRIALS AND
JOY WILL
COME

1 PETER 4:12-13

Are you ready for Peter to help us fix our attitudes about trials?

He taught: **"Beloved, think it not strange concerning the fiery trial which is to try you, as though some strange thing happened unto you: But rejoice, inasmuch as ye are partakers of Christ's sufferings; that, when his glory shall be revealed, ye may be glad also with exceeding joy."**

Peter is very lovingly telling us to stop being so surprised when we have to deal with a big trial. And then he gives the sacred reminder of why we shouldn't think it is strange when we have these trials.

When we suffer, we are experiencing just a small part of what Christ experienced. Christ was blessed with great glory for what He suffered, which means that we, too, will have a small part of that glory for the trials that we suffer. This will result in exceeding joy!

Having a trial-free life isn't the kind of life that disciples of Christ should seek. We should expect tough times to find us. But we will always be able to access His joy!

– Cali

DAY 327

FEED
HIS
FLOCK

1 PETER 5:2

The first Thanksgiving that I was away from my family, I felt really sad. I missed the traditions that I was used to, I missed the dishes that we always ate, and I missed the people. I wasn't feeling very grateful at all!

As I sat pretty quietly at the dinner table, I tried to have a change of heart. How could I contribute to the atmosphere even if I didn't feel very grateful? Instead of feeling self-absorbed and sad, I decided to try and focus on making other people happy.

Gratitude is essential. But I love it when gratitude leads me to think, "How can I better feed or serve the people around me?"

Peter encouraged us: **"Feed the flock of God which is among you. . . ."**

I completely transformed how I felt on that Thanksgiving when I started trying to give happiness and joy to other people, even when I didn't totally feel it myself. Gratitude can help lead us to nourish others.

— Cali

YOU ARE NEVER FORGOTTEN

2 PETER 2:5-7

My daughter once wrote me a long list of reasons it's hard to be the youngest child. Growing up as the youngest in my own family, I could relate to much of what she wrote. The list included things such as:

- No one ever listens to you
- People forget about you
- You have no one to play with
- You are always the littlest and get left out of things

Have you ever felt this way? Have you ever felt lonely and forgotten? It has definitely happened to me! But the great news is that God sees and always remembers you. Always! Peter reminds us that even when the world was covered in wickedness, God remembered the very few who were being obedient. Peter said that God **"...spared not the old world, but saved Noah... And turning the cities of Sodom and Gomorrha into ashes... [He] delivered just Lot."**

Even amid the chaos of a worldwide flood and the total destruction of two cities, God remembered Noah, Lot, and their families. And He always remembers you. No matter how alone or forgotten you feel, God will never forget you!

- Kristen

DAY 329

2 PETER 3:18

My mother became a widow at 39. She had five daughters to raise, a full-time job as an elementary school teacher, and a difficult calling as the ward Young Women president.

Can you imagine the weight of all of those responsibilities? And yet, looking back, my mom did all of those things with incredible power. She was a wonderful mother, a fantastic teacher, and the best Young Women president ever!

How did she do it? Certainly not on her own! She reached out for and received God's grace through constant prayer, fasting, and temple attendance. She accessed God's unlimited power to make it possible to do more than she ever could on her own.

Peter instructed us to **"...grow in grace, and in the knowledge of our Lord and Saviour Jesus Christ."** Before my mom became a widow I'm sure she had sought God's grace. But as she faced the insurmountable challenges of life without a husband she grew in God's grace. She learned how to rely more on God's power and less on her own. And so can we! We can receive more grace as we seek more, and with God's help, we can be more righteous, more powerful, and more like Him than we ever thought possible!

— Kristen

DAY 330

1 JOHN 1:5

One time the power went out while I was in a room without windows, and the door was closed. I couldn't see anything except a faint strip of natural light coming from under the door. I didn't realize how much I needed light until it was gone!

If you've ever been in a pitch-black situation like this, you know that your first priority is always to get to a light source.

"This then is the message which we have heard of him, and declare unto you, that God is light, and in him is no darkness at all." God is light! I think we get so used to His presence and guiding hand in our lives that we begin to forget how essential He is in every moment of every day.

So what do we do when we can't see the light anymore? The natural light source itself didn't go anywhere so we yank open the door, climb over obstacles, and open windows to get back to the light. We are the ones who have to act!

And eventually, we will find the source of all things good and light!

– Cali

DAY 331

1 JOHN 1:8

I would love to be perfect. Really, it would be so nice.

But as my many mistakes and sins attest, I'm just not. And neither are you. (I hope that isn't a surprise!)

The fact is, we all mess up—every single day. We get lazy and fail to read our scriptures. We judge someone for the way they're dressed. We tell a white lie to avoid trouble.

It happens to everyone. We all need God's help—every single day.

John taught, **"If we say that we have no sin, we deceive ourselves, and the truth is not in us."**

So what does that mean? It means we need to repent—every single day.

Each of us needs to reset and recalibrate on a daily basis to get back to "good" with God and be in alignment with His will. And remember, if we think we don't need daily repentance, "we deceive ourselves." So let's get repenting!

- Kristen

DAY 332

1 JOHN 2:15

Why do you think the scriptures warn us not to "love the world"? I think it's because every second of time we spend loving the world is a second less to spend loving our family members and neighbors!

Every dollar we hoard because we love money is one less dollar we are willing to depart with as tithes and donations. Every moment we focus on our own vanity is a moment taken away from worshiping the Lord and serving others.

John taught, **"Love not the world, neither the things that are in the world. If any man love the world, the love of the Father is not in him."**

When we love the Lord first, and we love our families and our neighbors, then volunteering to donate our precious time and resources seems easy!

If you find that a love of the world might be preventing you from serving God fully, then you are not alone. This can be tough to eliminate completely while living in such a mortal world. Try starting small– what is one worldly possession you could give up to spend more meaningful time worshiping the Lord and loving your family?

– Cali

DAY 333

1 JOHN 3:18

When I taught middle school English, I would teach about the "third person objective" point of view in some stories.

"Third person" means the narrator is someone not in the story (thus using pronouns like "he, she, they"). "Objective" means the narrator can't see into anyone's thoughts at all. I taught my students that stories written in third person objective are just as if a drone was flying over and narrating everything it saw– it could describe actions, but never anyone's intentions or thoughts.

So if someone wrote a third-person objective story about my past week, would they be able to see me SHOWING my love to my family members, friends, and neighbors?

John taught: **"My little children, let us not love in word, neither in tongue; but in deed and in truth."**

Saying "I love you" and feeling love toward other people is amazing. But Jesus has also invited us to let those feelings change how we act! How would a "drone narrator" describe how you showed your love this week? And how could you find ways to show your love even more?

– Cali

DAY 334

GOD IS GREATER

1 JOHN 4:4

How would you describe your inner voice? You know, the voice in your head that critiques or applauds the things you do.

My inner voice tends to be a bit of a bully. It tells me things like, "You'll never be enough," or "You should just give up." Does your inner voice ever say those things to you?

If so, I've got some great news for you. That isn't God's voice. God's voice says things like, "With Me, you're more than enough," and "Never give up! You are so close!"

You see, on our own, that negative inner voice is right. We will never be enough, and we should just quit if we rely on our strength! But luckily, as followers of Christ, we aren't relying on us; we're relying on Him! John taught that, **"Ye are of God. . . and. . . greater is he that is in you, than he that is in the world."**

God is greater than any problem, any weakness, any sin! So when that inner voice starts bullying, we can remind it that we're partnered with God; and with Him, we simply cannot fail.

– Kristen

DAY 335

1 JOHN 4:19

It can be tempting to compare our righteousness with the righteousness of others. I know I've done it in the past and have to remind myself not to do it now!

We pat ourselves on the back because we show up to church early, or because we can answer all the questions in Sunday School, or because our family does scripture study every day of the week. Hooray for us! Aren't we so much better than everyone else?

While it's great to get to church early or answer questions in class, we can't honestly take full credit for doing those things. As John taught, **"We love him, because he first loved us."**

We are righteous because God first put the impulse to be righteous in us. We obey out of love because God loved us first! Without His goodness to motivate us, would we really be as anxiously engaged as we are?

So, though we should always do good things, we should also remember that we had some help doing them. Let's all judge others less and appreciate God's spiritual nudges more!

— Kristen

DAY 336

1 JOHN 5:3

As a little kid, having to attend church each Sunday seemed like a lot. As a teenager, many church media and language standards seemed restrictive. As a young adult, commandments about tithing and Sabbath day observance were really tough. Right now, consecrating my time to church efforts while dealing with a busy schedule takes a lot of effort.

"For this is the love of God, that we keep his commandments: and his commandments are not grievous." John teaches us that God's commandments are not meant to be grievous. In fact, we are encouraged to keep the commandments out of love for God!

Which commandments are easy for you to keep because you love God so much? Which commandments seem more like a grievous irritant right now?

When we turn to Jesus and learn to love God even more, it becomes easier to keep the commandments (yes, even the tough ones!) out of pure devotion to Him!

– Cali

DAY 337

REVELATION 1:3

I have fallen asleep while reading my scriptures more times than I can count! It's easy to see this as a "fail," but guess what? Falling asleep while reading your scriptures is infinitely better than not opening them at all!

The Lord loves the effort we put into keeping His commandments and drawing closer to Him. **"Blessed is he that readeth, and they that hear the words of this prophecy, and keep those things which are written therein."**

Are you not doing your best "studying" every time you open your scriptures? Do you ever fall asleep when you should be reading?

It's okay! We are blessed for any effort we make just to read. The Lord is filled with mercy and love, and when we give Him an inch, He blesses us with a mile in the best way possible!

– Cali

DAY 338

JESUS IS IN OUR MIDST

REVELATION 1:13

The Book of Revelation is wonderful because it teaches us how to speak God's language of symbolism. This is the same language God uses in His holy temples, so it's great to practice understanding it in the scriptures. However, symbolism can be confusing, so let's walk through some of it together.

In the first chapter of Revelation, we are shown the symbol of seven candlesticks which– luckily– is interpreted for us as symbolizing the church.

John tells us that he saw, **". . . in the midst of the seven candlesticks one like unto the Son of man. . . ."** In other words, John saw Jesus right in the middle of His church. Jesus wasn't off to the side, or far away in heaven, but right there with the church!

I love this reminder that Jesus is not an absent leader. Jesus did not establish His church, fulfill His atoning sacrifice, and then leave the world to its own devices. No! He is anxiously engaged in the work of the church right now, this very second!

You are part of a church that is being actively led by the Savior of the world who knows all, sees all, and is in our midst! What a blessing and comfort that is!

– Kristen

REVELATION 2:29

What is the most recent thing that the Holy Spirit taught you?

We have the unique privilege in our church that there are tons of opportunities to hear the revelation we need. Our prophet, stake leaders, and ward leaders can teach customized counsel. And then, of course, we can receive personal revelation for ourselves and our families.

The opportunities are everywhere. But are we taking the chance to actually hear what the Lord wants us to hear? Look at where John tells us the responsibility lies: **"He that hath an ear, let him hear what the Spirit saith unto the churches."**

How do we hear the word of the Lord even better? We can listen to counsel from prophets and then pray personally to receive our own confirmation. We can listen at church with the intent to act, no matter who is doing the teaching. We can keep our minds alert as we read the scriptures. We can limit the distractions around us so we are more in tune with the still, small voice.

The Lord is speaking to His children! But the responsibility is on us to do the hearing. How can we improve our capacity to hear Him?

– Cali

DAY 340

REVELATION 3:8

When I was in middle school, we had an assembly where we were told an "up and coming" band would be performing for us. My friends and I sat in the packed lunch room and watched as five teenage boys sang and danced on stage.

None of us were very impressed, and though the band members stayed behind selling their music and signing autographs, I don't think too many people took them up on it. Boy bands just weren't cool.

Fast forward a few years, and these five teenagers were now one of the most popular bands of all time. I was kicking myself for not meeting them and getting their autographs!

I had had an easy opportunity– there wasn't even a long line– and I had rejected it because I didn't see the value at the time.

The Lord has also given us an easy opportunity. He said, **"I have set before thee an open door, and no man can shut it. . . ."** Literally, anyone can be on Jesus' team. Anyone. The door is wide open for all of us, and no one can shut it. But it's up to us to see the value in it and take Jesus' invitation to walk through that open door to start and stay on the covenant path!

– Kristen

DAY 341

HOLD FAST
TO YOUR
FAITH

REVELATION 3:11

Our faith is not a tangible object! When it all comes down to it, I think our Heavenly Father wants us to have faith in His plan and His love, which means believing and trusting without concrete proof.

But what about when questions come? If you haven't had a "faith crisis" of any kind or magnitude yet, it will likely come at some point. You may wonder if God really loves you, you may question scriptures, or you may learn new information that doesn't seem to fit with what you already know about a prophet.

So what do we do when we hit a faith crisis? There is so much great advice out there, but I believe Jesus shares the most important piece: **"Behold, I come quickly: hold that fast which thou hast, that no man take thy crown."**

Hold fast to what we already have! It can be so tempting to throw away the faith we already have because there isn't anything tangible. We have to hold on to intangible spiritual experiences in our minds.

This can seem so difficult! But when we stick with it and hold fast to the faith-promoting and testimony-building experiences we've already gained, then nothing will take away our crown.

— Cali

DAY 342

REVELATION 3:20

A few years ago, I was driving home from work when one of "those songs" came on the radio. You know, the super catchy song that– if you listen too closely to the lyrics– you realize how completely inappropriate it is? My husband and I had plans to go to the temple for our date night that night. I had the thought, "I really should change the station." But I didn't. It was a fun song.

When I sat in the temple a few hours later, guess what popped into my head? "That song." I immediately prayed to have the song removed from my head so I could worship appropriately. But the reprimand I heard in the temple in my mind was clear as day: "You can't ignore the Spirit's promptings earlier in the day and then demand the Spirit to help take away the natural consequences later."

Jesus taught: **"Behold, I stand at the door, and knock: if any man hear my voice, and open the door, I will come in to him, and will sup with him, and he with me."** The Spirit knocked when I was prompted to turn off the radio. But I chose not to answer the door. And there were consequences for that choice! (After which I thoroughly repented and have been drastically better about my song choices ever since.)

The Spirit is knocking. He is waiting to help, inspire, guide, warn, and instruct. What are we doing to open that door and invite His presence into our lives?

– Cali

DAY 343

JESUS IS
WORTHY

REVELATION 5:12

Last year, my daughter won the elementary school spelling bee. I was so proud of her. I was especially proud, though, because she earned that winning spot! Without parental help or nudging, she faithfully studied the spelling bee words. She practiced them at school, at home, and even in bed.

My daughter was more than worthy of winning her school's spelling bee because she had worked so hard! With that in mind, what would you say Jesus is worthy of?

Is He worthy of five minutes of your time a day?

Is He worthy of your full attention during the sacrament?

Is He worthy of your whole Sunday?

John taught, **"Worthy is the Lamb that was slain to receive power, and riches, and wisdom, and strength, and honour, and glory, and blessing."** Christ is worthy of a spot next to God for eternity, which means that He is also worthy of as much worship as we can give Him! So this week, let's consider if we're showing Jesus how worthy He is of our time and attention!

– Kristen

REVELATION 6:15-16

The book of Revelation gives a brutally honest picture of what the end of the world will be like. John's writings speak of the sun becoming black, the moon becoming as blood, stars falling from heaven, and the entire earth shaking.

However, it only mentions one group of people who will feel afraid when this happens.

John says it will be **". . .the kings of the earth, and the great men, and the rich men. . . [who] hid themselves in the dens and in the rocks of the mountains; and said to the mountains and rocks, Fall on us, and hide us from the face of him that sitteth on the throne, and from the wrath of the Lamb."**

In other words, the unrighteous will be so afraid of standing in front of Jesus to be judged that they will beg for the mountains to crush them so they and their works can stay hidden.

Reading such scriptures is an excellent opportunity to self-reflect.

Which of our works would we want to stay hidden from Jesus at that last day? And if we don't want Jesus to see them then, why don't we take care of them now?

– Kristen

DAY 345

REVELATION 7:14

When I was in high school, I got a large glass of red juice and sat on the couch at home. I wasn't paying attention and spilled the entire glass of bright red juice all over our white carpet! My parents weren't home, and I panicked. I tried everything I could to wipe it up, but that stain wasn't going anywhere.

My mom walked in the door, and I sheepishly showed her what had happened. To my surprise, she laughed and said, "We are actually replacing the carpet with hardwood and the installers are coming in three days. Don't worry about it!"

This little experience of good timing gave me a small taste of how Jesus can make the sins and stains on our hearts disappear. **"These are they which came out of great tribulation, and have washed their robes, and made them white in the blood of the Lamb."**

It should be impossible to get a blood-red stain out of white robes. But Jesus did the impossible so that we could wash the stains, heartache, and pain out as often as we need. Every little evidence of red can be replaced with the purest white!

– Cali

DAY 346

REVELATION 7:17

Have you ever felt like life was just too hard?

I've been through trials that have left me emotionally, physically, and spiritually wrung out. It truly felt like I had nothing left to give, and then God asked me to do more.

Perhaps you have wept, like I have, for days, weeks, and even years over the trials you've faced. And during those long days, weeks, and years, it can feel like God has abandoned us, as if He is far away or unaware of our struggles.

But John teaches that the exact opposite is true. He taught that in the day we return home to Him, **". . . God shall wipe away all tears from their eyes."**

It doesn't say God will send angels to wipe the tears from our eyes but that He will do it Himself. That's one-on-one.

God will take however many days, months, or years it requires to minister to each child individually and wipe the tears from their eyes. Can you imagine the glory, love, and humility you will feel as you look into His eyes in that moment? I think we can all endure any trial for a God who loves us that much.

— Kristen

DAY 347

YOU ARE A WARRIOR!

REVELATION 12:7, 11

What words would you use to describe yourself? Really think about it. If you had to summarize your entire being in just three words, what would they be?

Even though we haven't met, I would summarize you with these three words: brave, righteous, devoted.

Don't believe me? John the Revelator saw you (and me) in a vision, and this vision shows who we truly are! He said, **"And there was war in heaven: Michael and his angels [that's you!] fought against the dragon [that's Satan]; and the dragon fought and his angels. . . and they [that's you!] overcame him by the blood of the Lamb, and by the word of their testimony; and they loved not their lives unto the death."**

You might not remember it, but you fought against an enemy so frightening he's called a dragon! Your testimony was so powerful, and your devotion so great that you overcame that dragon and earned a place on the earth in the last days.

So, when you face a temptation now, you can be absolutely certain that you can beat it! After all, you fought the creator of that temptation himself and came out the victor!

- Kristen

DAY 348

REVELATION 13:14

John reveals one of the biggest tactics the adversary will use in the last days: **"And deceiveth them that dwell on the earth."** He will try to deceive us!

What does it mean to be deceived? It means we believe something is <u>not</u> true even when it is! This means that deception will be a significant tool the adversary uses on people who already believe in Jesus Christ.

Think about the truths you know about Jesus Christ, what He does, and how much He loves you. Has the adversary ever tried to convince you that those things were actually false after you received your testimony?

Absolutely!

When it comes to the Savior, the adversary has been and always will be working overtime to make us doubt what we already know. To me, this means that it is always a good time to seek out more spiritual experiences and to increase my understanding of what Jesus can do for me!

— Cali

DAY 349

REVELATION 14:8

I've never had wine, but I've been told it feels great to drink! Those who get drunk on wine say that it tastes wonderful and makes them feel cozy and warm, like being next to a roaring fire. Sounds lovely, doesn't it?

However, they fail to mention that being wine drunk can also cause dizziness, blackouts, vomiting, and long-term health issues. Does that make you feel cozy and warm? Not so much.

Drinking wine is similar to the way Satan works. He gives us the illusion that sinning will feel great– it will be 100% rewarding. And to be honest, that is often how sin feels in the moment. The "wine" tastes great and feels warm and cozy. But then come the after-effects: the spiritual dizziness and long-term spiritual health issues.

In the last days, when Satan is finally beaten, an angel will announce that **"Babylon is fallen, is fallen that great city, because she made all nations drink of the wine of the wrath of her fornication."**

No matter how rewarding and fun sin may seem now, the after-effects are coming. And those who drink Satan's "wine" will fall with him into a pit of never-ending spiritual blackouts.

– Kristen

DAY 350

REVELATION 14:15

The joy that comes from growing your own garden is strangely powerful! You spend days, weeks, even months taking care of seeds, soil, water, shade, sunlight, temperature, and every other little condition possible. There is so much work behind the scenes, a lot of money spent, and some plants that are lost along the way.

But when it is time to finally eat and enjoy the harvest, the pride and happiness of enjoying the result of all your hard work is difficult to describe! So imagine how the Lord feels about the latter days when He reveals to John: **"And another angel came out of the temple, crying with a loud voice to him that sat on the cloud, Thrust in thy sickle, and reap: for the time is come for thee to reap; for the harvest of the earth is ripe."**

This is the time to reap the harvest! Right now is the time that the Lord is enjoying the fruits of thousands of years of preparation. How do we help in the harvest? We gather Israel, of course! We share our testimonies. We teach people about Jesus. We help children make and keep covenants. We volunteer our time in the temple. Jesus isn't just keeping all the joy to Himself– He wants each of us to feel the happiness that comes from reaping the reward of the gathering of Israel. How can you do your part to share your love of the gospel and join the harvest?

– Cali

DAY 351

REVELATION 16:15

Scientists have been studying our sleep habits for decades. Many of these studies have focused on the subject of nightmares and have helped scientists discover that certain nightmares are incredibly common; one of the most common is the nightmare of being naked in public.

Has that ever happened to you? Perhaps you dreamt that you had to stand up in front of your class only to look down and realize you'd forgotten to put on clothes! It's a terrifying dream!

We won't get into the psychology behind why this type of dream is so common, but suffice it to say, we all want to be fully clothed when we're around other people!

And yet the Lord warns, **"I come as a thief. Blessed is he that watcheth, and keepeth his garments, lest he walk naked, and they see his shame."** The Lord knows that if we aren't ready for His coming, our shame will be even more awful than standing physically naked in a crowd. So what can we do?

We need to have our spiritual clothing ready! Every day we need to put on the armor of God: the breastplate of righteousness, the shield of faith, and more! If we do that, we'll be ready to stand— fully clothed— when Christ comes!

— Kristen

DAY 352

REVELATION 19:7

As a pianist, I often get asked to accompany people singing or playing a solo instrument for church. Each time I am asked to do this, I put time and effort into learning the sometimes complicated piano piece, follow the soloist with precision, and perform with the best emotion or Spirit that I can bring.

And do you know who usually gets all the praise? The soloist! I always feel a sting of jealousy or sadness when someone compliments them without mentioning me. There have been many times, though, when the soloist has gone out of their way to make sure that I am recognized for my efforts.

It feels good to be acknowledged, and it sure doesn't feel great to be forgotten. John wrote: **"Let us be glad and rejoice, and give honour to him."** Jesus deserves every honor, credit, and praise. Anything that we do, we do because of Him. Do we acknowledge this? Do we show Him our gratitude for making everything possible and being the essential "accompanist" for the performance we sometimes take all the credit for?

I'm working on being better at giving all the glory to the Savior and not being afraid to point it out to other people, too! All the praise, honor, and credit belong to Jesus!

– Cali

DAY 353

REVELATION 19:11-13

In vision, John the Revelator **". . .saw heaven opened, and behold a white horse; and he that sat upon him was called Faithful and True. . . His eyes were as a flame of fire, and on his head were many crowns. . . And he was clothed with a vesture dipped in blood. . . ."**

I love that description of the Savior riding in glory and wearing clothing of deepest red. You don't hear of other heavenly beings wearing red clothing; it is reserved only for the Savior. Why is that?

Well, imagine the Savior at a different moment in history: the moment He exited the Garden of Gethsemane. Though it isn't portrayed this way in church films or art, we know that in the Garden Jesus bled from every single pore on His body. Can you imagine how red and blood-soaked His clothing must have been after that experience?

No wonder He wears a cloak of red to remind us of all He sacrificed for us!

And that is how we will see our Savior when He comes in red again, not being met by a crowd that will bind Him, but in glory to judge those who rejected Him!

– Kristen

DAY 354

REVELATION 20:2

"And he laid hold on the dragon, that old serpent, which is the Devil, and Satan, and bound him a thousand years." Are you excited for that time when Satan will be bound for a thousand years?

Unfortunately, we've still got to deal with him right now. While we can't get rid of him completely, I have been looking for ways to make Satan's temptations less powerful in my life. Want to know my top two ways right now?

First, I call him out on the temptation. Whenever the thought crosses my mind that I am too tired to pray, I'll think, "Wait a second, really? I can't even muster up a minute-long prayer?"

My second favorite strategy is to fill my life with so many good things that there is hardly any room for distraction from my eternal goals. I try to add so much goodness that I don't have the room or energy to do anything differently!

How can you try to "bind" the adversary in your life?

— Cali

DAY 355

REVELATION 21:4

Do you have sorrow in your life right now? It will be gone. Have you cried recently? There will be no need. Do you ever experience pain? There will be no more. Have you dealt with death? Completely gone.

"And God shall wipe away all tears from their eyes; and there shall be no more death, neither sorrow, nor crying, neither shall there be any more pain: for the former things are passed away."

It's hard even to imagine that. And yet, it sounds like exactly what I desire the most. Pain and sorrow will be gone. And in their place, the loving embrace of my God as I dwell with Him in His presence!

What would I be willing to sacrifice right now to gain this blessing someday? When I read this scripture and remember this perspective, absolutely anything!

It can be so easy to forget this. But God understands exactly how we feel. He will sit upon His throne and wipe away your tears!

– Cali

DAY 356

REVELATION 21:6

I think what sets me most apart from the general population is that I'm obsessed with drinking water. I thoroughly enjoy drinking water, and I crave it all the time! No flavorings or powders, just cold, refreshing water. If you ever see me in person, you will probably see me with my water bottle.

This is why I love these words from John: **"And he said unto me, It is done. I am Alpha and Omega, the beginning and the end. I will give unto him that is athirst of the fountain of the water of life freely."**

How long can I go without reconnecting with my Savior? Longer than I can go without a drink of water? That's a piercing question for me!

I want the Savior's loving and peaceful influence in my life, but do I always thirst for it?

I'm working on building up that desire on a consistent basis. Instead of forgetting prayers or scriptures, I want to feel a longing and a need to not go without them, just as I wouldn't go to bed without my water bottle.

– Cali

OBEDIENCE
PREPARES US FOR
HEAVEN

REVELATION 22:14

If we can't earn our way to heaven (after all, our actions will never be enough on their own), what is the point of keeping the commandments?

The scriptures teach, **"Blessed are they that do his commandments, that they may have right to the tree of life, and may enter in through the gates into the city."**

That scripture makes it sound like our tiny efforts in righteousness give us the "right to the tree of life." But how is that possible? It's possible because those small actions prepare us for life with God!

You see, in order to live with God, we have to learn to live like Him. And how does God live? Perfectly! He thinks, acts, serves, lives, and loves without error or sin.

And so that is what we're practicing here on earth. We are learning (however imperfectly) to be patient, honest, hard-working, righteous, selfless, and kindhearted just like God.

Though we won't ever get it completely right in this life, we are still preparing, and that is all God has asked us to do!

— Kristen

EASTER

EASTER PALM SUNDAY

WORSHIP JESUS WITH JOY

MATTHEW 21:8

About one week before He would conquer the grave and be resurrected, Christ rode into Jerusalem on a donkey. Did you know that kings would often ride horses during times of war and donkeys during times of peace?

Here's what the people did: **"And a very great multitude spread their garments in the way; others cut down branches from the trees, and strawed them in the way."**

The people of Jerusalem waved branches and set down coats as a reverent but joyful greeting to the person they recognized as their Savior! It was one of the only times Christ was recognized for who He truly was while He was here on the earth.

Spreading out your clothes or going to cut down a branch from a tree may not be things you commonly do, but how do you worship Jesus? How do you find joy in celebrating what He has done and who He is?

When we find happy, meaningful ways to recognize Jesus as our King, we can join with the saints in Jerusalem in shouting "Hosanna!"

— Cali

EASTER MONDAY

KEEP YOUR HEART RIGHT

MATTHEW 21:12-13

On the last Monday of Jesus' life, He went to the temple. Of all the places on earth He could go, this was supposed to be where Jesus could feel closest to His Father.

And yet what did Jesus find? He found the temple full of unrepentant sinners.

The scriptures tell us that, **"Jesus went into the temple of God, and cast out all them that sold and bought in the temple, and overthrew the tables of the moneychangers, and the seats of them that sold doves, and said unto them, It is written, My house shall be called the house of prayer; but ye have made it a den of thieves."**

Those who congregated at the temple weren't there to worship God but to worship their own gain. And that was incredibly displeasing to Jesus.

But what does that have to do with us? Perhaps we need to be more careful about where our thoughts and hearts are when we are in God's holy houses. When we go to church, do we do it with a heart intent on learning and serving? When we attend the temple, are we doing it out of love or a sense of obligation?

Though it is always pleasing to God for us to be in the right place, we should also make sure we are there for the right reasons!

— Kristen

EASTER TUESDAY

RESPECT GOD'S SERVANTS

MATTHEW 21:42

On the Tuesday of Passover week, Jesus spent His day teaching. As He taught, Jesus told a parable about a householder (or "lord of the vineyard") who rented out his land.

The lord of the vineyard moved far away and sent servants to check on the status of his land. But when the servants arrived, the man renting the vineyard beat and killed them. When the servants didn't return, the lord of the vineyard sent more servants whom the renter also killed. When these men didn't return, the lord of the vineyard decided to send his son, who he was sure the renter would respect and send back with a fair report. And yet this young son was also killed.

When Jesus questioned His listeners about what they thought the lord of the vineyard would do to his violent renter, they answered that he and his men should be killed! Then **"Jesus saith unto them, Did ye never read in the scriptures, The stone which the builders rejected, the same is become the head of the corner. . . ?"** Or in other words, this story is about Me! I am the Son of the Lord of the Vineyard, and you're planning to kill Me!

God sends us His servants– or prophets– that some reject. He sent His Son– God's greatest offering– and He was also rejected. We need to ensure that we aren't like the wicked vineyard renter. We need to accept the Son and the servants God sends by listening to and obeying their counsel!

- Kristen

EASTER WEDNESDAY

LUKE 5:16

The scriptures are silent regarding the Lord's final Wednesday on Passover week. Though we have no written record of what He did, we can learn from this scriptural silence.

It means that Jesus was not out in public. He was not teaching. He was not calling to repentance. He was not healing the sick. That means He was probably resting in anticipation of the intense days ahead.

As He had done at other times during His mortal ministry, Jesus likely **"...withdrew himself into the wilderness, and prayed."**

This is a great lesson for all of us: spiritual rest is important for everyone– even for the Savior!

Though Jesus could have filled that last Wednesday with miracles and messages, He didn't. And though there are many wonderful things we could do to fill all of our time, it isn't necessary.

What is necessary is running our race wisely and making time for spiritual rest-- for personally connecting with God-- so we don't become too weary.

– Kristen

EASTER THURSDAY

REPENT OVER AND OVER

MATTHEW 26:33-34

Have you ever taken the sacrament with the intent to do better the next week and not make the same mistakes again? But then, the following Sunday rolls around, and you find yourself repenting of the same sin?

Peter can relate! Right after Jesus showed His disciples the sacrament and how partaking of it would give them a remission of their sins, Peter and Jesus had this conversation: **"Peter answered and said unto him, Though all men shall be offended because of thee, yet will I never be offended. Jesus said unto him, Verily I say unto thee, That this night, before the cock crow, thou shalt deny me thrice."**

Peter promised Jesus that he would never be offended by or deny the Savior. But Jesus knew Peter would break that promise! And Jesus knows we won't be able to keep every commandment, commitment, or covenant perfectly.

I wonder if Jesus had this conversation with Peter in mind as He entered the Garden of Gethsemane that evening, prepared to make the greatest personal sacrifice so that Peter– and all of us– could break our promises over and over. He willingly gave us the chance to have those mistakes wiped clean as often as we need, as long as we turn to Him with pure intent each time. What a blessing His atoning sacrifice can be to each of us!

– Cali

EASTER FRIDAY

MATTHEW 27:24

Before Jesus was taken to be crucified, He had one last chance to be saved: Pontius Pilate. Pilate was the Roman governor of Jerusalem, and without his permission, the Jews could not put anyone to death.

And so the chief priests and elders brought Jesus to Pilate to be condemned.

Yet Pilate could find no reason for Jesus to be put to death. There was no fault in this Man whom the Jewish leaders seemed to hate so much. And so Pilate told the people that Jesus was innocent and should be set free. But the people disagreed, and **"When Pilate saw that he could prevail nothing, but that rather a tumult was made, he took water, and washed his hands before the multitude, saying, I am innocent of the blood of this just person: see ye to it."**

Pilate physically washed his hands of the situation, but spiritually that was impossible.

Not making a decision about Jesus <u>is</u> making a decision about Him! If we are not for Him, we are against Him!

Have you made a decision about Jesus yet? Have you decided to be for Him no matter how unpopular or what kind of "tumult" it creates?

- Kristen

EASTER SATURDAY

SUNDAY WILL ALWAYS COME

MATTHEW 27:62-64

What a horrible day Saturday must have been for Jesus' disciples. Their beloved friend, teacher, and Savior was dead. He had promised never to leave them but now, He was gone. Forever it seemed!

Christ had been buried in a tomb, and His enemies wanted to make sure He stayed there. They came to Pilate once more and said, **"Sir, we remember that that deceiver said, while he was yet alive, After three days I will rise again. Command therefore that the sepulchre be made sure until the third day, lest his disciples come by night, and steal him away, and say unto the people, He is risen from the dead. . . ."**

And so they sealed the tomb shut and set a watch over it.

The tomb was closed. Christ was gone. There was no sign that He would return. But we know what happened the next day. Resurrection Sunday came! But Christ's disciples didn't know that. In fact, they were shocked to hear of it that Sunday morning.

Christ's resurrection reminds us that when life seems dark and hopeless, God sees the light we cannot. When trials seem impossible to overcome, God sees the way out that we cannot. We can keep hoping and trusting that God will always provide a way. We can trust in good things to come.

– Kristen

EASTER RESURRECTION SUNDAY

TELL OTHERS HE LIVES

MATTHEW 28:6, 8

When did you first believe that Jesus was real? Were you young? Old? In a church building? In nature? What truths did the Spirit teach you about Jesus?

When Mary Magdalene and Mary arrived at the unexpectedly empty tomb, the angel boldly taught them: **"He is not here: for he is risen."**

What did these women do after learning this powerful truth? **"And they departed quickly from the sepulchre with fear and great joy; and did run to bring his disciples word."**

These women were converted to a new truth about Jesus, and then they ran quickly to share that news with others! Jesus lives, and His miraculous resurrection means that sins can be forgiven, love can be restored, and priesthood power is real.

Do you feel converted to these truths about Jesus? If so, you can take the example of these faithful women and run with joy to tell others about this life-changing message, too! What will you do because you know that He lives?

— Cali

CHRISTMAS

CHRISTMAS DAY 1

BE A
WILLING
SERVANT

MATTHEW 1:23

The Christmas story about the baby Jesus actually begins with a girl and a miracle.

Mary was a young female Israelite, which in and of itself means that in normal circumstances, she would be forgotten by history. But because of the miracle surrounding her, she has become the most famous woman in all history.

Even before her birth, the scriptures bore witness of Mary saying, **"Behold, a virgin shall be with child, and shall bring forth a son, and they shall call his name Emmanuel, which being interpreted is, God with us."**

This unknown and unimportant virgin girl would experience the miracle of carrying and giving birth to the Savior of the world. It seemed impossible! Medically and logically speaking it was. But with God, even this impossible miracle was made possible.

As we know, the miracle of the virgin Mary is true! And it happened to and through a girl of no particular importance who was willing to let God's will prevail.

Perhaps when we feel unimportant, we can remember that God can work miracles through willing servants!

- Kristen

CHRISTMAS DAY 2

GIVE GOD
YOUR
ALL

LUKE 1:30-31, 38

Mary was going about her day like usual. As an unmarried Israelite girl, she was likely helping with household chores: cleaning, cooking, washing, or fetching water.

Then, suddenly, in the middle of this ordinary day, came an absolutely extraordinary sight: an angel! It's hard to imagine her feelings of shock. The angel quickly reassured her, saying, **"Fear not, Mary: for thou hast found favour with God. And, behold, thou shalt conceive in thy womb, and bring forth a son, and shalt call his name JESUS."**

Those sentences seem to be totally contradictory. The angel told Mary to "fear not" and then explained that her life was about to be turned upside down! However, that is how revelation often works. God gives us spiritual inspiration that feels peaceful because it's from Him but scary because it changes all our plans.

Mary's response to the angel's announcement — which would have serious social, spiritual, emotional, and physical implications for the rest of her life— is how we too should respond to God's revelations. She said, **"... be it unto me according to thy word."** In other words, "I'll do whatever God wants!"

The next time we receive a revelation that might make life uncomfortable, let's remember Mary and her humble willingness to give God her all!

— Kristen

CHRISTMAS DAY 3

LET SACRIFICE BRING JOY

LUKE 2:4-5

When I was very pregnant, I participated in a large Christmas choir concert that required me to stand for long periods of time. I complained pretty much constantly during our rehearsals and the first few performances. I was miserable!

Right before our final night of concerts, our director invited everyone to choose to make sacrifices to bring the audience joy from the Savior. I realized that while I had good reason to complain, I was focused too much on myself!

What if I could stop thinking about how much I had to endure and instead focused on Jesus? That final concert transformed my spirit as I turned my focus from "poor me" to "Jesus brings me joy!"

I can't help but think of the parallels to young Mary, who had to endure tough travels at the end of her pregnancy. **"And Joseph also went up from Galilee. . .To be taxed with Mary his espoused wife, being great with child."**

We don't know Mary's attitude during their journey. I'm sure she was in pain. I'm sure she ached and worried about the safety of her unborn child. But Mary still sacrificed. And because of her great sacrifice, we all have reason to find joy! Sacrificing can turn us inward, focusing on how rough we have it, or it can help turn us to the Savior of the world to find everlasting joy!

— Cali

CHRISTMAS DAY 4

LUKE 2:6-7

Mary and Joseph were far from home. They had traveled ninety miles through the desert while Mary was at the most uncomfortable stage of pregnancy. They arrived in Bethlehem, where there was no room to stay in a comfortable and private spot. **"And so it was, that, while they were there, the days were accomplished that she should be delivered."**

Seriously? Now?! Of all the times for Mary to have her baby, this was probably the most inconvenient. Surely at home she had her mother and sisters, a bed to lie on, blankets and medical aid. And yet the scriptures say that **". . . she brought forth her firstborn son, and wrapped him in swaddling clothes, and laid him in a manger; because there was no room for them in the inn."**

In one of the filthiest places imaginable, in the humblest of conditions, God asked Mary to go through one of her most difficult physical experiences. And yet she did so with faith.

The truth is doing God's will is often inconvenient. God might ask us to bear our testimony, move across the country, or quit a job during times that feel incredibly difficult. But no matter what we think or how hard it might be, God's will and His timing are always perfect.

– Kristen

CHRISTMAS DAY 5

BE AN
ANGEL TO
SHEPHERDS

LUKE 2:8-9

Can you imagine being a shepherd and having the night shift? Those late hours of watching must have left the shepherds exhausted. Yes, it was their job, but that didn't make it any less taxing on their bodies or minds.

These shepherds probably needed a reminder that someone knew who they were. That they were making a contribution. That their tiring efforts mattered.

"And there were in the same country shepherds abiding in the field, keeping watch over their flock by night. And, lo, the angel of the Lord came upon them, and the glory of the Lord shone round about them."

God sent an angel to the shepherds to announce the divine birth of His Son! He let them join in the joy of the occasion! He knew that they needed a reminder that they mattered.

Who needs you to be an angel? Who is tired, forgotten, or feels like they've lost their purpose? At this Christmas season, how can you share love and remind others that they are seen and known?

— Cali

CHRISTMAS DAY 6

MATTHEW 2:11

One of my favorite poems is the Christmas poem by Christina Rossetti, "In the Bleak Midwinter."

I love how she describes the cold but miraculous evening of Christ's birth at the beginning of her poem, but the final stanza is the one that touches my heart every time I read or hear it.

"What can I give Him, poor as I am?
If I were a shepherd, I would bring a lamb;
If I were a Wise Man, I would do my part;
Yet what I can I give Him: give my heart."*

"And when they were come into the house, they saw the young child with Mary his mother, and fell down, and worshipped him: and when they had opened their treasures, they presented unto him gifts; gold, and frankincense, and myrrh."

The wise men presented their gifts to the Savior in person. While we can't do that right now, what gift could we ever possibly give Jesus? It's our heart. He wants our desires, our obedience, and our love. What gift can you give the Savior this year?

— Cali

*"In the Bleak Midwinter" by Christina Rossetti, Scribner's Monthly, January 1872

CHRISTMAS DAY 7

JOHN 3:16

Presents are fun.

Candy canes are delicious.

Christmas trees are beautiful.

But they're temporary.

Whatever you gave or received this Christmas, it has an expiration date. It might last for years, but it won't last forever. But what will last forever is Jesus' gift to you. His atoning sacrifice has eternal ramifications that are truly life-changing. And that is why we celebrate Christmas! That's what it's all about, that first and best Christmas gift of all: God's perfect Son, Jesus Christ.

"For God so loved the world, that he gave his only begotten Son, that whosoever believeth in him should not perish, but have everlasting life."

As we finish our Christmas celebrations, let's make sure that we give a gift in return to our Father and His Son: the gift of remembering the true reason we celebrate.

— Kristen

Thanks for coming closer to Christ with us, one minute at a time.

— Kristen & Cali